Interpreting the Legacy

Interpreting the Legacy
JOHN NEIHARDT AND *BLACK ELK SPEAKS*

BRIAN HOLLOWAY

UNIVERSITY PRESS OF COLORADO

Published by the University Press of Colorado
5589 Arapahoe Avenue, Suite 206C
Boulder, Colorado 80303

Printed in the United States of America

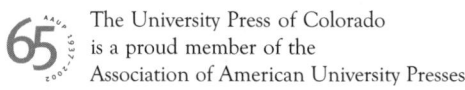

The University Press of Colorado
is a proud member of the
Association of American University Presses.

The University Press of Colorado is a cooperative publishing enterprise supported, in part, by Adams State College, Colorado State University, Fort Lewis College, Mesa State College, Metropolitan State College of Denver, University of Colorado, University of Northern Colorado, University of Southern Colorado, and Western State College of Colorado.

The paper used in this publication meets the minimum requirements of the American National Standard for Information Sciences—Permanence of Paper for Printed Library Materials. ANSI Z39.48-1992

Library of Congress Cataloging-in-Publication Data

Holloway, Brian R., 1952–
Interpreting the legacy : John Neihardt and Black Elk speaks / Brian R. Holloway.
p. cm.
Includes bibliographical references and index.
ISBN 0-87081-679-9 (alk. paper)
1. Black Elk, 1863–1950. Black Elk speaks. 2. Neihardt, John Gneisenau, 1881–1973. 3. Oglala Indians—Biography 4. Oglala Indians—Religion. 5. Teton Indians. I. Title.

E99.O3 B4835 2002
978.004'9752–dc21

2002011501

Design by Daniel Pratt
Typesetting by Laura Furney

12 11 10 09 08 07 06 05 04 03   10 9 8 7 6 5 4 3 2 1

For the next generation reading
John Neihardt and Nicholas Black Elk
in a new and challenging century

Contents

List of Figures

Preface and Acknowledgments

THIS VOLUME EMERGED FROM RESEARCHING PRIMARY AND SECONDARY MATERIALS connected with *Black Elk Speaks* and from a process of thinking about that book that began while I attended the University of Missouri–Columbia in the 1970s. At that time and in that place, Neihardt's works were conspicuous, although the Neihardt ambiance has receded today. The personal library Neihardt donated to the university has been moved from Ellis Library to Tate Hall, and although Mona Martinsen Neihardt's bust of the poet still surveys patrons with a warm, majestic look, the clerks tell me few students now use the collection. Neihardt's treasured Stockdale *Shakespeare* is there for perusal, and one may still find photographs and Neihardt's letters to posterity inserted between the leaves of other volumes. These annotations, however, rest between unturned pages.

It appears that a clinical and often cynical approach to Neihardt arose for a time to replace much former enthusiasm. Not all dissection is bad, of course, but a tone of indictment and scorn may prejudice well-intentioned commentary. One might get the impression that some would prefer that Black Elk's vision had perished under the heel of the dominant culture instead of flourishing, nurtured by Neihardt's accomplishment and the dialogue it has inspired. But Neihardt's writing is in no sense a Victorian curiosity ready to be relegated to the museum like piano-leg pantaloons or Macassar Oil, nor is it scientific anthro-ethnography dedicated to reproducing the least-literary belch of an "informant." For readers of literature, Neihardt's legacy includes *Black Elk Speaks* and *When the Tree Flowered.* For ethnographic use, Neihardt preserved transcriptions of interviews that led to these important works.

Lately, interest in Neihardt seems to be increasing, and several current writers provide fresh interpretations of Neihardt's legacy. Family and personal reminiscences of both John Neihardt and Black Elk have appeared. An exhaustive biography and an edition of Neihardt's essays are among the projects currently approaching print. Of course, the typical hiatus between creation and publication means those currently interested in Neihardt's role in *Black Elk Speaks* may be using one of the older critical approaches as a foundation. There is value in even the problematic examples of these, as they provide good indications of the dominant culture's reactions to *Black Elk Speaks.*

My goal in this book is not to recapitulate Raymond J. DeMallie, who has provided an outstanding service to ethnography by editing, reproducing, and commenting upon John Neihardt's field notes in *The Sixth Grandfather: Black Elk's Teachings Given to John G. Neihardt.* Nor when discussing the collaboration that produced *Black Elk Speaks* do I want to declaim about Lakota culture, which is best written about by the current generation of Lakota scholars. Instead I wish to explore *Black Elk Speaks* as literature, using drafts and transcriptions to achieve an understanding of how that literature was created. Other manuscripts and works will help illuminate Neihardt's writing, editing, and thinking process as well. Biographical references underpin certain sections, but I leave comprehensive biographical discussions to those writing that type of commentary: Hilda Neihardt in her book *Black Elk and Flaming Rainbow: Personal Memories of the Lakota Holy Man and John Neihardt,* Esther Black Elk DeSersa, Olivia Black Elk Pourier, and others in *Black Elk Lives,* Tim Anderson in his new biography of Neihardt, Lori Utecht in her study of Neihardt as public essayist. These projects will enhance the dialogue about the makers of *Black Elk Speaks.*

In a project involving this much source material, several organizations have been the generous custodians of much that I cite or reproduce, and I wish to acknowledge them.

Passages from *Black Elk Speaks* are reprinted from *Black Elk Speaks* by John G. Neihardt by permission of the University of Nebraska Press. Copyright 1932, 1959, 1972 by John G. Neihardt. Copyright 1961 by the John G. Neihardt Trust.

Quotations from *The Twilight of the Sioux* are reprinted from *The Twilight of the Sioux* by John G. Neihardt by permission of the University of Nebraska Press. Copyright 1943, 1946, 1953 by John G. Neihardt.

Several collections of papers were key to this work and receive credit as follows:

John G. Neihardt Papers, c. 1858–1974, Western Historical Manuscript Collection, Columbia, Missouri.

Huntington Library, Sterling Letters, San Marino, California.

Stanley C. Smith Papers, 1951–1971, Western Historical Manuscript Collection, Columbia, Missouri.

M. Slade Kendrick Papers, 1951–1973, Western Historical Manuscript Collection, Columbia, Missouri.

Permission to quote from or reproduce images in the Neihardt Collection, portions of *Black Elk Speaks,* and parts of *Twilight of the Sioux* has been granted by the John G. Neihardt Trust.

In addition, I wish to thank those whose help has been exemplary as I worked on this long project. The West Virginia Humanities Council, and through it the National Endowment for the Humanities (NEH), supported my research with a scholar's grant in 1996. A second scholar's grant from the NEH–West Virginia Humanities Council provided further support in 1999. The energetic personnel of the Western Historical Manuscript Collection, University of Missouri, including past and present members Laura Bullion, David Moore, Nancy Lankford, Randy Roberts, Diane Ayotte, and Cindy Stewart, have provided outstanding assistance. David Archer and the University Press of Colorado have believed in this book and made it happen. Howard Hinkel, chair of the English Department at the University of Missouri–Columbia, made me feel at home again. Mountain State University's administration provided encouragement, and its students lent me some of their dynamic energy. Doug and Mary Leigh Burns supplied gracious hospitality during my research sojourn. Kathleen, Rachel, and Hazel Holloway exhibited the patience born of love as this project engulfed my free time. The John G. Neihardt Center and the John G. Neihardt Trust have been wonderfully supportive of my endeavors. The manuscript has benefited from expert and insightful reviewing by Professor William Urbrock of the Department of Religious Studies at the University of Wisconsin–Oshkosh and Charles Trimble, past president of the John G. Neihardt Foundation. Finally, Hilda Neihardt, Charles Trimble, Nancy Gillis, Robin Neihardt, Joy Neihardt, Jon Fiechtner, and Janyce Hunt—you are wonderful hosts. Thank you for adopting me into your spiritual family.

Interpreting the Legacy

Introduction

THIS BOOK EXPLORES *BLACK ELK SPEAKS* WITHIN LITERATURE'S CONTEXT AND as a consciously created work of art. Although *Black Elk Speaks* has been used as a political document, for example, in the Native American civil rights struggles of the 1970s, it was created with other intentions that do not necessarily exclude this single use. Although *Black Elk Speaks* has been cited as if it were a collection of anthropological field notes, it is not an anthropological study, and the chapters derived from exchanges between Neihardt and Black Elk are not ethnography. Nor were they intended to be. But neither was it Neihardt's function to impose Marxism, Puritanism, neo-new-age paganism, or the doctrines of Plato upon Black Elk's telling; nor was it Black Elk's imperative to enforce European Catholicism or a frozen-in-time view of Lakota spirituality echoing the redactions of James Walker on the text. It is also highly unlikely that Black Elk, in 1931, discussed all of his knowledge with John Neihardt, since more was related in 1944 to become part of *When the*

Tree Flowered and since Black Elk later talked about other aspects of Lakota spirituality with Joseph Brown.

For Neihardt, Black Elk was a seer whose articulated, detailed visions of the "outer world" embodied much of Neihardt's own theory of consciousness and the role of art as a means to, or expression of, an advanced state of awareness. Neihardt felt Black Elk's engulfing vision possessed great aesthetic value and embraced the diverse particulars of different religions. For Neihardt, in fact, this unitary, visionary consciousness was activated through the intuition unleashed by art—potentially the art of the poet collaborating with the mystic. Neihardt's goal, then, was to use his art to induce a transcendent experience in his readers. To follow Neihardt's understanding, the proper way to examine a work uniting poetry and mysticism is to study its crafting. That is, we need to examine the sources of such art's production, the particulars of literary craft in action, the reactions to and implications of such art. This type of study will reveal how and why *Black Elk Speaks* successfully conveys the spiritual content of the unique collaboration that produced it.

AS ART, *BLACK ELK SPEAKS* ENGAGES US IN A VARIETY OF WAYS. FOR EXAMPLE, the book has roots, origins in a special collaboration, that can be studied for its impact on the work. In this regard, philosophical and historical contexts are important in showing how Neihardt made artistic choices in presenting Black Elk's material and in revealing how Black Elk helped him. Neihardt's *Poetic Values* and other key texts explain the poet's approach to art as a medium of the sacred.[1] We will also consider items of Neihardt's correspondence, notes, other books, and even marginalia to understand his approach.[2] We may learn about ways in which the values reinforced by Neihardt's collaboration with Black Elk, who controlled the circumstances and methods of transmitting his knowledge, constituted for Neihardt a "sacred obligation" influencing subsequent efforts. Social and communitarian ambiances are also important to comprehend, since Black Elk and his friends taught John Neihardt through ceremony and displays of community, as well as through speech.

Also, close attention to Neihardt's craft in relating Black Elk's telling to an audience from the dominant culture will reveal a philosophy, an aesthetic, and a knowledge displayed in practice by a master mediator. Comparative examination of drafts with final copy and attention to the construction of *Black Elk Speaks* from the material produced during the interviews will demonstrate the ways Neihardt innovated, using techniques of discourse familiar to white readers to present Black Elk's telling to the largest possible audience and to kindle within that audience an expanded perception. Even contemplating successive strikeovers in the manuscript of *Black Elk Speaks* will assist us in this undertaking. An explication of craft might suggest ways in which Neihardt's poetics live on.

Moreover, examining the interaction between *Black Elk Speaks* and some critics foregrounds the relationship between the book's poetics and the work's sometimes resistant readership, revealing much about both entities. Neither the arcana of neoscholastic deconstruction nor the colonialist desire to appropriate *Black Elk Speaks* for sectarian causes has produced much more than sets of opposites annihilating themselves. To fit all molds, Black Elk must be Lakota, Protestant, and Catholic; whereas Neihardt must become Marxist, Calvinist, Establishment, and proto-new-age. He must be both a cynic and an ardent awaiter of the Rapture. Opinions are plentiful, but they should stand the test of "Occam's Razor" in seeking the simplest explanation for phenomena. Perhaps the least complex explanation of *Black Elk Speaks* is simply that Black Elk's material is presented in literary form, not as ethnography, using strategies of discourse familiar to general readers so that the vision and its context will find a larger audience. Only the specialist reads ethnography, and John Neihardt dedicated his life to writing intended to elevate the awareness of a larger, reflective public.

Finally, the study of Neihardt's emulators among that very audience suggests the enduring quality of the language of North American prose epic emerging from the collaboration between Neihardt and Black Elk, showing how significantly the tone and tenor of *Black Elk Speaks* have established themselves in writing about the American West. Seeing how other writers have resisted or incorporated Neihardt's innovations in *Black Elk Speaks* will help us appreciate his influence on contemporary literature.

NOTES

1. To distinguish between the two editions of *Poetic Values* used, I will cite the Ghose edition as Ghose and the 1989 printing as *Poetic.*

2. In referring to the Neihardt papers in the Western Historical Manuscript Collection, I use the collection designation (e.g., c3716) followed by the folder or audiocassette numbering, if necessary. All such documents are courtesy of the Western Historical Manuscript Collection, 23 Ellis Library, University of Missouri–Columbia, Columbia, MO 65201. They are used by permission of the Western Historical Manuscript Collection and the John G. Neihardt Trust. Copies of the Sterling correspondence, referred to later in the book, appear in the Western Historical Manuscript Collection (c3074); originals are located in the Huntington Library, San Marino, California, and are used by permission of all parties.

Some material in this book is derived in part from two articles and one presentation of mine, supported in part by the NEH and West Virginia Humanities Council grants described in the Preface and Acknowledgments: "Black Elk and Neihardt Speak—If We Would Listen," *People and Mountains* (January 1997): 4, 8; "Black Elk and Some Discontents," presentation to the Spring Neihardt Conference, "John Neihardt the Writer: New Critical Perspectives," Bancroft, Nebraska, April 25, 1998; and "Working with the Legacy," *Neihardt Foundation News* (November 1996): 2. These are not listed in the bibliography.

1
SEEING *Black Elk Speaks*

BLACK ELK SPEAKS, THE PRODUCT OF UNPRETENTIOUS TALKS BETWEEN JOHN Neihardt and Nicholas Black Elk in 1931, has frequently been cited as one of the most notable writings of the twentieth century. It even occupies a place on the HarperSanFrancisco list of the top ten spiritual books of that hundred-year period (Zaleski 9). The book spans American history of the West from the middle to the end of the nineteenth century, using material from Black Elk and others to render that history both personal and poignant. But the work is remarkable spiritual literature as well, filled with the tension between inspiration and action, the conflict over modes of belief, the voices of prophecy in a confusing wilderness of exile—all animated by a great vision, part of which is described. Certainly, in both its content and the public reaction to it, *Black Elk Speaks* reflects the diversity and anxieties within North America, qualities also manifested in the lives and backgrounds of its cocreators. In constructing this text, though, John Neihardt served its subjects and cultures far better than is sometimes acknowledged and in fact opened the path for later efforts depending upon the accomplishments of this enduring book.

Black Elk Speaks is often conceived of as an image of Neihardt or Black Elk in totality, although these men and their life situations were much more complicated than their book and neither intended their collaboration to be a sole, definitive summation of Native American beliefs. Neihardt, although often discussed as if he were in the mainstream of Euro-American society, was decidedly opposed to that society and was in fact a nonconformist and socialist—rejecting the capitalism, mass culture, and materialism of his time and possessing a spiritual orientation far different from that of the dominant culture surrounding him. Black Elk, although sometimes presented as a "reconstructed" catechist in the European Catholic mode, perplexes that view because of his continuing orientation to traditional Native American practices and his ability to reconcile beliefs from different traditions within an overarching spiritual view. These men—and the time and space they lived in and in which they produced their book—influence the discussions of *Black Elk Speaks* within the present volume.

IN PREPARATION FOR THE SECTIONS OF THIS BOOK TO FOLLOW, A BRIEF OVERVIEW of history might help to clarify aspects of the persons, location, era, and production of *Black Elk Speaks.* Since this material will be amplified in later chapters, reference annotations appear sparingly here. But we must remember that John Neihardt's writing, philosophy, spirituality, and art energized him and impelled him to that first meeting with Black Elk and are crucial considerations. Black Elk's past, aspirations, and control over the manner and content of his meetings with Neihardt are equally critical. Moreover, we must realize that the contexts that shaped this project often still fail to be appreciated.

John G. Neihardt, who was born in Illinois in 1881 and graduated from Nebraska Normal College at age sixteen, had accomplished many things before meeting Black Elk. He had overcome physical limitations and poverty. Through strenuous conditioning he had developed a pugilist's punch and a wrestler's tenacity. He had been a manual laborer; a marble polisher's helper; a trader's assistant in Bancroft, Nebraska, near the Omaha Reservation; a schoolteacher; a writer of lyrics, epics, stories, drama, and newspaper pieces; and a lecturer. Neihardt's biographical narratives *All Is But a Beginning* and *Patterns and Coincidences* depict some of that author's many careers. Neihardt was even runner-up for the Pulitzer Prize, and Ralph Pulitzer himself believed the prize had been awarded to him, only to have been rescinded for political reasons (Anderson 10). Neihardt was also an artist who believed art was the conduit to spirituality and the "higher values," who distrusted institutional religion but was reverent. He believed in the visionary and the paranormal. He was fifty years old, busy working on completing the epic *Cycle of the West* and seeking to interview some of those who had been present when the U.S. military crushed the Ghost Dancers at Wounded Knee. That personal contact was vital because for Neihardt the historical facts were not enough to produce art; emotion was also important. In seeking that contact Neihardt went to the Pine Ridge Reservation to discuss the past with some old-timers and encountered Black Elk.

Black Elk (Hehaka Sapa) also had a significant background. He had been a child and a young man during a time of turbulence. Born in 1863 into a band headed by his father, a medicine man related to Crazy Horse, young Black Elk experienced the triumphs and misfortunes of his people as the United States pressed in upon them to dispossess them of their lands. Black Elk's birth date is to be noted: shortly thereafter the Civil War ended, and the United States deployed increasing energy in driving westward—building roads and railroads across the land, mining for gold, settling, and homesteading. The problem was that this newfound land was already occupied. As "legal" cession and illegal turf grabbing proceeded, original inhabitants were pushed off. Some moved to more remote regions of tribal territory, increasing friction with competing tribes contesting those areas. Some acquiesced, gathering at forts, agencies, and areas of concentration designated "reservations." Others fought for their homelands. The Lakota and allied tribes forced closure of the "thieves' road," the Bozeman Trail, and instituted a guarantee of land boundaries in the Treaty of 1868—made when Black Elk was five years old.

The treaty, however, which provided punishment for infractions committed against it, was soon shamefully violated by the United States—and with impunity. Gold had been discovered in the Black Hills, igniting further land lust. By the last decade of the nineteenth century the vast territory was gone except for the reservations, themselves dwindling in size. Illness, insufficient food, and the psychological and cultural shock of the loss of their homeland all preyed upon the Plains people. Many were receptive to what is usually called the Ghost Dance, a pan-Indian movement to pray a new world into being that provoked government reaction—culminating in the slaughter of about 300 Minneconjou at Wounded Knee in 1890, when Black Elk was a twenty-seven-year-old spiritual leader, a healer, and himself an adherent of the Ghost Dance.

Fourteen years later, in 1904, when Black Elk was forty-one, he became a Roman Catholic, and accounts differ regarding his participation in traditional religion after that point. The extent to which Black Elk retained, maintained, or modified his prior beliefs with Christianity has become a subject of academic conjecture. Significantly, Black Elk did educate outsiders about traditional culture during his Catholic years—in working with Neihardt on two books, *Black Elk Speaks* and *When the Tree Flowered*; in collaborating with Joseph Brown on *The Sacred Pipe*; in teaching ceremonies to Reginald and Gladys Laubin; and in the Duhamel pageants of Native American culture held in the Black Hills in the 1930s (DeMallie, *Sixth*). In these aspects Black Elk paralleled a relative and protégé, Frank Fools Crow, who was also traditional and a Catholic, who worked with writer and artist Thomas Mails on a biography, *Fools Crow,* and who assumed a very public role as spokesman and negotiator during the 1973 Wounded Knee protest.

The agreement the sixty-eight-year-old Black Elk made with Neihardt in 1931 was that Neihardt would tell Black Elk's story from his youth through the Wounded Knee massacre, using as much material from Black Elk as he could. The agreement is memorialized in a letter initiating the project. Neihardt would, then, write a personal story set against the background of the final thirty years of struggle by the Lakota people to remain independent of the encroaching United States. It is this account of spirituality and seeking, shaped and threaded through the larger historical events, that constitutes *Black Elk Speaks.*

We must consider further historical issues in contemplating the 1931 collaboration. The location was profoundly important, for Pine Ridge was then a closed world in which a Washington-appointed bureaucrat could impose restrictions by fiat. Neihardt had to apply to the government for permission to go onto the reservation to interview Black Elk and his friends, and documents suggest that bureaucrats may have debated Neihardt's clearance to do so. In some places agents monitored the private lives of Indians and others residing on reservations, as illustrated by government correspondence regarding the Ghost Dance prophet Wovoka later in life. In this correspondence officials are depicted tracking Wovoka's movement on and off the reservations, recording the prices of his train tickets, documenting his visitors, and planning ways to discourage any dancing that might revive his religious movement (Hittman 269–291).

Of course, the official religion at Black Elk's Pine Ridge Reservation was missionary Christianity, chiefly Catholic and Episcopalian, and native beliefs had long been officially suppressed. Not until John Collier became commissioner of Indian Affairs in 1933—two years after Neihardt's first series of interviews with Black Elk—were a number of limitations rescinded, although the legality of ceremonies such as the full Sun Dances remained doubtful. Finally, in mid-1978, twenty-eight years after Black Elk's death, Congress guaranteed liberty of religion for Native Americans in the American Indian Religious Freedom Act.

In addition to being born in a troubled place, *Black Elk Speaks* originated in a troubled era. The early 1930s were historically significant in assessing the initial lack of impact of *Black Elk Speaks.* The depression ground on, forestalling the sale and distribution of the book, which quickly became remaindered. The American people, entangled in economic problems and about to be engulfed by global conflict, were not ready to pay attention to spiritual messages conveyed from such then-unlikely places as Black Elk's Manderson, South Dakota, or Neihardt's Branson, Missouri.

The history of the book's production is also important to our understanding of its origin. The fact that *Black Elk Speaks* became a book in print is remarkable, for Neihardt's regular publisher—the stodgy Macmillan Company—wanted nothing to do with a Neihardt project featuring Native American voices. Hilda Neihardt related to me a family belief that Macmillan was trying to "kill" John Neihardt's works by letting them languish, perhaps for political reasons (Interview). After Macmillan's repeated off-puttings and rebuffs, William Morrow underwrote the project but died before the book was finished, leaving an unsympathetic successor to contend with Neihardt over the book's content—including wanting to delete the Great Vision or insert it as end matter. And although *Black Elk Speaks* influenced skilled American writers such as Mari Sandoz, the book was not reprinted in the United States during Black Elk's lifetime.

We must understand that the interviews that produced the book were conducted on Black Elk's turf and were the products of people not trained to be or interested in being anthropologists. Instead these discussions were the outcome of a spiritual leader talking with a poet. The format of the talks seemed clear to participants and is described in the prefaces to *Black Elk Speaks.* There were formal sessions during which Black Elk would speak; his bilingual son, Ben, would translate; and John Neihardt's oldest daughter, Enid, would take stenographic notes. Black Elk's lifelong friend, Standing Bear, stood by to vouch for the integrity of what was said; other friends also attended at different times. John Neihardt's daughter Hilda, exempted from her schoolwork, was present as a counterpart to Standing Bear (see Hilda Neihardt's comments on this process in *Black Elk and Flaming Rainbow* and in *Black Elk*

Lives ix). Hilda Neihardt has told me that the collaboration included material not written down in the notes, and it is evident that the elaborate ceremonials held for and with the Neihardts were also intended to influence John Neihardt's understanding of the issues discussed. Questions about Neihardt's cultural preparedness or receptivity, not voiced by participants at the time, later became part of the academic debate over *Black Elk Speaks.*

The very act of organizing and writing from the material gleaned during this collaboration, as John Neihardt performed it, is a main theme of this book. The stenographic notes, their typed transcriptions, and the handwritten draft that became *Black Elk Speaks* all provide insight into how the book was created, as does Enid Neihardt's scrapbook containing photographs of the ceremonies and the entire encounter. The transcriptions' nuances are often visually different from their edited counterparts in Raymond DeMallie's book *The Sixth Grandfather*; and the draft manuscript contains directions, signs, and clues to the book's design that are equally not apparent in the typeset *Black Elk Speaks.* This study will explore such literary nuances. They are important.

Finally, over time and inevitably, the finished book has been put to a number of uses that are often not literary and often to its detriment. *Black Elk Speaks* has been employed in anthropology classes and has been cited as an example of ethnography, although the book was not intended as an anthropological study. Its prefaces clearly identify *Black Elk Speaks* as other than ethnography. The book has been used as a repository of cultural and spiritual information, and although much is contained within, *Black Elk Speaks* is not a descriptive manual of practices and concepts universal among the first peoples of North America or even among all Lakota. Nor was its function to be such a compendium. The book, however, has directed a generation of young Native Americans toward their particular and often differing roots during the flowering of the Native American civil rights movement. The book does constitute fascinating spiritual literature, the refashioning of a reverent Lakota's eloquence into a near-epic free verse that in fact has been borrowed stylistically by Neihardt's successors, although without the same consistent effect. It is no accident that this prose epic was written as Neihardt also completed his verse epic, *A Cycle of the West.*

THIS CROWDED AND COMPLICATED HISTORY OF *BLACK ELK SPEAKS* HAS LED A number of academics to attempt analytical simplification. Categorization is the academic response to many phenomena, and other writers have classified both Neihardt and Black Elk in self-contradictory ways. Some argue that

Neihardt was too sympathetic to his own Christianity and too unaware of Native American cultures to appreciate Black Elk's message. Others assert that Black Elk's Catholicism should be viewed as the primary feature of his life, unfortunately obscured by Neihardt's lack of sympathy for Christianity and his fascination with traditional Lakota spirituality. The function of Black Elk's communication with Neihardt is also questioned: some believe Black Elk's discourse was essentially a performance or that his telling was so profound that it was impossible for the Caucasian Neihardt to understand. Still others see in the substance of Black Elk's talks only a recapitulation of a time gone by and a belief no longer active. These issues, calling into question Neihardt's or Black Elk's integrity, will be explored later as they affect analysis of the text of *Black Elk Speaks*.

Perhaps a way to begin putting these questions of textual interpretation into perspective is to examine basic responses to the contact between Native American and Christian beliefs, whether expressed in literature or in interpersonal dynamics. These responses vary in ways analogous to the manner in which critics react to *Black Elk Speaks* itself, a point discussed by religious studies professor Bruce David Forbes.

In his article "Which Religion Is Right? Five Answers in the Historical Encounter Between Christianity and Traditional Native American Spiritualities," Forbes outlines what he perceives to be five operational viewpoints likely to result from such an interaction between religions: a denial of all but Christianity, a belief that other spiritualities culminate in Christianity, a view that only the traditional Native American beliefs are correct, a sense that both beliefs are right but that they should remain apart, and the feeling that both beliefs—being tenable—can enhance each other (19). Forbes sees these categories of response at work in the minds of academics who have approached the question of Black Elk's relationship to Christianity in *Black Elk Speaks* (24). Forbes also notes that "Black Elk has been placed by various interpreters in almost all of the positions" he outlines and speculates that "many of the historical interpretations of Black Elk's religious views reveal more about the assumptions of the interpreters than about Black Elk" (25).

Even without following Forbes's schematic completely, a summary of certain critical responses to *Black Elk Speaks* does reveal some ways in which critical perceptions align with its different positions. Such a review may also provide a synopsis of various "lenses" through which critics perceive the book. Of interest is that many such responses do not treat *Black Elk Speaks* as literature with a literary context and intent and a literary legacy of appropriation and reaction.

In 1984 Raymond J. DeMallie published *The Sixth Grandfather: Black Elk's Teachings Given to John G. Neihardt.* The book contains, as DeMallie puts it, "the combined efforts of the interpreters and of Neihardt to express in English the meaning of the old man's Lakota words," that is to say, the notes on which Neihardt depended to write *Black Elk Speaks* and the later *When the Tree Flowered* (xxii). Preceding the edited presentation of these notes is a large section that discusses historical and biographical material relevant to their interpretation. DeMallie reminds us that Black Elk converted to Catholicism after a career as a traditional healer, that he then served as a catechist and missionary, and that, while so doing, he also presented Lakota traditional life in his role in the Black Hills pageants. DeMallie tells us that Black Elk embraced Catholicism after a prolonged investigation of Christianity. DeMallie states that Black Elk's doing so was sincere and speculates that it freed Black Elk from the unpleasant aspects of his vision. These involved the potential to unleash destruction by using the "soldier weed," discussed in a section of the transcripts not present in *Black Elk Speaks*—perhaps in keeping with Black Elk's attitude of nonviolence at the time he met Neihardt. Furthermore, the conversion conferred the benefit of belonging to the church organizations that had supplanted the traditional societies suppressed by the government. As DeMallie relates, participation in missionary and benevolent work fostered by the church could also be a dual cultural expression, as Black Elk could receive small sums for his efforts that he then gave away—to the apparent exasperation of Father Eugene Buechel of Holy Rosary Mission who cautioned his priestly cohort not to give Black Elk any money directly. DeMallie remarks of Black Elk that "on the one hand, holding to Christian doctrine, he practiced the virtue of charity to its fullest. On the other hand, he was able at the same time to fulfill the traditional role of a Lakota leader, poor himself but ever generous to his people" (22–23).

For DeMallie, Black Elk's meeting with Neihardt revivified an interest in traditional Lakota spirituality: "It was as if something long bound up inside the old man had broken free at last, an impulse to save that entire system of knowledge that his vision represented and that for more than twenty-five years he had denied" (28). DeMallie reviews the editorial changes Neihardt made to the material in the transcripts and sees him as an active shaper, editor, and summarizer in *Black Elk Speaks*—"an extraordinarily faithful spokesman for Black Elk; what he wrote was an interpretation of Black Elk's life, but not one that was embellished in any way" (51). For DeMallie, then, Black Elk grew up in the traditional Lakota way, became a Catholic, and then became interested again in his pre-Catholic beliefs. The religions remained essentially separate, though.

For Julian Rice, it is rather the traditional element in Black Elk and his message that predominates: even when Black Elk uses the discourse of Catholicism, he is still Black Elk the traditionalist in his original role. In other words, Catholicism may function as a mask behind which the speaker can use the discourse of tradition. In *Black Elk's Story: Distinguishing Its Lakota Purpose* (1991), Rice seeks to illuminate the context of Black Elk's telling by depicting the Lakota elements referenced in it. For instance, Rice discusses Lakota ritual, multiple souls, the role of the *heyoka,* the development of a traditional holy man, buffalo symbolism, and other subjects—drawing on accounts including those of James Walker, edited by Raymond DeMallie and Elaine A. Jahner in 1980. Rice views Black Elk's telling as obscured and thwarted by John Neihardt, who Rice believes could not distinguish the message from its vehicle because he was captivated by the idea of progress and was inextricably acculturated within an orthodox Christian heritage. Rice refers the reader to Neihardt's *Song of the Messiah* as an example of a Christian providentialist view in which the Lakota are destroyed so they can be "saved." This view sees Neihardt as partaking of the same missionary zeal that impelled a cultural genocide in order to "save" the Indian. For Rice, then, a blinded and programmed Neihardt failed in his task if his task is seen from the Lakota point of view, whereas Black Elk remained ever vigilant for his people as the terms of his calling dictated.

In contrast, Michael F. Steltenkamp's *Black Elk: Holy Man of the Oglala* (1993) posits that Black Elk had a singular conversion experience and then dedicated his entire life to promulgating a Christian, Catholic message. For Steltenkamp, traditional references in the text of *Black Elk Speaks* may actually point to Catholic instruction, not to traditional beliefs, as when he suggests that Black Elk's comments on the truth-bringing role of sacred clowns, or *heyoka,* might be influenced by the writings of St. Ignatius Loyola (24). In Steltenkamp's view, even the two intersecting roads of Black Elk's vision appear to be derived from a chart with parallel roads used as a teaching tool by missionaries and catechists beginning in 1911 (97–101). Steltenkamp does not say what would influence members of a preceding generation, including Black Elk's father, to construct a traditional hoop with red and black roads intersecting at a sacred center. But for Steltenkamp, Neihardt was simply too absorbed in Native American traditionalism to be receptive to the Catholic element predominating in Black Elk's life and discussion, and he used a poetic approach to alter key elements of Black Elk's Christian philosophy. Of interest, though, is Steltenkamp's remark that despite these perceived shortcomings of Neihardt, "he still managed to discover and reveal much of the substance that made the holy man who he was" (88).

Partly in response to these writers, Clyde Holler has provided detailed critiques of the positions of DeMallie, Rice, and Steltenkamp—most thoroughly in *Black Elk's Religion: The Sun Dance and Lakota Catholicism* (1995). For Holler, *Black Elk Speaks* is tarnished by what he thinks is John Neihardt's perception that Black Elk's story ends in irretrievable despair. In other words, for Holler *Black Elk Speaks* effectively terminates with the account of Wounded Knee, which is exactly where a lesser writer would have ended such a book. Holler's reading of *Black Elk Speaks* here resembles Rice's, since for both writers Neihardt is depicting the end of the Lakota. Holler, however, grapples with the sincerity of Black Elk's several "religions," believing that rather than being Rice's covert traditionalist, using the forms of Catholicism to assist his people; rather than being a conventional Catholic convert, as Steltenkamp would see Black Elk; and rather than being an on-again, off-again Catholic/traditionalist, as DeMallie interprets him, Black Elk was able to absorb both religions into his spiritual view. Furthermore, Holler argues, Black Elk's discussion in Joseph Brown's *The Sacred Pipe* contains a recipe for a modernized and revitalized religion and displays Lakota rites within a seven-sacrament matrix informed by Catholicism. For Holler, then, Black Elk was a religious innovator, able to employ different vehicles to articulate the sacred. It is odd that Holler does not perceive John Neihardt in much the same way, for a historical look at Neihardt might reveal the diversity of his views and methods.

One can discern Forbes's paradigm in the assessment of *Black Elk Speaks* by these and other critics—the beliefs we have reviewed favor either one religion or another but not at the same time: a Native American traditionalist view, an orthodox Christian view, and the perception of simultaneous religions. And although it might be easy to confute one secondary work with another as a dialectic exercise, it is not the fault of these books that Black Elk is greater and more complex than the critical works he has inspired or that *Black Elk Speaks* is more powerful and engulfing than any critical work. But these commentators and their like have performed several valuable services by wrestling with their questions.

Rice, for example, identifies a tendency within the dominant culture to incorporate what historian Francis Jennings cites as the conqueror's discourse, which Jennings thoroughly dissects in *The Invasion of America: Indians, Colonialism, and the Cant of Conquest*. Although Rice interprets Neihardt's *Song of the Messiah* as literal instead of ironic—a position not congruent with Neihardt's actions and writings, as we will observe later—Rice is correct in sounding the alert to colonial misappropriation of subjects in multicultural works. Some of this misappropriation, though, is derived from academic commentators seeking a one-size-fits-all explanation for a bicultural expression, but only an explanation that emerges from Western tradition. Rice's presentation of Lakota contexts for Black Elk's telling is also informative, providing us with a fuller picture of the traditional Black Elk. Of particular importance is Rice's directing the reader to the Walker material, which helps contextualize Black Elk's formative background.

Steltenkamp's book, although fired with the zeal of true belief, nevertheless also gives us a fuller picture of Black Elk—a man operating in a reconstructed social world and an expressive system of reservation Catholicism, in many ways different from its European counterpart. Steltenkamp's own findings, moreover, show us how fluid the boundaries were between that system and traditional belief: Black Elk, the aged catechist, is cured of his stroke in a traditional ghost ceremony held by his friend Little Warrior (123–125), bending the boundaries of orthodox Catholicism quite a bit in the days before modern ecumenism.

Holler's desire to see the points of mediation among disparate views of Black Elk reflects the natural impulse of the intellectual in the Euro-American tradition to seek and understand the point at which thesis converges on antithesis. For that alone it is valuable, since it reflects what scholars within this culture often do when confronted with opposites that seem plausible. In his informative study Holler eschews DeMallie's conjecture that Black Elk was first one kind of believer and then another. Instead, Holler proposes that for Black Elk, Lakota traditionalism and Lakota Catholicism may simply have fulfilled different aspects and that Black Elk may not have been thinking in terms of mutually incompatible assertions, each claiming to be true. Rather he was working within different means of manifesting the spiritual.

THIS ABILITY OF BLACK ELK'S (AND NEIHARDT'S) SPIRITUALITIES TO SURMOUNT and embrace different traditions has, then, caused difficulties for many in the academic world seeking to distill a certain "canonical" view—a single Lakota religion, a single Caucasian point of view, even a single Catholicism. Such thinking in discrete, abstract categories may not be the best way to approach complex examples incorporating non-European cultures, let alone European ones. For example, many commentators on *Black Elk Speaks* rely on the Walker documents. Walker, a government doctor at Pine Ridge, collected narratives from men who often belonged to the generation senior to Black Elk. These men did not agree on all points regarding spiritual practices and ceremonies, a point that troubled Walker himself as he tried to construct a canonical depiction of the Sun Dance, for instance (see 25–26, 29–32, 37, 50, 65). So those who study the Walker material must allow for the diverse beliefs of its Lakota contributors. Yet in discussions of *Black Elk Speaks* one may hear the term *Lakota religion* or *Oglala religion* as if there were a single, catechizable doctrine applying to all. Even Christianity's influence on the Lakota is part of a centuries-long process of filtration, absorption, and contact rather than an instantaneous appearance and construction within a newly instituted reservation system, as missionaries and traders had long been in contact with the Lakota and their allies. The question of whether there is one type of Christianity has at times riven the European Church to its core: we should not be surprised, then, if gradations, modifications, and adaptations of traditional and Christian beliefs have appeared during the history of Pine Ridge. In certain cases we may not even be able to identify whether something is wholly Christian or traditionally Lakota in its intent.

Now let us further cloud Euro-American categorizations by recalling the problems historically besetting government officials, Euro-American observers, and scholars struggling even to understand not religion but polity—the seeming fluidity of an entire tribe or band as it responded to its external environment and answered its internal needs. Different leaders and configurations emerged depending on circumstance. Who was the "chief"? Who decided what, and when? Through what governing construct was consensus about social action achieved? Who represented the nation? These questions affected anthropology, negotiation, and treaties. For example, U.S. history is replete with examples of government commissioners failing to identify the band fathers and assuming that generals were chiefs. With functions determined by custom, bands possessed different social organizations that came into operation to respond to different contingencies. These modes of organization have been called *poses*—an unfortunate term suggesting insincerity—but in *The Indian in America*, Wilcomb E. Washburn reviews the positive, responsive nature of these different structural modes and how populations were cued to employ them or make them effective (47–51). The important point is that whatever configuration a tribe or band assumed to meet a specific task, it was still a unity, a whole. It was true to its internal needs, values, and aspirations, although from the viewpoint of the Eurocentric outsider its external appearances changed radically.

Similarly, one might say that Lakota individuals who exhibit Christianity in one mode and traditional beliefs in another are perhaps expressing parts of a unified spiritual vision greater in scope than any sectarianism. A particular expression of spirituality might emerge for one purpose and a different expression for another, but these expressions proceed from a unified perception. This unity can obtain even if a Euro-American construction such as a monolithic "Lakota religion" is absent. For instance, Thomas Lewis, a physician at Pine Ridge during the 1960s and 1970s, writes of an informant whose spiritual dimension expressed itself in a variety of ways. He "not only retained a working position in the Catholic Church; conducted Sun Dances; and officiated at frequent Eagle pipe ceremonies, sweat bath ceremonies, and weddings, but also, with some uneasiness, I thought, was an officer in the Native American Church" (105). If no single viewpoint can represent "all" Lakota belief, one must not assume that Black Elk's beliefs could be represented that way.

THESE ISSUES ENTANGLE WITH LITERARY PROBLEMS ELEGANTLY ANALYZED BY Sally McCluskey and Michael Castro, whose responses to *Black Elk Speaks* will be taken up later in this book. Essentially, though, John Neihardt must have perceived the force and coherence in Black Elk's spiritual perceptions, and he strove to evoke that engulfing unity in literature in a way European Americans could assimilate. What Neihardt sought in presenting Black Elk (and others) was to give readers a glimpse of a total, powerful, ineffable world—a world that could not be described simply by the everyday language of history and observation but that could be accessed through the medium of poetry and other arts that, Neihardt believed, served as conduits to enhanced consciousness. Neihardt wished to recapture the speaker's discourse—a formal eloquence Black Elk's granddaughter Esther DeSersa remembered (*Lives* 132). To do so he tried to fashion an appropriate literary style that would employ Euro-American techniques of poetry. This enhanced perception was not to be achieved through verbal art alone, for Standing Bear's paintings formed an important part of the first edition of Neihardt's book. These paintings portray historical and visionary events in a vivid ledger-art style, uniting the pictograph with paper.

It is unfortunate that the 1932 preface, explaining Black Elk's contact with what Neihardt called the higher values, and the 1972 preface, which related Neihardt's desire to absorb and relate the emotional impact of the interviews rather than to provide ethnography, remained absent from the edition of *Black Elk Speaks* often cited for academic reference—the Bison edition of 1988 and its reprints. As well, it is regrettable that the portfolio of paintings by Standing Bear was incompletely represented. The book's original design fusing collaborative voices, narrative in the old high style of rhetorical eloquence, lyric, song, and picture was thus partly lost and with it the impact of Neihardt's effort.

From 1996 through 1999 I discussed with Hilda and Robin Neihardt the necessity of returning these items to the text of the book so its audience could understand the holistic goals and achievements of *Black Elk Speaks,* accomplishments we will examine further in the present volume. The "Twenty-First Century Edition" of *Black Elk Speaks,* released in the fall of 2000, has such additions, returning to the text material necessary to appreciate it. In addition, Esther Black Elk DeSersa and Olivia Black Elk Pourier—granddaughters of Black Elk—have described the Black Elks' home life, interaction with the Neihardts, and Black Elk's integrity within spiritual traditions in their book *Black Elk Lives,* edited by Hilda Neihardt and Lori Utecht. The sisters have chosen not to respond directly to a number of extraneous comments made about Black Elk, John Neihardt, and their families that are the by-products of emotionally charged presentations within the academy.

Discussions with the Neihardts also indicated the importance of the photographs documenting the Black Elk family's education and cultural integration of the Neihardts through ceremony. Several such photographs are retained in the new edition of *Black Elk Speaks,* and extensive coverage of this part of John Neihardt's interviews of Black Elk can be found in Hilda Neihardt's *Black Elk and Flaming Rainbow.* Readers will note that these interviews took place in an atmosphere of sharing, community, and cultural immersion, the totality of which affected the production of *Black Elk Speaks* as a work of art.

INDEED IT IS NO WONDER THAT *BLACK ELK SPEAKS* LOOKS LIKE ART AND READS as poetry, for John Neihardt believed the arts conducted one to spiritual understanding—for him the preeminent value. As we examine *Black Elk Speaks* through studying its context, its craft, and the reactions to it, we will observe different aspects of Black Elk's vision as perceived by Neihardt and expressed in diverse ways by both collaborators. And we may recognize in *Black Elk Speaks* a work of literature with a distinctive language and a linguistic heritage that still has impact for those of diverse traditions. Clearing away the critical brambles and focusing on the book itself, we may begin to see *Black Elk Speaks.*

2
OTHERS *Speak*

WE MIGHT BEGIN BY STRIVING FOR BALANCE IN ASSESSING *BLACK ELK SPEAKS*, attainable if we understand both the book's role as a literary expression and the author's artistic challenges in creating it. John Neihardt faced the literary task of presenting Black Elk's vision-talk and other discourse so it would have an appropriate impact on readers from the dominant culture. Now Ben Black Elk, hearing what his father was discussing for the first time, pronounced it

---

Portions of this chapter are taken from my presentation at the Spring Neihardt Conference in Bancroft, Nebraska, on April 25, 1998. The theme of that gathering was "John Neihardt, the Writer: New Critical Perspectives." Thanks to my copresenters, Lori Utecht and Tim Anderson, for stimulating discussion regarding Neihardt the literary and public writer. An article derived from this presentation appeared as "*Black Elk Speaks* and Some Discontents" in the *Neihardt Journal* and is listed in the bibliography.

"wonderful" (H. Neihardt, *Black Elk* 53), and according to Hilda Neihardt, Nick Black Elk's speech in that context was for his granddaughters also poetic (Interview). Esther Black Elk DeSersa recalls that during the interviews "I'd sit there and listen to them talk, because the words sounded like rhymes, music—a rhythm. . . . Mom was giving me the cups and I'd take the coffee and pour it out very slow, just to listen to them." She states:

> What fascinated me was the rhythm in the way my grandfather talked in Lakota. It just had a rhythm, the way he talked. And then the way my dad [Ben Black Elk] brought it out in English, it rhymed now and then. The language sounded like a rhythm. I always wanted to bring the coffee to them, because I wanted to listen. (*Lives* 132)

John Neihardt needed to cast Ben's translation into poetic language again, into words that would evoke the spirit of the original. "I would use as much of your language in it as possible," Neihardt had assured Black Elk in the November 6, 1930, letter that set the project going; "I want to tell the things that you and your friends know, and I can promise you that it will be an honest and a loving book" (c3716 f39).

Analyzing crucial and "poetic" parts of *Black Elk Speaks,* former Neihardt student Sally McCluskey[1] wrote an article that, although upholding Neihardt in his task, has in many ways been as misunderstood as the misunderstanding she was trying to correct. McCluskey and Neihardt wanted us to realize that Neihardt was not a mere recorder or transcriber but a coauthor of *Black Elk Speaks* in a collaborative context. Neihardt, in fact, had provided McCluskey with this statement:

> *Black Elk Speaks* is a work of art with two collaborators, the chief one being Black Elk. My function was both creative and editorial. I think he knew the kind of person I was when I came to see him—I am referring to the mystical strain in me and all my work. . . . And I think he knew I was the tool—no, the medium—he needed for what he wanted to get said. And my attitude toward what he has said to me is one of religious obligation.
>
> But it is absurd to suppose that the use of the first person singular is not a literary device, by which I mean that Black Elk did not sit and tell me his story in chronological order. At times considerable editing was necessary, but it was always worth the editing. The beginning and the ending are mine; they are what he would have said if he had been able. At times I changed a word, a sentence, sometimes created a

> paragraph. And the translation—or rather the *transformation*—of what was given me was expressed so that it could be understood by the white world.[2] (quoted in McCluskey 238–239; italics in the original)

For McCluskey, the editorial choices John Neihardt made, for example the arrangement of interview material that emerged topically into chronological order, are as important to the artistic unity of the work as is Neihardt's choice of diction: the use of strong, non-Latinate words and simple, active phrasing (240–241). For her, *Black Elk Speaks* is, as Neihardt had expressed to his publisher, a book as "written through" Neihardt (234–235). This is a book that, like a conventional poem, can select material for presentation in an English heightened to reflect the eloquence and point of its telling.

Black Elk Speaks is also a text that at its outset disclaims being a conventional autobiography or ethnographical document—"orthodox" by dominant culture standards. The beginning declares the book a synecdoche, a part reflecting a universal whole or a small experience reflecting a great one. The title explains that the book is "as told through." Remember the beginning of *Black Elk Speaks,* which states that the book is not a personal biography but the "story of all life that is holy"; that early in the text the reader is reminded that the personal elements such as hunting, traveling, and warfare are only seemingly important next to the spiritual issues (1–2). This is as close to a qualifying thesis statement as a work of literature will likely provide. It posits a "holographic" quality in which the particular is a reflection of the universal, and the personal is only relevant as an expression of a larger group.

Such an emphasis, which Neihardt distilled from his interaction with Black Elk and presented in the opening of *Black Elk Speaks,* is characteristic of Native American accounts, as Arnold Krupat, a student of the form, has noticed: "So far as one may generalize . . . it does seem to be the case that Native American autobiography is marked by the figure of synecdoche in its presentation of the self" (231). H. David Brumble also notes that the task of such an "autobiography" may involve suppressing the personal (182). And Ruth Rosenberg reminds us that "the contents of the medicine bag are synecdoches," as is Lame Deer's biography (xix–x).

Resembling that later book, *Black Elk Speaks* is not the norm for autobiography in the dominant culture, to be sure, but at its very beginning Neihardt describes editorial choices to avoid compromising the material:

> My friend, I am going to tell you the story of my life, as you wish; and if it were only the story of my life I think I would not tell it; for what is

> one man that he should make much of his winters, even when they bend him like a heavy snow? So many other men have lived and shall live that story, to be grass upon the hills.
>
> It is the story of all life that is holy and is good to tell, and of us two-leggeds sharing in it with the four-leggeds and the wings of the air and all green things; for these are children of one mother and their father is one Spirit.
>
> This, then, is not the tale of a great hunter or of a great warrior, or of a great traveler, although I have made much meat in my time and fought for my people both as boy and man, and have gone far and seen strange lands and men. (1)

Although these editorial delimitations are effective, some have tasked Neihardt with various types of textual colonialism in words such as these:

1. "Raymond DeMallie's transcripts show how much the original diction was heightened into biblical cadences" (Ruth Rosenberg, introduction to Washington Square "Enriched" edition of *Lame Deer, Seeker of Visions* xii).
2. "As an artist, Neihardt was a descendant of such thoroughly Christian writers as John Milton and Nathaniel Hawthorne" (Julian Rice, associating Neihardt with a Christian idea of progress in *Black Elk's Story: Distinguishing Its Lakota Purpose* 43).
3. "Even more surprising, as Michael Castro has noted, is that Neihardt invented parts of Black Elk's vision, such as the fourth ascent" (Hertha Wong, in *Sending My Heart Back Across the Years: Tradition and Innovation in Native American Autobiography* 121).

Did John Neihardt transform the "original diction" into King Jamesean prose? Does the ominous specter of Puritan providentialism loom behind *Black Elk Speaks*? Do the DeMallie presentations or the original transcripts reveal that there was no "Fourth Ascent"?

First, let us consider the issue of diction and what has been said about it. McCluskey compares the diction in *Black Elk Speaks* with that of a part of *The Sacred Pipe*, "Recorded and Edited by Joseph Epes Brown," and finds that Brown's diction and cadence, although conveying Black Elk's message, are prosaic while Neihardt's are poetic (240–241). The assumption is that since Brown views himself as a transcriber and that since Neihardt is a poet, we will see a more actively poetic diction in *Black Elk Speaks*. Yet recall that profound statements tend to sound poetic and that in both cases Black Elk is conveying his message to his son, Ben, for translation—which, at least in its early stage, is "unpoetic." In fact, the text of *Black Elk Speaks* actually shares certain similarities with the text of *The Sacred Pipe*. Breaking up the text into free-verse paragraphs may help us notice just how "poetic" Brown's text becomes.

FROM "THE GIFT OF THE SACRED PIPE"
This round rock,
which is made of the same red stone as the bowl of the pipe,
your Father *Wakan-Tanka* has also given to you.
It is the Earth,
your Grandmother and Mother,
and it is where you will live and increase.
This Earth which He has given you is red,
and the two-leggeds who live upon the Earth are red;
and the Great Spirit has also given to you a red day,
and a red road. (7)

FROM "INIPI: THE RITE OF PURIFICATION"
And as we light the fire,
always on the side facing east,
we pray:
"O *Wakan-Tanka*, this is Your eternal fire
that has been given to us on this great island!
It is Your will
that we build this place in a sacred manner." (33)

Other examples abound; see pages 53, 129, and 130 for "poetic" language in Brown. Did Brown, too, "heighten" the language of the holy man, making it biblical in cadence? Or is the truth perhaps that religious expression tends to be formal and incantatory in tone? Compare the curing prayer on page 201 of the 1988 Bison edition of *Black Elk Speaks*, but now set into the same kind of free-verse pattern with strong percussive beats behind each line (Black Elk is relating that he accompanies this prayer with the drum):

My Grandfather, Great Spirit,
you are the only one
and to no other
can any one send voices.
You have made everything, they say,
and you have made it good and beautiful.
The four quarters and the two roads

> crossing each other,
> you have made. Also you have set
> a power where the sun goes down.
> The two-leggeds on earth
> are in despair.
> For them, my Grandfather,
> I send a voice to you.

McCluskey notices that Neihardt emphasizes the poetic over the unpoetic in his telling but perhaps needs to elaborate on the origin of this style, which she implicitly defines as the free verse it approaches. She states that "Neihardt, throughout the book, used parallelism and other means to insure the rhythm of his prose, and he often began sentences with 'And,' a device that often makes the prose echo the King James version of the Bible" (241); perhaps this is the origin of Rosenberg's comment quoted earlier. Such "ands" could have arrived through the influence of Whitman as well. Yet the 1931 transcription of the stenographic notes also contains the same device of speech, fresh from the interview. Note the cumulative repetition, rhythm, parallelism, and use of "and," as we saw in the material recorded by Brown:

> The bay horse said to me: "Behold them, your horses come dancing." I looked around and saw millions of horses circling around me—a sky full of horses. Then the bay horse said: "Make haste." The horse began to go beside me and the forty-eight horses followed us.
>
> I looked around and all the horses that were running changed into buffalo, elk, and all kinds of animals and fowls and they all went back to the four corners.
>
> I followed the bay horse and it took me to a place on a cloud under a rainbow gate and there were sitting my six grandfathers sitting inside of a rainbow door and the horses stopped behind me. (c3716 f414, 3)

Page 16 of the same folder of transcriptions even contains a King Jamesean second-person "thy" (used twice) when the southern spirit is about to reveal to Black Elk how badly his people were faring.

Now DeMallie tells us that in his presentation of the transcript material he has edited out the run-ons from the sentence structure, has organized material into paragraphs, and has converted second-person "thy/thou" to "you/your" (*Sixth* xxv). Yet Father Buechel's *Grammar of Lakota,* printed initially in 1939, lists second-person personal pronouns as translated into thou/thee

(20–21). In many ways, then, the DeMallie renditions are less "poetic" than the actual transcripts, which reflect bursts of thought, use run-on constructions, and vary in pronoun choice. The point is that Neihardt found license for what he did in what was already there. Secondarily, we see that Ben as interpreter was sensitive to the second-person plural and that Neihardt appears to have toned it down because of, not in spite of, its archaic quality.

Next let us consider the issue of latent Puritanism and the Idea of Progress. Does John Neihardt impart a providential scheme of Christian evolution, a version of the Idea of Progress in which the first peoples must be eliminated on the course to Salvation? Did he believe in such in the first place? Julian Rice sees Neihardt as a rabid Christian convinced that the Native American must be crucified on the cross of progressive modernity (xi). For Rice, Neihardt was an evangelical racist who believed the Indians must die to effect apocalyptic renewal (xi, 49–50, 60–61). As Neihardt has commented, however, the real victors of the conflict between Indians and the United States were Sitanka's Ghost Dancers massacred at Wounded Knee because "they'd seen the greatest vision that man has seen, of the relation of man to man, and to all life" (undated transcript of interview 11, c3716 f498). Furthermore, Neihardt's address at Wayne State College, on June 25, 1954, explains that the victors at Wounded Knee in December 1890 "were the defeated," since "they had seen the great vision of the unity and holiness of all life and the brotherhood of man" (c3716 ac 52). In that same talk Neihardt proclaims Native American religion "fundamentally true"—hardly the sentiments of a Puritan believer in the dominant culture's Idea of Progress.

And we might recall that the *Cycle of the West* ends with an assault on an indigenous culture that is spiritually advanced and socially cohesive. By contrast, the conquering culture's spiritual barbarity is characterized by extreme individualism reinforced by its technology, emblematic of the modern problem as a whole, as Neihardt elsewhere reminds us: "Science saves thousands upon thousands of bodies, yet the bland cruelties of our barbaric social system continue; and periodically we destroy human bodies in wholesale quantities by strictly scientific methods" (*Poetic* 43). For Neihardt, the literatures of oppressed cultures might in fact embody the best values; since the dominant culture only rewards grasping materialism, heedless of human consequences, then "in that scramble of the acquisitive instincts, to cherish the higher values as evolved through ages of race experience, is to ensure defeat" (*Laureate Address* 16). For Neihardt, there was no "progress" toward an end-time event on earth, no certainty that spirituality would ensure a comfortable temporal existence, and no providential evolution.

Several writers about *Black Elk Speaks* have assumed that *A Cycle of the West*, and *The Twilight of the Sioux* within it, demonstrate otherwise and suggest that those beliefs appear in *Black Elk Speaks*. Both Clyde Holler and Rice, for example, subscribe to the view that *Black Elk Speaks* depicts the end of the Indian. Rice references *Twilight* to delineate what he believes is Neihardt's interpretation of history as a typologically marked annihilation of the Indian along the evolutionary path to an end-time glory. But these ideas are not Neihardt's.

In *A Cycle of the West*, *The Twilight of the Sioux* fulfills its histories using a language and form familiar to the Euro-American reader, but its intent is not to reassure that reader. Instead, with its patterns, repetitions, and elaborations, *A Cycle of the West* presents alternative views of the American experience, and *The Twilight of the Sioux*—its very title suggesting diurnal cycles—well demonstrates the reverse side of that westward expansion so glorified as triumph.

Twilight is written in response to such triumphant images, written to teach the dominant culture of John Neihardt's day and beyond. It lulls, startles, and then shames the Euro-American reader by using Euro-American culture's language, symbol, and very typology—its expected templates of situation—to communicate through irony and reversal a view of history quite different from the mainstream, canonical propaganda and to help guide that reader to a broader understanding of the issues implicit in a not-so-tidy or manifest or inevitable destiny. Throughout, the reader from the dominant culture may discover that the values he or she professes are those of the original residents, not the invaders.

We recall that the seizure and domination of the lands of the Americas had very early on caused European theorists to develop a unitary, linear concept of social evolution—the "argument" of which, as historian J. H. Elliott remarks, "postulated a sequence of development from barbarism to civility" and that was current although by no means universally accepted by the end of the sixteenth century (50). Of course, it was the European cultures that considered themselves "civil" both spiritually and materially, despite their thirst for land, gold, and domination over the supposedly barbarous. This "evolutionary" model continued to inform propaganda justifying expansionism and appropriation of the lands of indigenous peoples.

In contrast, *The Twilight of the Sioux* shows us repeated examples of Indians fighting for home, hearth, and the highest spiritual values, those

Who saw the end of sacred things and dear
In all this wild beginning; saw with fear

Ancestral pastures gutted by the plow,
The bison harried ceaselessly, and how
They dwindled moon by moon; with pious dread
Beheld the holy places of their dead
The mock of aliens. (*Wars* 3)

And *The Twilight* depicts the barbarous invaders, characterized thus by Sitting Bull:

Tireless in toil,
These madmen think it good to till the soil,
And love for endless getting marks them fools.
Behold, they bind their poor with many rules
And let their rich go free! They even steal
The poor man's little for the rich man's weal!
Their feeble have a god their strong may flout!
They cut the land in pieces, fencing out
Their neighbors from the mother of all men!
When she is sick, they make her bear again
With medicines they give her with the seed!
All this is sacrilegious! Yet they heed
No word, and like a river in the spring
They flood the country, sweeping everything
Before them! (*Wars* 33)

These "madmen" create the westwarding, restless, moving broken lines of the frontiers advancing across the new continent from the subdued old world—a gothic invasion indeed, a colonizing of a people whose metaphor for relationship with the world is natural and organic by a people whose social metaphor is the machine. Consider the types of mechanisms enumerated in *The Twilight* as characteristic of the invaders: the mowing machine, the mechanical saw, the train, the steamboat, the Gatling and the Hotchkiss gun. The gold-crazed invaders even arrive clanking like automatons and thundering like factories:

Then yonder on the Yellowstone was heard
The clank of sabers; and the red men saw
How Long Hair, still the Wolf of Washita,
Went spying with his pack along the stream,
While others, bitten with a crazy dream,

Were driving stakes and peeping up the flat.
Just so it was that summer on the Platte
Before the evil came. And devil boats
Came up with stinking thunder in their throats
To scare the elk and make the bison shy. (*Wars* 105–106)

Neihardt tells us in the introduction to *The Twilight* that in devising his epic he had "no thought of synthetic *Iliads* and *Odysseys*, but only of the richly human saga-stuff" of the land with which he is acquainted (vi). Yet consistent reminders of those epics appear in *The Twilight of the Sioux*, such as echoes of Troy in the opening of part ten of the *Song of the Indian Wars* in which men gather in a holy cause to repulse the mad, gold-crazed invaders:

And, mightier than any maiden's eyes,
The Lilith-lure of Perilous Emprise
Was setting all the young men's blood astir.
How fair the more than woman face of her
Whose smile has gulfed how many a daring prow!
What cities burn for jewels on her brow;
Upon her lips what vintages are red!
Her lovers are the tallest of the dead
Forever. When the streams of Troas rolled
So many heroes seaward, she was old;
Yet she is young forever to the young. (121)

Neihardt's choice of epic form and allusion is most useful in this context. It is a style of narrative traditional in Euro-American culture and is familiar to Neihardt's readers from school-day studies of the *Iliad* and the *Odyssey*, for that form is the narrative vehicle of those very Indo-Europeans who swept westward, consuming and conquering, like the prairie locusts early in *The Song of the Indian Wars* (37–38). Here, however, epic is at the service of those whom the dominant culture invades, thus achieving an editorial irony but also demonstrating the worthiness of the Indian position—an epic cause well worth fighting and dying for.

A similar use of artistic irony and reversal appears in the deployment of typology to present this epic history. In the Euro-American tradition, typology ponders scriptural parallelism and foreshadowing, occurrences in the Old Testament that prefigure events in the New. Euro-American sermon making and religious literature have a rich and sometimes tortuous heritage of the study of such prefiguring: one recurring example is that of Adam's fall as it relates to a tree foreshadowing Christ's redemption of humanity while crucified on a tree. Another pairing is that of Adam and Eve succumbing to temptation in Paradise and Jesus resisting temptation in the wilderness. And such Christian providentialism does indeed employ typology to justify God's ways to Man.

Although Neihardt employs parallels resembling the typology familiar to the dominant culture, he uses them to demonstrate the thrusting of a world into bondage rather than to illustrate its deliverance. Little Big Man holds Crazy Horse, the thirty-year-old Man of Sorrows, from behind so he can be pierced with a bayonet. Later, Sitting Bull is seized by some of his own people and pierced with a bullet. Finally, Sitanka is sequestered by the apparently friendly Forsyth so his skull can be pierced with a rifle butt. Sitanka's sacrifice occurs at a moment of epiphany during which time stops: he sees into the heart of things and knows the brotherhood of all humanity—an epiphany denied the conquerors, whose humanity has vanished. Reinforcing these prefigurings, parallels, and repetitions is religious phraseology previously used by Sitanka that references the wounding of the Messiah (of the Spirit Dance or the Bible)—"The Savior's wound grows beautiful in you! / Lift up your hearts made holy with the spear!" (*Messiah* 94)—as well as the narrator's earlier remark that "the frail flesh, crucified, / Forgot the Spirit" (*Messiah* 91).

Another and heavily ironic use of such pairings unfolds because the Spirit Dancers are looking westward to Wovoka for spiritual guidance even as the invaders hearken westward for gold, their spiritual destruction. Dissolution is prefigured right at the outset, since when Good Thunder, Kicking Bear, and the rest go to investigate the messiah religion, the poem remarks, "So once again the man-compelling West, / Sad mother of dissolving worlds, lured on" (*Messiah* 13). There is also the extension of typology itself through Wovoka, as interpreted by Kicking Bear in the poem:

> I tell you He is Jesus come again!
> I saw the marks upon Him! It is so!
> Have not the Black Robes told how long ago
> One came to save the people? It is He!
> Did not Wasichus nail Him to a tree? (*Messiah* 29)

The undulating, recursive qualities of this epic narrative are not unlike Nebraska's rolling hills or the undulating Missouri River, and they suggest Neihardt's views on historiography. Deeply embedded in that European notion of "evolution" from hunting to agrarian to industrial culture—the latter two often termed *civilization* by those who reside in them—has been the concept Neihardt distrusted that civilization is an upward-climbing path, that humanity is progressing toward a better state. But Neihardt's idea that history is built of cycles, shared by many writers of the premodern periods, resonates in the title *Cycle of the West.* It is certainly within the context of Neihardt's narrative that we witness the ascendancy of materialism and the trampling of spirituality. It may be possible for conditions to reverse.

Definitely, Neihardt's letters to the poet George Sterling, pondering the repeating rise and fall of humanity throughout time, and statements in "The White Radiance" (October 30, 1926) dovetail with Neihardt's perception of history and refute the sometimes postulated image of Neihardt as awaiting salvation as one of the Elect or even as believer in the rapture of a dialectical materialism. For these letters to Sterling, written during the teens through the 1920s—that is, prior to Neihardt's meeting Black Elk—contain discussions of philosophy and worldviews in which Sterling, it seems, is an optimist. But to Sterling, Neihardt expresses the view that the heights of human achievement may repeat as well as the depths. Neihardt disagrees with Sterling's conventional idea of progress as an upward-moving straight line or curve. Neihardt insists that humanity's experience is instead a continual rise and fall of looped script, L-shaped oval lines. At different places and times humanity has reached heights and may do so again—but the depths too will repeat:

> Progress seems to me an illusion. As I conceive it, we do not proceed toward perfection upon an ascending straight line; not even upon an upward curve. I would diagram the course of Civilization like this: ℓℓℓℓℓℓℓℓℓ etc.
>
> The height has already been reached often; often we have fallen. This is a world of endless struggle. If anything like the Ideal is ever to be attained, it will be in some spiritual existence—certainly not in a world where guts are so important. (July 17, 1916; c3074)

Perhaps Neihardt's early education in the classics disposed him to consider the present age as a decline or degeneration, not an inevitable rung on the ladder of progress. As Neihardt speculates in *Poetic Values,* likely the past was golden, and the materialist present, dross (Ghose 4–5).

Significantly, Rice remarks that the missionaries who induced Black Elk's temporary "recantation" did not notice any of Neihardt's alleged "almost heavy-handed urging of a doctrine of spiritual evolution in harmony with their own" (42). In contrast, something made the missionaries very uneasy. It was not a doctrine of such evolution, for Neihardt did not embrace that idea. It was something else. In fact, as Hilda Neihardt relates, trouble occurred right after *Black Elk Speaks* was published. Black Elk was terrified because the missionaries (who could invoke civil authority against the old beliefs as "Indian Offenses") pressured him, told him he had apostatized, that he was going to hell. Notwithstanding the pressure to recant and the difficult situation it engendered, the problem dissipated, and the Neihardt and Black Elk families remained friends (Interview). What made the missionaries jumpy, in an age predating ecumenism, were definitely not Christian overtones in *Black Elk Speaks*.

If there were explicitly Puritan overtones, we should see them. Black Elk is not punished with guilt for his affair with the young woman in Paris. His admirer neither gives birth nor wears a scarlet "A." We might, then, dismiss baleful Hawthornian influence in *Black Elk Speaks*. There is a sense of regret, as when Black Elk remarks that he should have followed his great vision instead of being confused by a lesser one: "I have thought much about this since, and I have thought that this was where I made my great mistake. I had had a very great vision, and I should have depended only upon that to guide me to the good" (249–250). But there is no sense of damnation, original sin, worry over salvation and grace. At the end, in spite of everything, Black Elk hopes the tree will yet flower, and the rain he requests does come.

We must be careful as well with assertions that a Miltonic cast pervades Neihardt, such as Rice's understanding that since Neihardt undoubtedly read Milton, he must be influenced by the old Puritan (43). In fact, Rice conjectures that "Neihardt was a self-professed man of letters. His education would almost certainly have included the English and American authors most widely accepted as major, and as models for serious poetry" (42).

But this cannot be stated categorically. Neihardt's education, whether formal or self-directed, almost certainly included some English and American authors disfavored as "models for serious poetry" as well, for Neihardt read extensively. His personal collection of approximately 5,000 books, preserved as the Neihardt Memorial Library at the University of Missouri, may represent a fraction of the intellectual input Neihardt devoured. These books include works by logical positivists such as Bertrand Russell, spiritualists, historians, literati, even writings on practical farming. And it is very tendentious, if not Puritanically deterministic, to argue that simply because a writer encounters a particular book, a worldview and behavior are inexorably determined by that text. After fifty active years of life, most spent reading, reviewing, and writing, the mature collaborator with Black Elk would hardly be the disciple of the profligate Swinburne he recited or the moody, brooding Tennyson he read as a boy—let alone a twisted version of Milton or Hawthorne.

Even the youthful Neihardt, allegedly steeped in the thin, bitter gruel of Puritanism but actually in the employ of a freethinking stonecutter interested in Hinduism, authored a madcap satire on revivalism in which the hellfire preacher and his venue meet with ironic demise (Neihardt, *All* 73–75). It would be well to recall Neihardt's strongly worded reaction to pompous partisanship in general, especially as it affects the production of art. Writing to George Sterling on September 30, 1924, Neihardt rejects Upton Sinclair's notion of "all art being inescapably propaganda" and declares that it is wrong "for a man to tie himself to any dogmatic belief in this shifting cosmos" (c3074).

It *is* worthwhile to consider whether any technical influences on Neihardt emerge from his familiarity with other writers, but even there one must be cautious when thinking of Milton, and one cannot assume that an ideology accompanies a technique. Within John Neihardt's epic, formalism is not quite the epic style of Milton. Note this often-circulated passage from *Paradise Lost*:

> Would thou hadst heark'nd to my words, and stayed
> With me, as I besought thee, when that strange
> Desire of wandring this unhappy Morn,
> I know not whence possessd thee; we had then
> Remaind still happy, not as now, despoild
> Of all our good, sham'd, naked, miserable. (IX. 1134–1139)

In Milton's verse paragraph, the sense runs past light caesuras all the way to the strong stop at the semicolon in line 1137; the caesura assumes a different position in each line or may become multiple, as in line 1139; compression of dropped vowels is indicated by contraction; and a tone of declamation, not wistfulness, characterizes the statement.

Now compare that passage to the treatment of loss in *The Song of the Messiah* in a verse paragraph describing events before the advent of Wovoka's message:

> "There is no hope for us," the old men said,
> "For we have sold our Mother to the lust
> Of strangers, and her breast is bitter dust,
> Her thousand laps are empty! She was kind
> Before the white men's seeing made us blind
> And greedy for the shadows they pursue.

> The fed-on shadows shall be shadows too;
> Their trails shall end in darkness. We have sinned;
> And all our story is a midnight wind
> That moans a little longer and is still.
> There was a time when every gazing hill
> Was holy with the wonder that it saw,
> And every valley was a place of awe,
> And what the grass knew never could be told.
> It was the living Spirit that we sold—
> And what can help us?" (*Messiah* 6–7)

This is epic but not necessarily Miltonic. It avoids Latinisms, speaking in plain diction, using mono- and disyllabic words that are not contractions. Enjambment does occur in that the sentences carry lightly through the rhyme and caesuras to their conclusion and move more freely than those in Milton's passage, the first line of which is particularly thumpy in declamatory cadence. In architecture and in rhythm, though, the passage's last six lines evoke Wordsworth more than Milton. Consider the "Ode on Intimations of Immortality" and its treatment of glory faded from the world:

> There was a time when meadow, grove, and stream,
> The earth, and every common sight
>   To me did seem
>   Apparell'd in celestial light,
> The glory and the freshness of a dream.
> It is not now as it hath been of yore;—
>   Turn wheresoe'er I may,
>   By night or day,
> The things which I have seen I now can see no more. (lines 1–9)

Although Wordsworth is obviously more in tune with the tradition of English poetry since Milton and uses archaisms and contractions as well as a different form, a degree of parallelism exists between the poems commencing with the "There was a time" lines. And this is true not just in word choice or initial cadence; both writers speak of a perceived alteration in nature, discuss a vanishing of spiritual power from an earth held in material thrall, and retrospect catastrophe. In the passage quoted, Neihardt is likely using features of the "Intimations Ode" to elicit recognition in readers familiar with Wordsworth's poem. This faint shadow of Wordsworth behind Neihardt's verse functions as a code reinforcing the loss of the paradisal. The construction of

Neihardt's epic lines does build upon the English iambic and conception of the epic, but Neihardt's approach is his own. It is hardly evangelical rant. And *Black Elk Speaks* is not the same as the *Cycle of the West,* nor is it in iambic pentameter. As McCluskey has deduced, in *Black Elk Speaks* the text resembles free verse.

Finally, let us consider Neihardt's editing practices as they relate to the notion that Neihardt installed an alien verbal citadel in Black Elk's text. Hertha Wong's apprehension that the Fourth Ascent is a fabrication not present in Black Elk's telling seems to derive from misunderstanding another critic's comment rather than from an inspection of DeMallie's edition of the transcripts of the 1931 interviews of Black Elk, for she claims that Michael Castro has proven Neihardt's falsification. We need, then, to have two points of departure in analysis. We need to see what Castro *did* say, then we need to look at the transcripts.

First, Castro notes that the transcripts of interviews do not constitute the complete body of information Black Elk presented to John Neihardt. Rather, contributing elements also included rapport, background, Black Elk's agenda, and ceremonial or casual interactions. These embraced even the everyday, ongoing aspects of Black Elk's behavior (82). All these encounters may have distilled the essence for Neihardt; the entire experience was a powerful communication about spirituality, values, endurance, and community and was so received—not just by John Neihardt but by the family as well. Enid's scrapbook records the total immersion in this physical and symbolic world of their hosts—the special tipi, meals, dance, and ceremonials (c3716 f468a)—as does Hilda Neihardt's book *Black Elk and Flaming Rainbow.* Black Elk used this total immersion in the Duhamel pageants as well, teaching Lakota children about their own culture by having them participate in it.

Neither was *Black Elk Speaks* a Neihardtian intrusion into Black Elk's life, but rather, as Castro reminds us, "the project was agreed upon by both men, and in a very real sense it had been initiated by Black Elk himself when he proposed to teach Neihardt, whom he knew to be a writer, 'the secrets of the Other World'" (84). Castro concludes that "Neihardt did, in fact, follow closely the English translation of Black Elk's narrative, as recorded in a transcript prepared from the original interviews by his daughter Enid" (85–86)—not Hilda, as Rice states in his introduction (ix)—and that such "stylistic heightening" as that McCluskey notices "represents a further tribute to Neihardt's ear for Indian idiom, even if it meant that, for the most part, he had the good sense to leave well enough alone" (86). And Castro notes that both those emendations that added to the text and those that compressed it were motivated by a profound desire to clarify the essence of Black Elk's message (89).

Castro then presents a passage in *Black Elk Speaks* that occurs "after the fourth and final ascent in which Black Elk sees himself restoring his fractured and fragmented nation to health with the aid of a sacred healing herb of power" (89). The added passage, which describes seeing the flowering tree in the center of a hoop of hoops, is, as Castro indicates, a distillation of Black Elk's expression rather than an "impressionistic judgment" (90). Castro warmly praises Neihardt's work and its affinity with the consciousness of its cocreator, even in its necessary condensation of digressions.

A copy of the 1931 transcript (c3716 f414, 14–23) shows that Black Elk discussed the Fourth Ascent, although his digressive presentation lacks the tautness of Neihardt's. An annotated copy follows the text of this chapter, so the reader may observe its existence as a part of the vision independent from John Neihardt (Figure 2.1). One may also find this chart of interest. It compares the pagination of the transcripts as presented by DeMallie in *The Sixth Grandfather: Black Elk's Teachings Given to John G. Neihardt,* the text of the 1931 transcriptions, and the 1988 University of Nebraska edition of *Black Elk Speaks,* the one most commonly cited in critical studies in recent years.

DEMALLIE, *THE SIXTH GRANDFATHER*

FIRST ASCENT, PAGES 125–126

Unified, prosperous people

SECOND ASCENT, PAGES 126–127

Traveling the "good road," unity with nature, people transformed into animals; closes with restlessness and fear

THIRD ASCENT, PAGE 127

Fear and difficulty—no one gets along

FOURTH ASCENT, PAGES 127–133

"Terrible" (127); poor, sick humans, destroyed village (128); but Black Elk heals the hoop (129)

BLACK ELK SPEAKS, 1988 BISON EDITION

FIRST ASCENT, PAGE 36

Happy, unified people

SECOND ASCENT, PAGES 36–37

A little harder going, people as animals, transition to Third Ascent (even this foreshadowing transition is in the original)

THIRD ASCENT, PAGES 37–38

Fearfulness, rugged climb, destruction of unity, war

FOURTH ASCENT, PAGES 38–42

Animals change back to humans, destruction; Black Elk heals the hoop (38-40)

1931 TRANSCRIPT BY ENID NEIHARDT

FIRST ASCENT, PAGES 14–15

SECOND ASCENT, PAGE 15

THIRD ASCENT, PAGES 15–16

FOURTH ASCENT, PAGES 16–22

Michael Castro's remarks should also caution critics who rely on the transcripts of the interviews as though they were the entire teaching Black Elk communicated to John Neihardt. We must recall several points. First, the typed transcripts Enid Neihardt made convert her shorthand, taken in the field, into regular orthography. This shorthand often employs "short forms" and contains explanatory annotations in normal handwriting (see examples in Figure 2.2). This is not necessarily clear from reading DeMallie's edited collation. Second, the transcripts do not reflect other situations intended or created by Black Elk to teach John Neihardt: elaborate Lakota ceremonials and candid discussions not set down in writing, such as Black Elk's first encounter with Neihardt, his commentary as they walked at the Wounded Knee site, or his actions and statements on the final hike up Harney Peak; changes in tone or voice; and conversations at home (see H. Neihardt, *Black Elk* throughout for examples). Third, John Neihardt possessed a phenomenal recall, as displayed late in life when he recited hundreds of lines of poetry from memory. Fourth, Neihardt relied on the entire experience—not just the transcript prepared by Enid, which he carefully employed—in writing *Black Elk Speaks* and in determining how the presentation could best fulfill Black Elk's wishes. Certainly, in so doing John Neihardt repoeticized the often tangled transcripts and reinforced chronological order to ensure that the visionary experience appeared as the book's core. And naturally, sections of *Black Elk Speaks* receive emphasis or the reverse with respect to the transcripts but with a poet's regard for the holy man's feelings. The final result is a book that, like a medicine bundle or a hologram, is a bit of the whole it represents. That Neihardt's abilities withstood the demanding obligation is astonishing and wonderful. That some have misunderstood is regrettable but understandable. Not ethnography, autobiography, biography, or history, although touching all, *Black Elk Speaks* must be appreciated on its own literary terms.

NOTES

1. Not "McClusky," as seen in Brumble x, 21.
2. Not "whole world," as appears in Castro 87.

Figure 2.1 (overleaf) c3716 f414 Pages 14–23, 1931 transcript of stenographic notes by Enid Neihardt: the Fourth Ascent and its aftermath (annotations mine). Courtesy, the John G. Neihardt Papers, c. 1858–1974, Western Historical Manuscript Collection, Columbia, Missouri; the John G. Neihardt Trust.

of the sacred hope." "This nation shall send a voice for their children." (means these people will prosper and increase.)
Song about the people increasing. (Words sung by the southern spirit.) :

"A voice I am sending as I walk. (twice)
A sacred hoop I wore.
Thus, a voice I send as I walk."(twice)

(to future generations) The first child they called for was by thename of Spotted Deer Woman. The next one I called for was Young Buffalo Woman. "Behold thy nation as they walk and to the first ascent they shall step as they walk." (meaning they are going to take them to the first ascent.) When they get to the first generation (ascent) all the creatures on the earth and in the air shall rejoice because the first ascents represent the people here on earth and they are going to multiply and increase and at the same time prosper. One of the old men said (showing me the sacred hoop): "Behold a good nation, a sacred nation, again they will walk towards good land, the land of plenty, and no suffering shall there be." "A nation you shall create and it shall be a sacred nation. " (meaning that he was given the power to raise a nation.) Song in 1st ascent:

First Ascent

"May you behold this I have asked to be made over. (twice
A good nation I have asked to be made over.
May you behold this I have asked to be made over. (twice
A sacred nation I have asked to be made over.
May you behold this I have asked to be made over."(twice

After singing this song, the people went on. When they got to the end, the men and women began sending voices for their children and again they stopped. (at the 2nd generation).
Note--(Black Elk says at this point he has a queer feeling all the time he is telling this, and that he is giving his power away, he feels--that he will die very soon afterward. His dream has been coming true. The first and second ascents were both good and the 3rd is to be a fearful thing and perhaps we're in that time now--something is going to happen. In the 3rd ascent people are going to transform themselves into all kinds of beasts. He knew something was going to happen in the war, so he didn't allow his son to go even tho' he wanted to. In Black Elk's days, he has

Note Black Elk's digression—discusses next two Ascents

seen the second generation and in the third he thinks something fearful is going to happen.)

The man of the south says: "Behold, thou shalt prevent the making of the clouds." (They were now at the second ascent and B. E. was given the power to defend his people at all dangerous times and to keep them from destruction.) South man says: "Behold thy nation they have given thee, for they ~~it~~ shall be like unto the animals and the fowls; thus they shall walk." As they started, the men and women were sending voices for their children again. At this moment the whole people walking on the Good Road transformed into buffaloes and elks and even fowls of the air and were travelling on the Good Road towards the north. As the beasts walked along, I saw that the Indians from thence on would be like unto the animals and will have rules of their own. As I noticed this, all the animals became restless and were all in fear and were afraid that they weren't what they were. This nation was walking in a sacred manner. Just before the people ~~beasts~~ stopped, I could hear them callings for their chiefs. They were scared and wanted the chiefs to come at once. After sending voices for their chiefs they stopped. The southern spirit said: "Behold thy nation walking in a sacred manner, from thence they shall walk in difficulty. Now you shall go forth to the center of thy nation's hoop." "Behold this, for you shall go forth to the center of the nation's hoop, with this you shall have power."

Second Ascent

(Wakan Shasha--Holy Man)

Note--(The third ascent represented all kinds of animals and fowls and from there on every man has his own vision and his own rules. The fourth ascent will be terrible.)

Third Ascent

They couldn't get along with us and they did not look after us. The birds and other animals are the only race that we really get along with. We, Indian race, and the beings on this earth--the buffalo, elk and birds in the air--they are just like relatives to us and we get along finely with them, for we get our power from them and from them we live. The white peo le came on this continent and put we Indians in a fence and they put another fence somewhere else and put our game into it. When the buffaloes and elks are all gone, the Great Spirit will look upon the whites for this and perhaps something will happen."

"Behold when you shall go forth to the center of the nation's hoop you shall run to the four quarters." (Nobody should be sacred before him. Wherever he goes, in front of him there will be no hard task for him. Every task he undertakes he will push through. It won't be hard for him either.)

Then the spirit sang a powerful song:

"The four quarters may you run to. (meaning that he will get his power from them.) No man will be sacred before thee. They have said to me."

At this time, everything that was given to me by the spirits I had. The man of the south said again to me: "Behold they grandfathers who have given thee the sacred relics." "Whenever you lo k upon an enemy, it shall tremble." (meaning that he shall conquer any kind of opposition.) "Remember this (meaning the cup of water he got), for from this the people shall have strength and power." As they stood ready to go on the fourth ascent of the earth, the south spirit said: "Look upon thy nati on." (the beasts transformed themselves into humans and they were all very poor.) ("Oh Gee, it was a sight!" says Black Elk.) There were lots of sick children--all pale, and it looked like a dying nation. They showed me a circle village and all the people were very poor in there. All the horses were hide and bones and here and there you could hear the wail of women and also men. Some of them were dying and some were dead. Quite an epidemic there. Again the southern spirit said: "Behold thy nation." (meaning they were going to show him something terrible. I am now ready to return to the earth after being in the air with the

Fourth Ascent Begins

fowls. The three ascents were all spiritual, but now I am to see the fourth quarter and in this they were showing me the difficulties. As I looked down upon the people, there stood on the north side a man nted red all over his body and he had with him a lance (Indian spear) he walked into the center of the sacred nation's hoop and lay down rolled himself on the ground and when he got up he was a buffalo tanding right in the center of the nation's hoop. The buffalo rolled and when he got up there was an herb there in his place. This herb plant grew up and bloomed so that I could see what it looked like--what kind of a herb it was from the bloom. After the buffalo's arrival the people looked better and then when the buffalo turned into a herb, the people all got up and seemed to be well. Even the horses got up and stretched themselve s and neighed. Then a little breeze came from the north and I could see that the wind was in the form of a spirit and as it went over the people all the dead things came to life. All the horses pulled up their tails and neighed and began to prace around. Spirit said: "Behold, you have seen the powers of the north in the forms of man, buffalo and herb and wind. The people shall follow the man's steps, like him they shall walk and like the buffalo they shall live and with thy herb they shall have knowledge. They shall be like relatives to the wind." (From the man in the illustration they should be healthy, from the buffalo they shall have meat, from the herb they shall have knowledge of diseases. The north wind will give them strong endurance.)

Spirit speaks again:

"Behold him they have sent forth to the center of the nation's hoop." (Then I saw the pipe with the spotted eagle flying to the center of the nation's hoop. The morning star went along with the pipe. They flew from the east to the center.) "With this thy nation's offering as they walk. They will be like unto him. With the pipe they shall have peace in everything." "Behold thy eagle, for your nation like relatives they shall be. Behold the morning star, relative-like they shall be. From whence they shall have wisdom." (Just then the morning star appeared and all the people looked up to it and the horses neighed and dogs barked.) (The flowering stick was in the middle of the nation's hoop again.)

Spirit said: "Behold the circle of the sacred hoop, for the people shall be like unto it; and if they are like unto this, they shall have power, because there is no end to this hoop and in the center of the hoop these raise their children." (the sacred hoop means the continents of the world and the people shall stand as one. Everything reproduces here inside the hoop.) They put the sacred stick into the center of the hoop and you could hear birds singing all kinds of songs by this flowering stick and the people and animals all rejoiced and hollered. The women were sending up their tremolos. The men said"Behold it, from there we shall multiply, for it is the greatest of the grestest sticks. " This stick will take care of the people and at the same time it will multiply. We live under it like chickens under the wing. They live under their flowering stick like under the wing of a hen. Depending on the sacred stick we shall walk and it will be with them always. From this they will raise their children and under the flowering stick they will communicate with their relatives --beast and bird--as one people. This is the center of the life of the nation. The sacred stick is the cottonwood tree. (rustling tree--waga chun) The nation represents this tree. This tree never had a chance to bloom, because the white men came. The trunk is the chief of the peo le. If this tree had seen a bloom probably Black Elk or some of his descendants would be great chiefs.)

The people camped there. I was on the bay horse again on the west side and was with another man. This man is still living today and probably I could have made him medicine man, but I never did it as yet, because I have never seen him. This man lives at Grass Creek, andhe knows nothing about this, nevertheless. This man's name was One Side.

One Side had bow and arrow in one hand and a cup of water in the other. I saw that the people were getting ready for a storm and they were fixing their teepees to make them stronger for the storm. The storm cloud was approaching and swallows were coming under the cloud, and I, myself, and One Side were coming on top of the cloud. (We were travelling on the fourth ascent and I saw the people on the 3rd ascent from the fourth ascent.) It was raining on earth now. A spirit said to me that they had shown me everything there was to do on earth and that I was to do it myself now. He sang this song and it went like this:

Still on Fourth Ascent—can look back and see Third Ascent

"A good nation I will make over.
The nation above has said this to me.
They have given me the power to make over this nation."

The cloud then swept over the village and they stood in the west. When they turned around, the cloud was all gone. The cloud christened them with water. They all hollered: "Eagle-Wing-Stretches, A-ha-hey!" (meaning thanks to Eagle Wing Stretches.) The people on earth started on the good road again, the Red Road, and I was forced to give all my relics to the people with the exception of the bow and arrows. The horses were all very fat now, so the people began to break camp. The people accepted what I gave them and I went ahead on the Good Road. (bow and arrows represents lightning)

Starting on the good road again

Western spirit said: (people turning towards the west) "Behold where the sun goes down, thou shalt walk. Everything that lacks strength you shall make over as you walk." I was on the bay horse and with "One Side" on a bay also, we led the black, white, sorrel, and buckskin westward. As they went into formation one of the black horse riders, Left Hand Charges, said: "Behold thy grandfathers, they will seek thy enemy. Take courage, you shall be the leader." Just as he said this he called for someone by the name of Red One Horn and someone by the name of Brave Thunder and they all three hollered for Black Elk.

Soon I could see a flame coming up from the earth. They went around the it and Left Hand Charges went around the left instead of rightand we followed. They were on the West side of the flame when they stopped. When we got around it, it was a sight. You could hear the crashing of the thunder and lightning. Left Hand Charges was ready to charge and he saw the flame of it. The horse's tail was lightning and the falmes were coming out of his horse's nose. As I went I could see nothing but I could only hear the thunder and lighning and of course I heardx could see the flames. All the rest of the troops went around this enemy. Left Hand Charges made a vain attempt to kill the enemy. a spirit said: "Eagle Wing Stretches, take courage; your turn has come." We got ready and started down on the cloud on our bay horses. One Side and I were coming down together. I could see the lightning comingoff of my arrows as I descended. Just as we were about to hit the earth, we struck something. I could hear thunder rolling and everyone cheered for me saying: "Unhee!" (kill). I could hear my people on the Good Road saying: "Who killed that enemy?" I heard someone say then that Eagle Wing Stretches has done it and they all cheered again, "Un hah hey." I made a swoop again on the west side of the enemy, whatever it was, and when I killed it, I looked at it and it was a dog, which had a very funny color. One side of him was white and the other side was black. Each one of them struck the dog (couped), meaning that they all had a hand in killing it. (This meant that when you go to war you should kill your enemy like a dog. Wheneyver an Indian gets hungry he kills the dog and then whenever you call someone a dog it means you don't like them and you want to fight.)

The western spirit said: "We are now going to show you a flipping." "Behold him," (they showed him a black horse that was brown-like and he was very poor, like skin and bones.) "for you shall make him over." Then the west spirit presented me with a herb and said "Take this and go forth in haste."

I took the herb and made a circle over the horse and as I did this they all said: "A-hey, a-hey, a-hey!" (calling for spirit power.) After I had made the circle over the horse, the horse neighed and began to roll. It was a beautiful shiney black stallion. His mane was streaming in the form of a cloud all around him and he had dapples all over him. Every time he snorted there was a flash of lightning and his eyes were as bright as stars. Then the stallion went forth and stopped. suddenly, facing the west. He neighed and you could see the dust flying over there as he neighed. In this dust there were a million horses coming. These horses were happy and full of pep. This stallion dashed towards the north and stopped and neighed. Then you could see millions of horses coming out of the dust from this stalions neighing dust in front of him. The stallion then dashed at the east and faced it and neighed and saw some more horses and then he did the same thing towards the south. Then the black spirit said: "Behold them, for these are your horses. Your horses shall come neighing to you. Your horses shall dance and you shall see." "Behold them, all over the universe you have finished." Then there appeared before him four beautiful virgins standing there dressed in red. One of the virgins held the sacred pipe! "Behold thy virgins all over the universe; through them the earth shall be happy. From all over the universe they are coming to see them."

The Black spirit sang a song:

"My horses prancing they are coming from all over the universe.
My horses neighing they are coming, prancing they are coming.
All over the universe my horses are coming."

The dappled black stallion sang this song now:

"They will dance, may you behold them. (four times) .
A horst nation will dance, may you behold them." (four times)

The horse's voice went all over the universe like a radio and everyone heard it. It was more beautiful than anything could be. All the fowls, beasts and every living thing heard this horse sing. The birds, horses, tree leaves and everything danced to the music of the horse's song.

It was so beautiful that they just couldn't help dancing.

After singing the black stallion spoke saying: "All over the Universe everything is finished and thy nation of nations is rejoicing." (meaning that everything is living--trees flowers, grass and every animal is living now.) (In the vision I was representing the earth and everything was giving me power. I was given power so that all creatures on earth would be happy.) (At the end of the 4th ascent I could see the horses all going back to their homes. The black stallion started back to the west where his home was.) The birds and everything sand and the women sang and the tree leaves sang as they went to the four quarters.

Reunification at the end of Fourth Ascent

The black horse rider from the west speaks:

"All over the universe they have finished a day of happiness." (as he said this the day was very beautiful, the day was green, the birds were singing, the creeks were singing, as they flowed clearly along, You could see the people down there very happy. The deer and the buffalo were leaping and running. The country was all very beautiful--fruit was growing up in great abundance.)

Western black spirit said:

"Behold this day, for this day is yours. Take courage, for we shall take you to the center of the earth." They said: "Behold the center of the earth for we are taking you there." As he looked he could see great mountains with rocks and forests on them. I could see all colors of light flashing out of the mountaints toward sthe four qurarters. They then took me on top of a high mountain where I could see all over the earth. Then they told he to take courage for they were taking me to the center of the earth. All the 16 riders of the four quarters were with me going to the center of the earth and also this man by the name of One Side. We were facing the East and I noticed something queer and found out that it was two men coming from the East and they had wings. On each one's breast was a bright star. The two men came and stood right in front of us and the west black spirit said: "Behold them, for you shall depend upon them." Then as ~~they~~ we stood there the daybreak star stood between the two men from the east. There was a little star beside the daybreak star also. They had a herb in their hands and they gave it to me, saying: "Behold this, with this on earth you shall undertake anything and accomplish it." As they presented the herb to me they told me to drop it on earth and when it hit the earth it took root and grew and flowered. You could see a ray of light coming up from the flower reaching the heavens and all the creatures of the universe saw this light.

Daybreak Star Herb

Note--(herbs used by Black Elk are in four colors--yellow, blue, red, white flowers all on one bush. The four colored flowers represent the four quraters of the earth. This herb is called daybreak star herb.)

Western black spirit said: "Behodl all over the universe."

As I looked around I could see the country full of sickness and in need of help. This was the future and I was going to cure these people. On the east and north people were rejoicing and on the south and west they were sick and there was a cloud over them. They said: "Behold them who need help. You shall make them over in the future." After a while I noticed the cloud over the people was a white one and it was probably the white people coming.

The western black spirit sang:

"Here and there may you behold. (twice)
All may you behold.
Here and there may you behold." (twice.)

They had taken me all over the world and showed me all the powers. Thad took me to the center of the earth and to the top of the peak they took me to review it all. This last song means that I have already seen it. I was to see the bad and the good. I was to see what is good for humans and what is not good for humans.

Summing up and reviewing

Black Horse riders says:

"Now your grandfathers, towards them may you walk." (meaning they are going back to the 6 grs. under the flaming rainbow.) "You shall now walk towards your grandfathers, but before thee there is a man with

Figure 2.2 c3716 f402 Pages 1–2, example of stenographic notes by Enid Neihardt, May 10, 1931. Courtesy, the John G. Neihardt Papers, c. 1858–1974, Western Historical Manuscript Collection, Columbia, Missouri; the John G. Neihardt Trust.

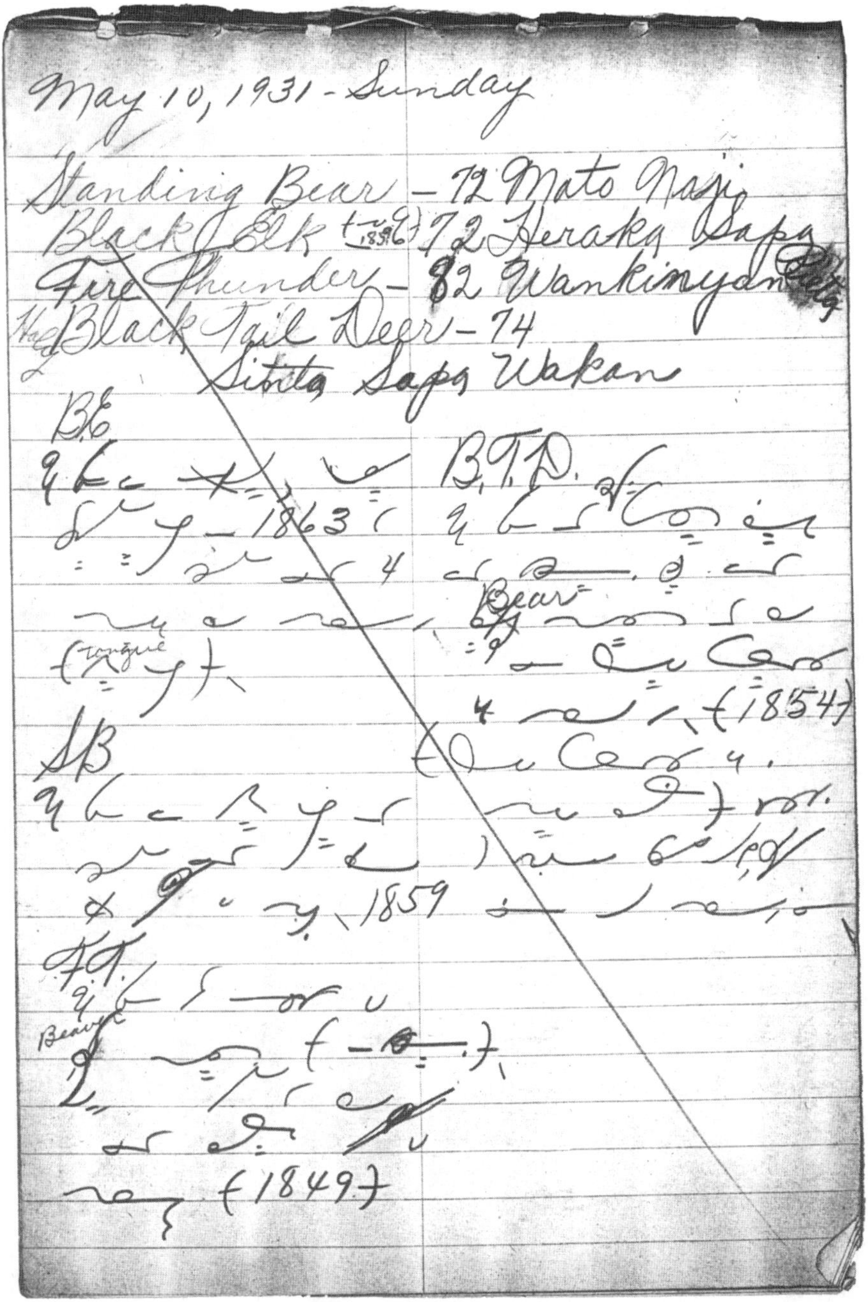
May 10, 1931 - Sunday

Standing Bear - 72 Mato Naji
Black Elk 72 Heraka Sapa
Fire Thunder - 82 Wankinyan Peta
Black Tail Deer - 74
Sinta Sapa Wakan

B.E.
1863

B.T.D.
Bear
(1854)

S.B.
1859

F.T.
(1849)

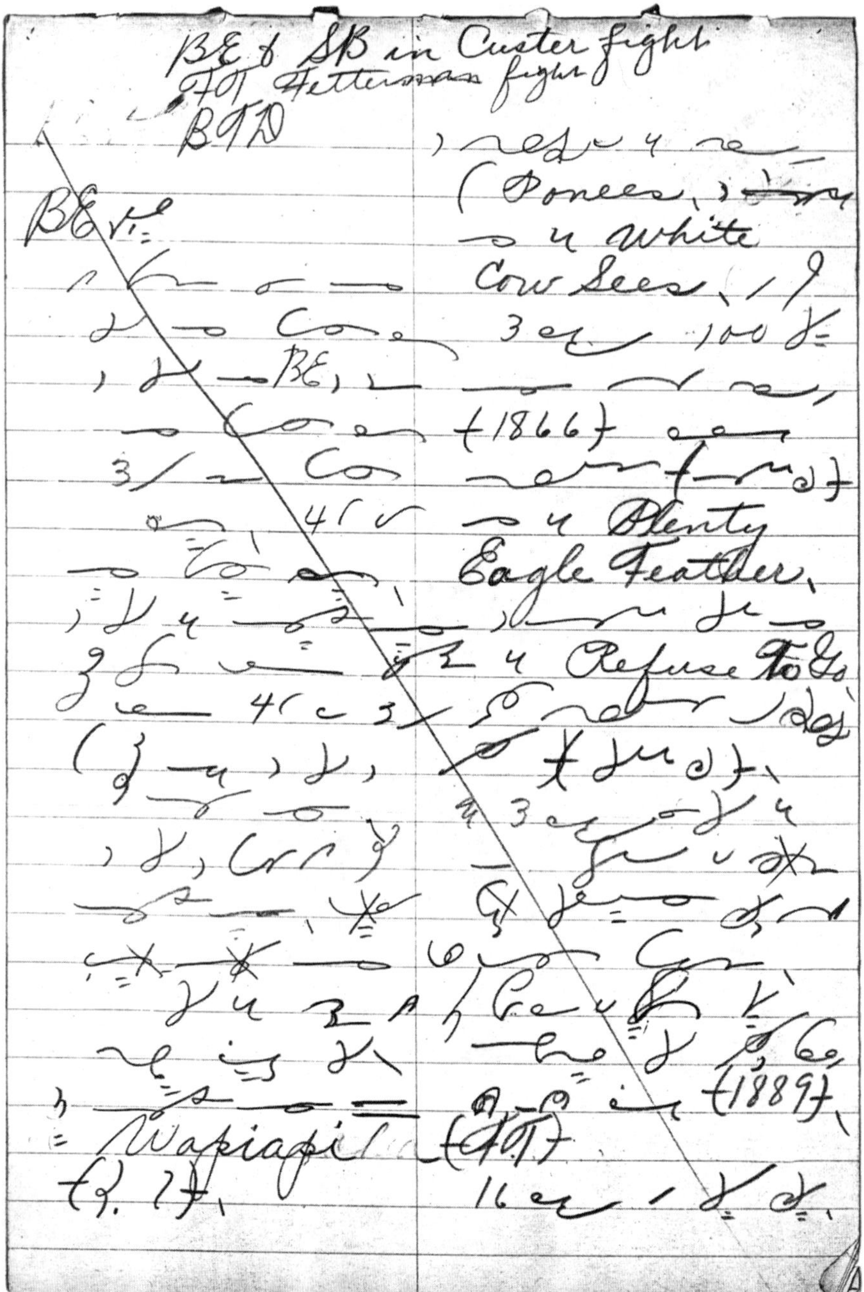
BE & SB in Custer fight
FT Fetterman fight
BTD
(Ponees
White
Cow Sees
3 100
BE
(1866)
4 Plenty
Eagle Feather
Refuse To Go
(1889)
Wapiapi (FT)
16

3
THE SACRED Collaboration

As an artistic vehicle for the sacred, *Black Elk Speaks* depended on two special collaborators working toward a common goal, yet from different backgrounds. A brief examination of what both Neihardt and Black Elk brought to their fateful first meeting will help to clarify features of their collaborative effort. The two men possessed striking similarities and differences, overlapping and complementary characteristics that helped shape the book they created.

John Neihardt, for example, did not set out to write *Black Elk Speaks* but in a way backed into the project. He had long wanted to write an extensive book of some kind about Native Americans. He had composed short stories with Native American themes, but he probably felt about them as he did about his early poetry—that they were stages to transcend. Just as the lyric poetry was self-reflective but not socially reflective, so the stories—although discussing a larger social context, as Jay Fultz has noted (xiv–xv)—tended to focus on a limited range of characters, including the outcast-hero. As a result of these stories, however, Neihardt received the incentive of admiration. He felt his work was validated. A note in Neihardt's script on the back of a photo of Mrs. Joseph La Flesche, "wife of the last chief of the Omaha tribe," states that one of her children, the famous Dr. Susan Picotte, "was the first to remark on my success in representing the Indian idiom in English. She said: 'all writers on Indians from Cooper to Remington have been offensive to me until Neihardt wrote his Indian stories, [sic] I cannot understand how it is possible for him to get the Indian idiom as he does'" (c3716 f474).

Neihardt was already interested as well in the literatures of all cultures as repositories of an enriched awareness, as his *Laureate Address* to Nebraska makes plain (c3716 f485). In this work he urges the study of "World Literature" and calls it "a record of the continuous consciousness" of humanity (18). Reacting to an age of rampant materialism, Neihardt may have felt a sense of urgency and mission to promote the values inherent in this timeless record of thought.

In addition, "The White Radiance" presents Neihardt decrying contemporary individualism and particularism, saying that they are of limited perception when contrasted with such timeless unity:

> More than once has the restless general consciousness of humans passed through all the shades and colors of the social spectrum, from the naive germinating violet on through the slowly maturing blues, the flowering greens, the mellowly fruiting yellows and the tempestuously revolting reds.
>
> But the truth about the light was never to be perceived by the split ray. (291)

That truth, or "white radiance," is engulfing, archetypal, unfragmented, "a vision of the larger truth about people and the human adventure in general" (291) to be sought and cherished now. This truth is not layered topmost on a stack of lesser platitudes, as in some linear neo-Platonist schematic, but instead, as Neihardt's *Poetic Values* explains, is composed of "outer" values—or values bordering, but not necessarily perceived by, the everyday world (*Poetic* 110–114). The function of art is to present this truth in the here and now. The function of a work of literature is to convey such verity using discourse analyzed in Chapter 4 as it emerges in *Black Elk Speaks*. Its strategies have more to do with poetry, the messenger from or translator of the outer values, than with reportage. And Neihardt very much wanted to express the "outer," spiritual truths. His notes and correspondence before writing *Black Elk Speaks* and his manuscripts during and after this endeavor provide evidence of the artist searching for and grappling with a proper medium.

For instance, Neihardt's desire to create a book about Native Americans plunged him into problems with his printers. Macmillan did not seem to want to fulfill Neihardt's wishes regarding such subject matter, but Morrow, which became the original publisher of *Black Elk Speaks*, broached a proposal that interested Neihardt. A May 11, 1926, letter to Neihardt from John Macy prospected for a book with Morrow to dispel misconceptions about Native Americans held by the dominant culture. Morrow desired a prose work from a poet, said Macy, and would even construct a pro forma outline as a point of departure (c3716 f28).

Neihardt forwarded Macy's letter to Macmillan, asking editor H. S. Latham for counsel. On May 19, 1926, Latham advised Neihardt that Macy's letter was a ploy to detach Neihardt from his association with Macmillan. Latham suggested Neihardt withhold publication of Native American subject matter for one or more years. Latham stated, however, that Macmillan would discuss the possibility of a Neihardt-written book about Indians later. He asked Neihardt to write Macy and refuse to do a book because of obligations to Macmillan (c3716 f28, 1–2).

Such documents chronicle a frustrating friction developing between Macmillan and Neihardt and also depict Neihardt struggling to find an artistic outlet. Something needed to get said, but Neihardt did not appear to be sure of what. As we know, however, Neihardt made a fateful choice, as Enid Neihardt's stenographic transcription of his 1930 letter to his friend U. S. Conn states: "In April I expect to go to the Pine Ridge Agency to get material for a prose book on the Sioux." William Morrow and Company would indeed be the publishers (in c3716 f38). A later letter to Julius Temple House, written in 1930, discusses Morrow's interest in a book on Black Elk and his people and mentions Black Elk's "uncanny . . . intuitions" (1930; transcription in c3716 f38); this must have been written after Neihardt's exploratory visit. The famous letter formally initiating the project—dated November 6, 1930, and presented in Figure 3.1 (in transcription; c3716 f39)—reveals a deep interest transcending mere storytelling. There would be no Morrow outline, no prose history. There would be something different.

Figure 3.1 (overleaf) c3716 f39 Transcript of the letter starting the project. Courtesy, the John G. Neihardt Papers, c. 1858–1974, Western Historical Manuscript Collection, Columbia, Missouri; the John G. Neihardt Trust.

(Transcript of stenographic notes for a letter written by John G. Neihardt to Nick Black Elk, November 6, 1930)

Nick Black Elk
Oglala, South Dakota

Dear Friend,

Your letter of November 3 has just reached me, and I am very happy to hear from you! I wondered why I did not hear from you. But I was sure that you would write to me, for I felt when we parted at your home in Manderson that we were friends and that you would not fail me. I see now why you did not write sooner.

I am glad to know that you are willing to make the picture story of the Messiah and of Wounded Knee for me. You say if I will send you $7 for the material, you can go ahead on this work, and I am sending you the money with this letter, so that you can get started. You did not tell me how much you will want for your work. Please do. I think that ____________ skin will be even better for the picture than rawhide.

Now I have something to tell you that I hope and believe will interest you as much as it does me. After talking with you four and a half hours and thinking over many things you told me, I feel that the whole story of your life ought to be written truthfully by somebody with the right feeling and understanding of your people and of their great history. My idea is to come back to the reservation next spring, probably in April, and have a number of meetings with you and your old friends among the Oglalas who have shared the great history of your race, during the past half century or more.

I would want you to tell the story of your life beginning at the beginning and going straight through to Wounded Knee. I would have my daughter, who is a shorthand writer, take down everything you would say, and I would want your friends to talk any time about, and share in, the different things that you would tell about. This would make a complete story of your people since your childhood.

So, you see, this book would be not only the story of your life, but the story of the life of your people. The fact that you have been both a warrior and a medicine man would be of great help in writing the book, because both religion and war are of great importance in history. The book that I sent you at Manderson (1.) is a poem dealing only with the wars between the Sioux and white men and does not tell everything that ought to be told. This book about you would be written in prose, and I would use as much of your language in it as possible. My publisher is eager to have me do this, for I have told him all about it.

I would, of course, expect to pay you well for all the time that you would give me. I would probably be necessary for us to have eight or ten meetings. Does this plan seem a good one to you, and if it seems good to you, will you not be willing to help me make it successful? I do feel that so much is known by you Indians that our

1. SONG OF THE INDIAN WARS

white people do not know and should know, that I am very eager to write this book if you will help me. Write and tell me how much you think you should be paid for each meeting, and there should be from six to ten meetings. And tell me if you think you could get three or four of the fine old men that you know to meet with us and talk about old times while you are telling your story to me.

This is not a money-making scheme for me. I can make money much faster and easier in other ways. I want to do this book because I want to tell the things that you and your friends know, and I can promise you that it will ba an honest and a loving book.

I often look at the beautiful ornaments you gave me, and I am very proud of them. And also when I look at them, I think of what they tell me, and that makes them more beautiful still.

With every kind thought for you and your family.

Your friend,

John G. Neihardt

The above letter is transcribed from stenographic notes taken by Enid Neihardt Fink on November 6, 1930, as attested by her signature below.

Enid Neihardt Fink

Enid Neihardt Fink

STATE OF MISSOURI)
)ss.
COUNTY OF BOONE)

Subscribed and sworn to before me this 11th day of May, 1978.

Elizabeth Jacobs Otradovsky

Notary Public

My commission expires: June 20, 1980

So far we see Neihardt impressed—a bit in awe because of Black Elk's prescience, his selection of Neihardt as a vehicle for his teachings, and the obligations of friendship sealed with the gift of the sacred ornaments. Neihardt promises that the book will not be a materialistic venture but will be concerned with what is good and beautiful, with what Black Elk and his friends have to teach the dominant culture. That is to say, Neihardt is consistent with his value system. He does, however, think of himself as in control of events. After all, he has navigated a difficult course around publishers, arranged to visit Pine Ridge, and found his way to Black Elk. The text of his letter contains the phrases "I want" and "I . . . expect." But soon Black Elk will direct events and open Neihardt's eyes to *his* view of the higher perceptions. At that point the true collaboration can begin, a collaboration intensifying Neihardt's sense of mission already noted. At this stage we continue to see Neihardt considering concepts and goals before the historic interviews take place.

Paralleling his frustrating relationship with publishers, Neihardt's extended interviewing of Black Elk was also subject to bureaucratic delay, suspicion, and evasion. A sequence of letters documents Neihardt's persistence in requesting permission to meet with Black Elk and others and the government's desire to investigate him to make sure he would not disturb the status quo. The exasperation of navigating the restrictiveness of the government mind-set appears in the following chronology of communiqués:

1. April 21, 1931—B. G. Courtright, agent, to Neihardt states that Neihardt must "secure the permission of the Secretary of the Interior and the Commissioner of Indian Affairs" for the project and notes that Courtright likes Neihardt's books.
2. May 1, 1931—Secretary of the Interior to Neihardt approves the trip but requests a "short report of your meetings with these Indians."
3. May 8, 1931—Malcolm McDowell (Board of Indian Commissioners) to Neihardt apologizes for inaction in handling Neihardt's letter to the chair of the board; McDowell says he had thought the trip to Pine Ridge would occur on June 8. McDowell notes that he has sent the agent a "night letter" clarifying the issue.
4. May 8, 1931—McDowell to Courtright explains that John Neihardt is a noted journalist and an epic poet and allays Courtright's apparent concerns about Neihardt "holding a series of meetings with Black Elk and his Sioux friends." McDowell explains his confusion about times and says he has sent a telegram that day to straighten things out. McDowell closes with a curious paragraph: "Mr. Neihardt is not

an investigator, an uplifter, nor anything of that kind and while I thoroughly appreciate the fact that it would be unwise for you to grant wide open permission to strangers to hold meetings in your jurisdiction, I think you need have no fear whatever about helping Mr. Neihardt to get in touch with some of the old fellows up there."

5. May 8, 1931—telegram to Courtright from McDowell regarding Neihardt. "He is all right," states McDowell.

Hilda Neihardt, in *Black Elk and Flaming Rainbow,* has speculated whether Courtright may have imposed the three-week limit on the Neihardt visit (29). One may read the foregoing and conjecture much. The government correspondence is in c3716 f40.

What, then, did Neihardt bring to this potentially suspicious and enduringly controversial collaboration? Fortunately, John Neihardt's voluminous writings allow the poet to speak for himself. Neihardt's own views emerge best in *Poetic Values, Patterns and Coincidences,* his essays, and his large correspondence and can be seen to express a wide-ranging eclecticism. As we examine these writings, we will encounter key attitudes Neihardt brought to the interviews of Black Elk that can legitimately be said to have influenced his work with the holy man. We can divide these attitudes into two main types: a religious or mystical inclination and the rational concern of the public scholar for truth and its fate in the modern world. I turn to these now.

First, Neihardt possessed an "activist" mysticism that originated in a visionary experience the poet had when he was young. As his wife relates in a biographical sketch,

> The birth of John in 1881 is of factual interest but his birth as a poet 12 years later is of far greater importance. It happened this way:
>
> John came home from the 9th grade of the grammar school in Wayne feeling sick. His mother, much excited over his feverish appearance, put the 12 year old lad to bed and called the town physician, an extravagance that showed her great apprehension. The fever lasting several days was a thrilling experience to the inwardness of the boy. In it he seemed to rise up from his bed and fly headlong through space, so fast that the air beneath him felt to his prone body like a sheet of glass upon which he skidded through infinite space. The memory and the mood of this flight stayed with him all through his life. (c3716 f515)

In fact, this experience initiated Neihardt's poetic career and generated the poem "The Calling Brother," or "The Ghostly Brother," as it was also titled. A draft of "The Calling Brother" (c3716 f203) expands the vision's theme of multiple selves and transcendent flight.

Aside from poetry, Neihardt's visionary outlook expressed itself in the writing of essays and book reviews for the general reader in which scientific materialism, the dominant culture's acquisitiveness, and an unfettered individualism all received rebuke; such essays posited that behind the material—and accessible to us all—was the larger spirituality of the universe. It had become Neihardt's goal to awaken this sense of the mystical interrelatedness of things not only through poetry but through expository documents as well, so we frequently find the poet endeavoring to put the quantitative at the service of the qualitative in discursive prose.

Neihardt's essay on Sir Arthur Eddington's book *The Exploding Universe* is a case in point. Eddington discusses the implication of the red shift that the universe is expanding at a heretofore unthinkable rate. Neihardt provides and reviews the numerical information, then links Eddington's bloated universe, its burst bubble, to the social problem of the inordinately bloated and expanding human ego. That is, for Neihardt scientific perception mirrors the social perception that is now a function of human self-absorption (c3716 f216). The universe, then, becomes ultimately qualitative despite its measurable quantities, for these quantities may themselves be functions of the observer. Again, conscious of living in a time of great scientific and social change, Neihardt reviews a work of Sir James Jeans, *The New Background of Science*; implying that the qualitative is the truly "real," Neihardt remarks that "science began destroying its old universe about 30 years before the breakdown of the society which was built upon its discarded conceptions. May not the present trend of science be regarded as equally prophetic?" Neihardt believes this change might betoken a more humane world (c3716 f228).

Neihardt's *Poetic Values*, begun as two talks presented at the University of Nebraska and subsequently edited by Dr. Sisirkumar Ghose, was published by Macmillan in 1925. In this document Neihardt discusses the very large, or relativistic, and the very small, or quantum, aspects of the universe as nonmaterial (*Poetic*, Ghose 4–5) and says:

> It is not to be assumed that anyone can predict just what the new science will find, but enough is known to justify the belief that the old hopelessly limiting notions will be destroyed and with them, sooner or later, will go the hideous superstition that we call materialism and its

> corollary, individualism. Then will be the time for poetry. (5; in c3716 f486)

Such themes also develop in Neihardt's address when proclaimed Poet Laureate of Nebraska (c3716 f485, published in 1921). Here the poet derides materialism and notes that this grasping world presently recognizes the "acquisitive instincts," defeating the "higher values" (16). But he remarks that "it is not Humanism that is impractical, but rather the debased ideals of our materialistic society" (18). Others recognized Neihardt's rejection of the materialism, reductionism, and cynicism of the modern age—for example, poet Lew Sarett, in an admiring letter dated December 28, 1928 (c3716 f31). Much later in life, dictating to biographer Lucile Aly in 1958, Neihardt again declares his consistent belief in a "qualitative," not a "quantitative," universe and states that current atomic physics provides direct proof of this to empiricists, since "the only reality is energy" (c3716 f517; two-page manuscript). Neihardt's views, then, remained consistent.

Of interest is that Neihardt's concept of a subjective, spiritual universe of energy inside which the quantitative may be perceived in a scientific but limited way resembles his concept of the creative act itself. First comes the overarching energy, the inspiration; next comes the attention to detail, or "science." The Stanley Smith papers in the Neihardt Collection at the Western Historical Manuscript Collection contain Neihardt's two-page, typed explication of his writing craft. Neihardt tells Smith:

> When I was writing *The Messiah* my desk caught fire and 900 lines of mms were burned up. I was able to restore those lines at a high rate of speed because every line was fitted to the lines before and after. Words too were fitted to words. Thus the sequence of words and lines made the restoration almost automatic. This is very characteristic of my verse, and the care with which it was put together.
>
> All this is clearly the mechanics of composition. First of all came the *conception, which is the poetry.* Then came the technique for expressing the conception. And there is science in my technique. That is to say, definite knowledge and control. (c3607 f16, April 2, 1970; emphasis original)

This exactitude is achieved as the antithesis of a chaotic, expansive egotism's production of what Neihardt calls in a lecture "the great wave of impressionism," which first crashed on the shores of the United States in 1912 and which has produced "a state of cultural anarchy." Such impressionism forgoes cumulative human wisdom for "individual caprice" (Neihardt program for interview with Ron Hull, c3607 f26). The fact that Neihardt was a mystic does not then mean, as some critics have suggested, that he was a nineteenth-century throwback trumpeting the platitude of an outworn egoistic romanticism. Neihardt regarded such hyperindividualism as a profound social problem.

In addition to focusing on the qualitative and mystical, Neihardt possessed the public scholar's interest in exactitude when dealing with the quantitative. Neihardt deemed it imperative to ascertain the precise appearances of settings for historical scenes in his writing. Mona Martinsen Neihardt tells us that "my thought here is that one should be told that even the state of the Heavenly Bodies at the time was correct! For instance in writing about the death of Sitting Bull the phase of the moon was ascertained by consulting the Naval Observatory in Washington" (c4910, undated, no folder).

A sense of this passion for detail can be seen in Neihardt's corresponding with Louisa Standing Bear to get her reaction to the Ghost Dancers Kicking Bear, Flat Iron, Good Thunder, and Yellow Breast. C3716 f197 contains her reply, describing the men's characters and appearances. Curiosity about detail also drove Neihardt to ask questions of Norma Kidd Green, who was working on a history of the descendants of Joseph La Flesche. C3716 f129 contains the answers to Neihardt's queries.[1] When painstakingly acquired information was distorted or devalued by others, Neihardt could be quick to retort. A hasty reviewer who misread part of the *Cycle of the West* and accused Neihardt of making a mistake received a testy response not only clarifying the issue but supplying a narrative résumé as well:

> I am well acquainted with the historical literature and government records of the period. Also, through the years I have known as friends many men, both white and Indian, who were themselves a part of the great drama. For instance, Major H. R. Lemly, who was General Crook's adjutant during the 1876 campaign against the Sioux, was a good friend of mine. Through his interest in my work I was elected the first civilian member of The Order of the Indian Wars of the United States. General Miles was then commander of the Order and most of the famous old Indian fighters of the Plains were still living. General Godfrey, who served as a lieutenant under Reno in the Little Big Horn battle, was a companion of the Order and helped me greatly. (c3716 f138)

The document continues, citing sources both Indian and white. A sample of Major Lemly's correspondence with the poet, dated 1922, appears in c3716 f20. Minutiae continued to be important; writing for information in 1969, Neihardt notes that "it is vitally important that anything I use be correct" (c3778 f35). Fine examples of Neihardt's meticulousness appear in the detailed marginalia of books in his personal library, now housed at the University of Missouri–Columbia. These sometimes include pages of handwritten summary and photographic documentation carefully inserted between leaves or attached to the inside covers. My annotated bibliography supplies specific information about three such books in the Neihardt Collection: Thomas Henry Tibbles's *Buckskin and Blanket Days*, Grace Raymond Hebard's *Sacajawea*, and Bertrand Russell's *Mysticism and Logic.*

John Neihardt remained concerned with the philosophy and preparation that influenced him during his work with Black Elk. He remained undogmatic, too. Back on July 6, 1918, he had written George Sterling that "my journal boss loves Jesus to distraction + he has the heart of a rat. Long ago I used to say, + I say it yet: Look out for an extremely religious person" (c3074). Writing to his friend Stanley Smith in 1964, Neihardt explains that "the essence of religion is *mystical experience.*" He states that "many, many times I have tried most sincerely to get an explanation of the salvation-through-Jesus affair, and *no one* has ever been able to give any sane explanation." But Neihardt adds that "I never speak against churches openly, because they *do* stand for spiritual aspiration for multitudes of people. For that reason I always feel reverent in any church" (c3607 f7). Commenting on science and materialism in a July 4, 1964, letter to Smith, Neihardt remarks that "what does surprise me is that *any* scientist, *of all people,* should insist upon materialism as an explanation of the wonder and mystery! Some do attempt such an explanation, but not many now. It's the mere technologist . . . who talks materialism" (c3607 f7).

Corresponding with Smith on July 27, 1964, Neihardt discusses the atomizing effect of individualism in every area of life and isolates as problematic "the dependence upon *reason as the means of understanding.*" Neihardt also decries an "*utter* dependence on *quantitative conceptions*" (my italics replace his underlining throughout) (c3607 f7). Writing to M. Slade Kendrick on June 5, 1959, Neihardt provides a synopsis of *Poetic Values* that discusses the spectrum of awareness from the commonsense perception of the material to that of mystical consciousness:

> In considering our scale of values from common sense, on thru science and the higher values (esthetics-religion) the vital error is the

> assumption that there is only *one valid state* of *awareness,* in which all values are conceived . . . the values of the lower *scale are created in consciousness in keeping with* the *sense-level of awareness*; and . . . the higher *values* (rising to *religious experience*) are created in consciousness *in keeping with a higher* (*or expanded*) *state of awareness. This is the source* of the universal error in regarding our *sense values* as *real,* and the higher values as *imaginary.* (c628 f2)

The purpose of craft in writing is to generate a musical bridge to this expanded state, Neihardt tells Stanley Smith on February 5, 1963. Speaking of Smith's elevated feelings induced by hearing poetry, Neihardt remarks that "it's the *song quality* as much as the meaning that moved you, and that song-quality is very important in helping to lift the level of awareness well above the common-sense level" (c3607 f6). Addressing a University of South Dakota seminar on teaching (February 15, 1962), Neihardt mentions the childhood dream "which changed everything," explains how dreams can supply one with the stuff of poetry, tells his audience that "later I learned how to dream awake," and reminds them that love is "inherent in the cosmos." And "in the deeps of sleep," he says, one may "touch the everlasting, the source of vitality of life" (c3716 ac56).

Neihardt's last book, *Patterns and Coincidences,* expresses his lifelong themes as it links the present with reminiscences of life in the years 1901–1908. The work documents the young Neihardt's shift in artistic focus from the personal to the universal (4–5); discusses the perception of the transcendent and the mystical as distilled by the experience of a sun dancer (34–35); sketches an account of Neihardt's Omaha friends, including evidence of his exposure to their language and customs (36–38, 39–41); displays a fascination with the roles of poetic and practical language (103–110); and finally provides a parable of the unity of all forms of life (116–117). Throughout his career, then, Neihardt expressed his mysticism through the practical vehicle of crafted, frequently reverent prose and poetry; in essence, art was his vehicle to and expression of the sacred. Raymond DeMallie has stated that "Neihardt perceived Black Elk's religion in terms of art; Black Elk perceived Neihardt's art in terms of religion. Both tried to use their special skills to enrich human life by merging it into something greater than the individual" (*Sixth* 37). Of course, Neihardt's art *was* his religion, just as Black Elk's religion *was* his art. When Black Elk learned of Neihardt's visionary experience as a youth, he said, "That was your power vision, that was your power vision, if you had not had that vision, you never would have done anything" (c3716 f498). The holy man recognized how intimately Neihardt's art and spirituality were entwined.

And because of Black Elk's and Neihardt's own vision, John Neihardt, too, felt the continuing pressure of a sacred obligation. Audiocassettes of Neihardt's "Introduction to *The Song of the Indian Wars* and *Song of the Messiah*"—a set of lectures for students—demonstrate constant and detailed reference to Black Elk's teachings, insist on the advanced spirituality and social structure of the Lakota, include corroborative material from Eagle Elk's narrative, explain that the Lakota were neither primitive nor idealized "noble savages," and stress the unity of all life (c3716 ac25–30). A letter to Dr. Harley H. Ziegler guides Ziegler through the steps of a lecture on Black Elk's teachings for classroom use (c3778 f57, February 21, 1972). Correspondence from Edwin A. Christ at the University of South Dakota–Vermillion (February 19, 1962) discloses Neihardt's intensive schedule of activities while visiting that campus. These included both tapings and live broadcasts with Ben Black Elk and programs for students and faculty (c3716 f127). In April 1967 Neihardt lectured on Nicholas Black Elk's teachings at the Warren Methodist Church in Lincoln, Nebraska. A photograph of the event shows a large hoop divided into four quarters (c3716 f452).

Then, of course, there is the famous set of interviews with Dick Cavett, first broadcast on April 27, 1971 (date is of showing on KETV), and repeated on ABC June 12 (see c3778 f9–76), in which Neihardt presents Black Elk's material and says, "He's a teacher. . . . And he's still teaching me" (tape of June 12 broadcast in the John G. Neihardt Center, Bancroft, Nebraska). Much moved by his meetings with Neihardt, Cavett wrote Neihardt on November 13, 1972, offering to buy at great cost one of the objects Black Elk had given him—preferably Black Elk's drum—so he could contemplate it and then donate it to the Museum of the American Indian (c3778 f64). Neihardt's gentle reply of November 21, 1972, states that he cannot do such a thing, that the holy artifacts must stay with Neihardt while he is alive and then be enshrined at the Neihardt Center as fulfillment of a sacred promise. Neihardt tells Cavett that although the Smithsonian Institution also wants the objects, he will not consider its inquiry (c3778 f65).

A corollary to Neihardt's sacred obligation is the poet's concern with the preservation of his papers as primary resources. Neihardt was both particular about their proper preservation and use and generous about sharing his material. He also encouraged collaborations between libraries and institutions, readily granting permission. Collection c3778 contains examples of correspondence related to such issues, including the release of tapes and papers.

Folder 33 shows tapes released to Eastern Kentucky University and Syracuse University; folder 75 contains the release sent to Nebraska Educational Television for duplication of *Twilight of the Sioux.* Folder 38 documents the Smithsonian's request for and receipt of the transcripts of the Neihardt–Black Elk interviews and includes a note from Neihardt saying he will forward any new material he finds. In addition, an item in c3716 f152 acknowledges Syracuse University's receipt of the microfilm of Neihardt's papers. And there is Neihardt's agreement with the University of Missouri to house his papers and books there (c3716 f112–113). Once while I was discussing the present volume with Nancy Lankford, formerly of the Western Historical Manuscript Collection at the University of Missouri, she remarked that Neihardt had been excited about a laminating process for conserving his materials.

Related to preservation is dissemination. One aspect of dissemination is Neihardt's teaching at the University of Missouri, in which he tirelessly explained Black Elk's work to his Epic America class and credited that material to "my old spiritual father, Black Elk, the great holy man of the Sioux" (c3716 f469). Although Neihardt spread the message in his popular classes, which survive on tape used in the university's extended learning program, he received minuscule wages for his task—being paid, for example, $4,000 for the period September 1, 1964–August 31, 1965, as a half-time appointee (c3716 f152) and $2,000 for February 1, 1966–June 30, 1966, as a half-time teacher. A note in Neihardt's hand on the latter contract reads: "This was a gratuity, I had no retirement pay" (c3716 f163). This miserly treatment outraged Neihardt's friend Stanley Smith, who catalogued what Neihardt had done for the university—giving a personal library, constructing the series of taped classes, donating his time, and teaching (c3716 f160)—but the paltry remuneration was not what motivated Neihardt to teach.

Like Black Elk, Neihardt worked to disperse his message in fulfillment of a spiritual, not a monetary, motivation. In the Preface to the best-selling 1972 Pocket Books edition of *Black Elk Speaks,* the poet plainly states his purpose of inducing spiritual insight through literature:

> It was my function to translate the old man's story, not only in the factual sense—for it was not the facts that mattered most—but rather to re-create in English the mood and manner of the old man's narrative. This was often a grueling and difficult task, requiring much patient effort and careful questioning of the interpreter.
>
> Always I felt it a sacred obligation to be true to the old man's meaning and manner of expression. (xii)

For *Black Elk Speaks* is a poetic synthesis reflecting as much of Black Elk's young vision and the Lakota life surrounding it as possible within the limits of a literary creation targeting all readers and using art to suggest the spiritual, in fulfillment of a sacred task.

FROM BLACK ELK'S PROFOUND POWER VISION IN CHILDHOOD, WHICH ALSO INDUCED the burden of obligation, accomplishments are still unfolding. Now that time has granted a more balanced perspective from which to assimilate the complex features of Black Elk's life, we may consider without dogmatism that Black Elk's interest and participation in traditional Lakota practices may not have been something that, having been dormant, flared up when he met Neihardt, only to be renounced forever after. And we need not be virulent partisans of one small hue within the holy man's spectrum of religious work. Consider the implications of this commentary from Black Elk's relative Frank Fools Crow, himself both Catholic and traditional Lakota healer: "I stayed with him quite often, and sometimes for long periods of time. We also made a few trips together, and over the years talked about many things. I learned a great deal about *Wakan-Tanka,* prophecy and medicine from him" (quoted in Mails, *Fools Crow* 53). And furthermore, says Fools Crow,

> Black Elk told me he had decided that the Sioux religious way of life was pretty much the same as that of the Christian churches, and there was no reason to change what the Sioux were doing. We could pick up some of the Christian ways and teachings, and just work them in with our own, so in the end both would be better. (45)

This mentoring of Fools Crow in the traditional ways took place after Black Elk joined the Catholic Church in 1904, since Fools Crow was only about twelve in 1904 and had his first quest for visions in 1905 (Mails 45, 49). Furthermore, Fools Crow states, it was not the Christian framework that Black Elk saw absorbing the Lakota but rather the Lakota traditional beliefs that could "pick up" and incorporate those Christian attributes desired.

Of profound significance is that when Black Elk was interviewed by Neihardt on December 7, 1944, for the book *When the Tree Flowered,* Black Elk referred to the former position of the medicine men in the tribe as an attribute of the past but referred to his being a medicine man in the present. He stated, as reproduced in the transcripts:

> The medicine men were the learned class, the scholars for the tribe. Later I will tell all about Drinks Water; that will be a long story.
>
> Sometimes we do make mistakes, but when we tell anything it has to be what we heard from the spirits (c3716 f434, 2).

Interviews of Bud Duhamel, Black Elk's employer subsequent to the holy man's initial collaboration with John Neihardt, cover Black Elk's participation in the Duhamel pageants and his use of traditional ceremony for the benefit of others—including actual healings and an effective ceremonial petition for rain to help fight the "McVey Burn," a devastating fire. Other evidence also exists of Black Elk's active role in teaching whites about the intricate and reverent aspects of Lakota culture. For Black Elk, like Neihardt, was also an "activist mystic."

First, note the way in which Black Elk and his family and friends established a communal context, a teaching arena, for the 1931 narrative work with Neihardt that produced *Black Elk Speaks.* Some of the preparations are recorded in that book, others in Hilda Neihardt's *Black Elk and Flaming Rainbow*; still more detail appears in Enid's diary and scrapbook in c3716 f406, f468a. Black Elk organized dances and feasts, decorated his home with pines, and supervised the creation of a special tipi with visionary symbols, including a flaming rainbow. He provided John, Enid, and Hilda Neihardt with a total cultural and communal immersion in which the visitors were active, physical participants. Informal interaction and traditional ceremony taught the visitors both intellectually and spiritually. The learning did not take place in the sterile classroom of the dominant culture's academe but was an experience activating senses and intuitions so the visitors would learn about culture, tradition, and the "outer world" (see Figure 3.2).

Although Neihardt originally intended to interview old men who knew about the past to acquire a greater feeling for the factual material of his epic and perhaps for a vaguely conceived descriptive book in prose, Black Elk's encounter with Neihardt changed the poet's direction and in important ways put Black Elk in control. The holy man selected the time for the next meeting, the agenda and locations of the telling, the interpreter, the corroborative

---

Figure 3.2 The context of Neihardt's learning. All images courtesy the John G. Neihardt Papers, c. 1858–1974, Western Historical Manuscript Collection, Columbia, Missouri; the John G. Neihardt Trust.

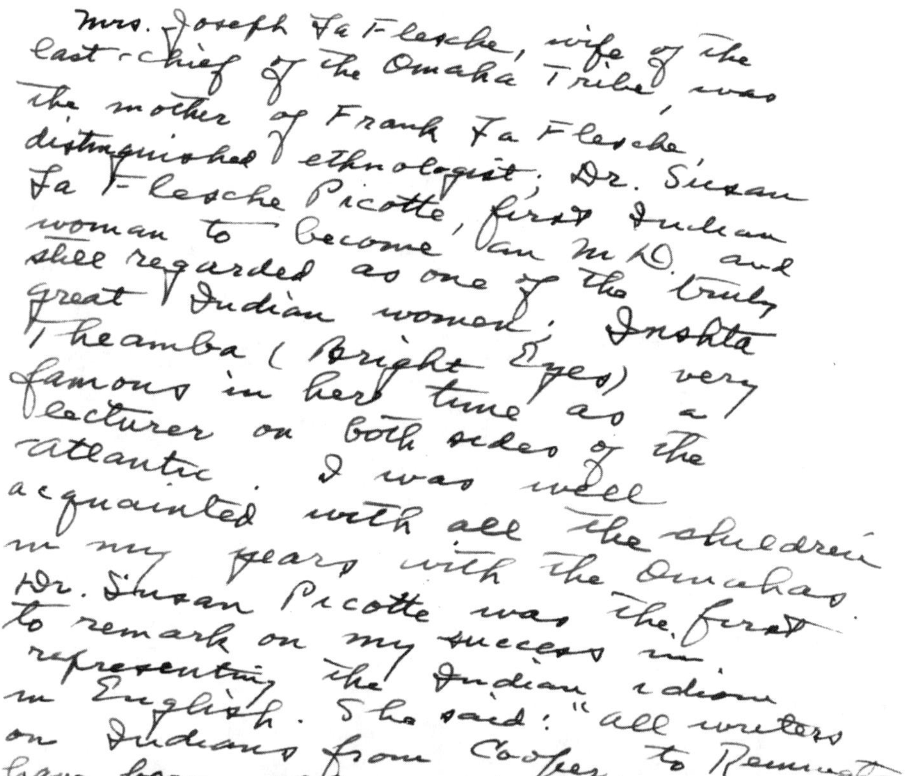
Mrs. Joseph La Flesche, wife of the last chief of the Omaha Tribe, was the mother of Frank La Flesche, distinguished ethnologist; Dr. Susan La Flesche Picotte, first Indian woman to become an M.D. and still regarded as one of the truly great Indian women; Inshta Theamba (Bright Eyes) very famous in her time as a lecturer on both sides of the Atlantic. I was well acquainted with all the children in my years with the Omahas. Dr. Susan Picotte was the first to remark on my success in representing the Indian idiom in English. She said: "All writers on Indians from Cooper to Remington have been offensive to me until Neihardt wrote his Indian stories. I cannot understand how it is possible for him to get the Indian idiom as he does".
Inshta Theamba (Bright Eyes) married my friend T.H. Tibbles (candidate for V-P when Watson ran). When she lay in her coffin, only Tibbles and I watched beside her through the night before her burial. She was truly a wonderful woman and beautiful to see. John G. Neihardt

Figure 3.2.1 Undated reminiscence of John G. Neihardt discussing his early acquaintance with Indians and the praise of Dr. Susan Picotte (c3716 f454).

Figure 3.2.2 Song and telling, from Enid's 1932 scrapbook (c3716 f466 #15).

Figure 3.2.3 Drum, voice, and pipe: song, narrative, and ceremony during the interviews (c3716 f464 #7).

Figure 3.2.4 Interviewing (c3716 f464 #6).

Figure 3.2.5 Ceremony (c3716 f465 #9).

Figure 3.2.6 Ceremony (c3716 f465 #11).

Figure 3.2.7 Women of the community (c3716 f465 #15).

Figure 3.2.8 Standing Bear in regalia; the ceremonial tipi is behind him (c3716 f467 #9).

Figure 3.2.9 The Black Elk family (and Neihardt's adopted family) in front of the tipi (c3716 f466 #7).

Figure 3.2.10 (right) Black Elk, left, *and friend (c3716 f466 #13).*

Figure 3.2.11 Black Elk's reminder to Enid: grandfather to granddaughter (c3716 f464 #5).

Figure 3.2.12 The two collaborators later in life (c3716 f443 #12).

witnesses, the form of the meetings, and the context in which the oral communication occurred. This is not the picture of a helpless old man being "colonized" by an invading, unsympathetic outsider.

After the encounter Black Elk dictated correspondence with the Neihardts that continued the theme of active participation. For example, Black Elk sent Enid a picture, dated October 8, 1933 [or 1935], "reminding" her that he was her "Tonkashila" (c3716 f468a, 20). Another letter from Black Elk, the spiritual father, to John Neihardt, the spiritual son—dictated at Oglala, South Dakota, and dated December 16, 1940—asked Neihardt to correspond more frequently, let him know the family was fine, and invoked a blessing from the Great Spirit (c3716 f64). A two-page dictated letter from Black Elk, dated October 11, 1945, from Manderson, South Dakota, was a response to an invitation from Neihardt. Black Elk wanted to know more details. The holy man said Neihardt's speech had delighted and uplifted the people (probably at the previous victory celebration) and that he hoped Neihardt could provide more assistance later (c3716 f72). Not humble but affectionate and a bit remonstrative at times, such correspondence befits a man in the role of father and grandfather, an elder dispensing love and advice.

Black Elk's long-term participation in the Duhamel pageants—for many years enacted annually at the Sitting Bull Crystal Caverns in the Black Hills—also demonstrates his traditional leadership and power, illustrates his desire to teach, and shows the holy man adapting new contexts to traditional ends. In *The Sixth Grandfather* DeMallie has provided a vignette of Black Elk's role in these presentations derived from a performance program and from talks in 1979–1981 with Bud Duhamel and others, including Emma Amiotte and Reginald and Gladys Laubin (63–71).

Further corroboration and clarification emerge from two striking documents amplifying Black Elk's role in the pageants. First, in 1994 David O. Born published the results of his extensive discussions with Bud Duhamel, conducted in 1991 and 1992. Born supplemented his material with family history provided by Charlotte Black Elk, a great-granddaughter of Nicholas Black Elk ("Black Elk" 23). Born accumulated evidence that Black Elk continued his role as a teacher, healer, and holy man while working at the pageants and living in the community of Indians residing at the pageant site. Second, Dale Stover's interview of Bud Duhamel (dated January 28, 1998, and produced by KOTA television in Rapid City) is consistent with Born's article in its explanation of Black Elk's role. Both Born and Stover agree with DeMallie with the exception of the latter's understanding that the pageant was initiated by Alex Duhamel, who asked Black Elk to join (63). Born, however, states:

> Bud Duhamel reports that at some point, prior to 1934 and possibly as early as 1927, Black Elk suggested the pageant to his father, Alex Duhamel, who was then running the family's enterprises, including the development of the caverns and the Duhamel Trading Post in Rapid City. The two men had known each other for many years as a result of their trading relationship. (24)

In fact, Born tells us, Bud Duhamel explained in 1994 that Alex Duhamel had solicited Black Elk's participation after hearing the latter's concept of the pageant (24). The idea would then have originated with Black Elk. DeMallie also offers the information—not found in Born or Stover—that in traveling to the pageant site, "Black Elk's party moved to the Black Hills, picking up children en route who had been attending boarding schools during the year" (*Sixth* 63). These children, participating in the summer encampment and the pageant, could then renew their contact with the very culture the schools were exerting themselves to extinguish. Black Elk, then, not only had rescued surviving children in the aftermath of Wounded Knee in 1890 by distracting the soldiers (*Black Elk Speaks* 257–259) but also had saved traditional culture for the young while working for the Duhamels more than two generations later.

As Born's article informs us, the Duhamel pageants began when tourists motored from Rapid City to the site of the Rushmore carving on a new state highway. Because of the potential for business, the Duhamel family—of old trading stock—opened the Sitting Bull Crystal Caverns to attract "geologists, natural historians, and tourists" (24). Black Elk's concept proposed holding a pageant of Oglala life there to employ the Indians but also to teach the dominant culture about the complexity, aesthetic integrity, and depth of Lakota culture (24, 29). As Bud Duhamel stated, "Black Elk was very sincere. It wasn't just a performance for him" (Interview with Stover). By 1934 the Crystal Caverns functioned as both pageant site and Indian campground; the Indians directed most aspects of the program themselves (Born 25). Born explains that Black Elk participated up to the late 1940s and that "from the very beginning, Black Elk was a central figure. His role as 'Medicine Man' made him a key performer in the presentations, and the Duhamels relied heavily on him in their dealings with the other singers and dancers. Duhamel reports that Black Elk generally determined which dances would be performed" (25).

Bud Duhamel told Born that although the enterprise rarely paid for itself, "it satisfied the Indians and it satisfied us, so what the heck" (26). Informative brochures accompanied the event and gave tourists details about Lakota culture. The program was offered two times a day, beginning with a procession, following with a pipe ceremony normally conducted by Black Elk, and presenting a series of dances including the Ghost Dance. After an intermission the Sun Dance was depicted without piercing. In between large events, aspects of Lakota life were displayed, including healing ceremonies and funeral rites (Interview with Stover; Born 27). The pageant served, then, as a safe haven for expressions of tradition and culture denied on the reservation. In all of this work, Bud Duhamel insisted, Black Elk "meant every word he was saying there," and the other Lakota were also "serious" about their activities (Interview with Stover). The Duhamels themselves acted as explainers and interpreters (Born 25; Interview with Stover).

Bud Duhamel remembered other features of Black Elk's role in the Crystal Cave community, such as conducting actual healings and a special dance with piercing. Born and Stover record Bud Duhamel's description of the healing of Henry Horse, a pageant participant written off as dying by the white doctors at the Sioux Sanitarium; after the doctors had given up, Black Elk administered a tea of herbs he had gathered, and after three days Henry Horse resumed dancing (Born 27; Interview with Stover). Black Elk also fixed Bud's aching tooth using slices of what Bud believed was purple coneflower. The healing was permanent, however, not the result of a topical numbing effect characteristic of a folk medicine application. Bud Duhamel remarked reverently that "Old Nick was no fake. He was a true medicine man" (Interview with Stover).

That Black Elk conducted real healings at times is remarkable enough, but Bud Duhamel also remembered that Black Elk petitioned Wakan Tanka in a spectacular ceremonial way. Duhamel noted that in 1937 the McVey Burn was raging—a terrible forest fire exacerbated by dusty, dry conditions. Firefighters were having trouble. Bud Duhamel said that Black Elk set up a "72-hour Sun Dance" praying for rain. The rain came, making the fire tractable (Interview with Stover; Born 28–29). Bud Duhamel was impressed by this event; asked to describe the dance, Duhamel noted that there was a tree with a flag, there were thongs to the dancers, and—he remembered with surprise—there was piercing (Interview with Stover). The law may have been subverted, but the prayers received a response.

As DeMallie notes, Black Elk's tipi in the Crystal Cave encampment was decorated with a flaming rainbow across its entrance, like the one his family made for John Neihardt (*Sixth* 64), which was symbolic of Neihardt's role as the gateway leading Black Elk's vision to the dominant culture. This flaming rainbow tipi, visible in a color postcard issued by the Duhamels (see Born 23, 29) and apparently a regular feature of the camp at Crystal Cave, reminds us that Black Elk's teaching of the public did not stop with Neihardt in 1931 but continued yearly and twice a day at the Duhamel pageants. It continues yet.

It also lives on in the memory of his granddaughters, Esther DeSersa and Olivia Pourier, who were interviewed about Black Elk's activities in a panel discussion moderated by Dale Stover. The panel, "Black Elk's Granddaughters Speak," was a special session of the 1998 Great Plains Regional Meeting of the American Academy of Religion. The sisters discussed the curing of Henry Horse at the Duhamel pageant, Black Elk's attendance at a large secret Sun Dance, and the drenching of the McVey Burn following the ceremony conducted by Black Elk—which was not described as a Sun Dance. The interview gives the date of the ceremony as 1939, not 1937 (tape viewed at the Neihardt Center, spring 1999).

Although Black Elk has been portrayed as thoroughly rejecting the traditional, events suggest otherwise. They show that Black Elk, too, felt the continuing pressure of a sacred obligation, as indicated even by the flaming rainbow on his lodge at the Duhamel pageant. Traditional exposition and explication, adapted to and in the very face of the dominant culture, appear at the Duhamel site; other types of exposition and adaptation appear in Black Elk's 1931 and 1944 interviews with Neihardt, his interviews with Joseph Brown in 1947 (xiii), and his teaching the pipe ceremony to Reginald and Gladys Laubin in hopes that disseminating it would educate and unify humanity (DeMallie, *Sixth* 66). DeMallie rightly indicates that Black Elk's desire to instruct the dominant culture about his vision and traditional ways, to share these spiritual concepts across cultural and religious boundaries, was an unusual idea at the time (*Sixth* 66).

In light of these aspects, it is important to note that a redefinition of Black Elk's "religion" may indeed be in order. Clyde Holler even points out the additional presence of Ghost Dance belief in Black Elk's material to emphasize his view of Black Elk as participating in several religions simultaneously (*Religion* 219). The "Ghost Dance" religion was certainly another way of accommodating Christianity to Native American beliefs and one present at the Duhamel pageant. And we do see Black Elk working with this accommodation in the foreword to *The Sacred Pipe*:

> We have been told by the white men, or at least by those who are Christian, that God sent to men His son, who would restore order and peace upon the earth; and we have been told that Jesus the Christ was crucified, but that he shall come again at the Last Judgement, the end

> of this world or cycle. This I understand and know that it is true, but the white men should know that for the red people too, it was the will of *Wakan-Tanka*, the Great Spirit, that an animal turn itself into a two-legged person in order to bring the most holy pipe to His people; and we too were taught that this White Buffalo Cow Woman who brought our sacred pipe will appear again at the end of this "world," a coming which we Indians know is now not very far off. (Brown xix–xx)

Perhaps the central issue is the Western or European definition of "religion"—literally, something that binds one or by which one is bound; a concept that influences attitudes and intellection, including Holler's use of the term *alternate,* with its connotation of separate religious media. Yet eclecticism, manifested in the panreligious, multitribal, traditional-Christian Ghost Dance and in other ways, has had a long history with the Lakota. Notice how Black Elk's quote from *The Sacred Pipe* unifies Lakota and Christian traditions and concludes with an apocalyptic statement reminiscent of the Ghost Dancers as well. And consider John Lame Deer's words:

> We believe all religions are really the same—all part of the Great Spirit. The trouble is not with Christianity, with religion, but with what you have made out of it. You have turned it upside down. You have made the religion of the protest leader and hippie Jesus into the religion of missionaries, army padres, Bureau of Indian Affairs officials. These are two altogether different religions, my friend. . . . Many of us Sioux go to a church on Sunday, to a peyote meeting on Saturday, and to a *yuwipi* man any day when we feel sick. (Lame Deer and Erdoes 216–217)

In practice, it is possible to have an interpretation of the issue that, like Lame Deer's, is less doctrinaire and more intuitive than that of the academics without using the linear metaphors of the professor, the dualist obsessions of Eurocentrism, or the "spiritual evolution" construct so popular with those who see European Christianity as a culmination into which so-called primitive religions will matriculate. Instead one might, as Black Elk did, receive an overarching vision, the parts of which could be expressed in different avenues of the sacred. Different "religions" could be subsumed by a greater spirituality. In such a light, religious forms—perhaps diverse—become means of expressing a central illumination; all go the same direction, and the road is wide. Recall that Black Elk's great vision itself discloses a complex, articulated universe in which different agencies of the sacred and unfathomable can be activated and made manifest through discrete actions and rituals. Recall, too, the verity of Joseph Brown's statement about Black Elk in *The Sacred Pipe.* Brown remarks that "he seemed a pitiful old man as he sat there hunched over, dressed in poor, cast-off clothing. But the beauty of his face and the reverent quality of his movements as he smoked the pipe revealed that Neihardt had given to us the essence of the man" (xiv).

The sacred collaboration between Neihardt and Black Elk indeed possessed special and reverent implications, including a panreligious aspect, that were noticed immediately. Native American anthropologist, story gatherer, and storyteller Ella C. Deloria was struck by *Black Elk Speaks* and responded strongly when it was first printed. Writing Neihardt on March 18, 1932, she offered emphatic support, explaining that she admired the book's innovation and integrity. She also connected the book, Black Elk, the visionary, and the social good in commenting on her grandfather's helping people through his own vision and her father's role as an Episcopalian minister whose children had to live in this world using a new religion as an agent of the traditionally sacred. For Deloria, *Black Elk Speaks* exemplified transmuting the personal vision into broader social and spiritual effectiveness. She assumed the value of literature concerned with such holistic issues. She told Neihardt that she had studied visions but found remarkable Neihardt's ability to convey the spiritual to the dominant culture (c3716 f42).

Impelling visionary re-creation is, as Joseph Campbell notes (117–118), a peak experience, an insight of such luminosity that it seems to proceed from an "other" or "outer" world. Psychologist Abraham Maslow explains that "what has been called the 'unitive consciousness' is often given in peak-experiences, i.e., a sense of the sacred glimpsed *in* and *through* the particular instance of the momentary, the secular, the worldly" (68)—as in Black Elk's vision of the Six Grandfathers, the two roads crossing in the sacred-hoop unity of the cosmos, the road of spiritual insight intersecting the road of time and difficulty, and unification at the spot of the Tree of Life.

The role of Black Elk and John Neihardt in producing *Black Elk Speaks* was to save and promulgate this great insight for all. As Maslow reminds us, this communication with the Mysterious can only be elicited, evoked, and lured by employing poetic language or action. In interviewing his subjects while studying peak experiences, Maslow said he

> "Learned," without realizing that I was learning, to shift over more and more to figures of speech, metaphors, similes, etc., and, in general, to use more and more poetic speech. It turns out that these are often more apt to "click," to touch off an echoing experience, a parallel,

isomorphic vibration than are sober, cool, carefully descriptive phrases. (78–79)

For Neihardt to propagate the vision required a poetics that Black Elk intuitively knew the writer possessed. Such artistry employs evocative, cadenced language close to (and sometimes reproducing parts of) ceremony: *Black Elk Speaks* simulates group tellings, describes ceremonies, provides the blueprint of rituals such as the Horse Dance. The book's rhythm and imagery are crafted to inspire; neither an academic nor a journalist could have helped Black Elk with this book the way Neihardt could. Only a poet who had received a vision could employ the language of imagination to achieve an effect impossible with the discursive, "cool phrases" to which Maslow refers. The stringy, digressive transcripts of Neihardt's interviews of Black Elk do not need to employ all these devices because Black Elk *knows* the truth of his telling. But Neihardt, writing for a skeptical mainstream audience, must conjure this truth using poetic strategies.

Our discussion of the two collaborators, then, places John Neihardt's poetry close to the influence of Black Elk's ceremonial presentation, using words to evoke the ineffable and poetic "music" to provide tones and cadence. *Black Elk Speaks* itself was created in a unitary collaboration that engaged words, music, dance, and art; the 1932 edition—with its paintings by Standing Bear, as well as its communal tellings and songs—reflected this aspect of the collaboration, as it added a pictorial dimension to the book, the text of which is then a synergy. Using his poetics, Neihardt sought to recapture his experience with Black Elk so that together these collaborators could present the sacred.

NOTE

1. Green's book provides much useful information about the Omaha during the time of transition experienced by Joseph La Flesche and his descendants, and it helps illuminate the milieu in which the young Neihardt became familiar with Native Americans.

4
THE ART OF *Black Elk Speaks*

Since you are interested, I will quote you what the Holy Man Black Elk said of me when he made me his spiritual son and named me Flaming Rainbow. . . . "He is a word-sender. This world is like a garden. Over this garden go his words like rain, and where they fall they leave it a little greener. And when his words have passed, the memory of them will stand long in the west like a flaming rainbow."

—NEIHARDT TO DR. AMADO M. YUZON, APRIL 9, 1971; C3778 F50

PREVIOUSLY, WE NOTICED SOME STRATEGIES USEFUL IN CONVEYING NEIHARDT'S text to a general but literate audience. This chapter explores the narrative art Neihardt used to turn the raw material of notes and remembrance into a book different from mainstream offerings and yet accessible to a mainstream readership. Looking at the original transcripts, the draft of *Black Elk Speaks* that shows Neihardt's editing, and the finished book will help us understand just how Neihardt employed poetic and editorial strategies to develop the art of *Black Elk Speaks.*[1]

WHAT LITERARY TECHNIQUES ASSIST NEIHARDT IN PRESENTING A UNIFIED TEXT? Regularizing the person or the address is one device. The transcripts record multiple speakers and forms of address, and the finished text simplifies them. First person—"I say"—and referential third person—"He says that . . ."—both become first person, as Raymond DeMallie (*Sixth* xxv) and Sally McCluskey

(238–239) indicate. The interviews also occur thematically: Enid Neihardt's steno books are labeled topically as "Black Elk's Vision," "Black Elk's Youth," and "Wounded Knee" (c3716 f402–405). But Neihardt organizes the material chronologically. Of interest is that Neihardt's publisher wanted chronological order except for the vision description, but Neihardt's organization places the vision solidly in its surrounding context. Note, for example, how the Great Vision is bracketed in the text, flanked on both sides by other visionary experiences and biographical-historical material. Within such a chronological framework, transitions must be intensified to impart a sense of continuity—unnecessary perhaps in oral communication, with its reliance on gesture and nuance, but important on the page. Therefore *Black Elk Speaks* contains strong transitions using time flow, repetition of concepts, and association. In other words, it employs the rhetoric of the written page made to look as though it were spoken.

Compressing the digressive features of oral communication while seeming to retain them imparts focus and minimizes the potential for deflecting the reader. For instance, the High Horse material seems to be an oral digression but in fact is placed strategically between two ominous sections, "At the Soldiers' Town" and "Wasichus in the Hills." The soldiers' town episode contains the story of the troops wanting to kill little Lakota boys because of their flagpole prank; Red Cloud intervenes, however. "Wasichus in the Hills" chronicles an unprovoked cavalry raid on a Lakota camp in which Crazy Horse intervenes to retaliate. Both episodes flanking "High Horse's Courting" thus contain auguries of conflict and trouble while depicting the corrupted values of the wasichu. "High Horse's Courting," in contrast, displays traditional Lakota values even as it foreshadows conflict in its ending raid on the Crows. Neihardt uses the High Horse episode to teach an uninformed mainstream audience about Lakota values and humor but also to provide important foreshadowing while slowing the pace to reinforce ideas. And those who believe the 1931 transcripts in the Western Historical Manuscript Collection constitute the entirety of Black Elk's teaching of Neihardt that produced *Black Elk Speaks* should consider this episode well. The High Horse telling, *not* in the 1931 transcripts, *is* discussed in the post–*Black Elk Speaks* 1944 transcripts and provides material for use in *When the Tree Flowered*, as DeMallie indicates (*Sixth* 77). Yet no transcription of this story, clearly told to Neihardt by Black Elk, exists in the 1931 collection of notes. In placing this tale in its crucial position in *Black Elk Speaks*, Neihardt employs a strategy used throughout the book—reinforcing a sense of forward movement through significant, even archetypal, elements.

In addition, Neihardt must retain features of diction and idiom both understandable and yet unique-sounding to a white audience. Key phrases appearing in Lakota (such as *wasichu, hoka hey,* and others) first strike the reader from the dominant culture as exotic but with continual use become familiar and expected. Such repetition is a key element in convincing the reader that the world of the text is internally self-referencing or verifiable. Wolfgang Iser, in *The Act of Reading,* reminds us that "the totality has to be assembled, and only then do the aspects take on their full significance, because only then can all the references carry their full weight. It is the reader who must conceive the totality which the aspects prestructure, and it is in his mind that the text coheres" (147).

These terms also resonate with the sound of the original language, something that concerned Neihardt in other writing. For example, Neihardt's early translation of the *Agamemnon* tries to duplicate the music and rhythm of the original and to retain the original's poetic qualities (c3716 f200). In *Black Elk Speaks* stylistic features that make the telling read as authentic include large phrases that collectively describe something or that act as nouns. These are features of the Lakota language and are what the grammarian Eugene Buechel calls "clausal substantives" (228). Also characteristic are a word ordering inverted with respect to English—for example, in adjectival placement; a non-Latinate vocabulary relatively free of polysyllabic words; and the use of repetition.

Mari Sandoz studied these aspects in *Black Elk Speaks,* learning the phrasing to enhance her terminology, vocabulary, and prose rhythm in writing *Crazy Horse: The Strange Man of the Oglalas* (Stauffer 9). Compare Sandoz—"Uncle, he said, you notice the way I act, but do not worry. There are caves and holes for me to live in, and perhaps out here the powers will help me. The time is short, and I must plan for the good of my people" (358)—with Neihardt on the same subject in *Black Elk Speaks*: "Uncle, you have noticed me the way I act. But do not worry; there are caves and holes for me to live in, and out here the spirits may help me. I am making plans for the good of my people" (136). Neihardt has traveled farther down the path of distinctive idiom, using, to Euro-American ears, a displaced phrase that is a noun cluster, or clausal substantive: "the way I act." Sandoz has learned about employing direct, monosyllabic speech from Neihardt while carrying over from her reading of *Black Elk Speaks* some repetition of "and" found in the original transcripts as well.

Reviewers have, of course, noticed many of the stylistic aspects of *Black Elk Speaks.* Sally McCluskey comments on the art of this book in her important article "Black Elk Speaks: And So Does John Neihardt" (1972). McCluskey focuses on aspects of *Black Elk Speaks* as literature: its characterization (232–233), the editing of material to provide clarity for a general reader (232–233), and the use of dramatic technique to relate events (233, 234, 239). McCluskey discusses synoptic passages in which Neihardt gathers separate but related issues into unified statements (237–238). She demonstrates Neihardt's skill at removing academic language from the text; Neihardt avoids passive, ornate, and multisyllabic constructions while using parallelism to emphasize points (240–241). She concludes with praise for Neihardt's approach (241–242).

Writing Neihardt in 1970, Robert Sayre notes that this approach is employed as an expression of affection and understanding. Sayre likens Black Elk to Socrates and Neihardt to Plato, remarking that Neihardt's artistry with the printed word complemented Black Elk's with the spoken word (c3778 f45). Raymond DeMallie adds that often "critics [have] missed the real dynamic of the book, the electric energy of the meeting of two like minds from two different cultures" ("Legacy" 111). Yet he reminds us that "Neihardt was an extraordinarily faithful spokesman for Black Elk. Although his psychic empathy for Black Elk might have led him to take great liberties with the material, he did not do so" (120). We can learn much about the specifics of Neihardt's part of the literary collaboration and his writing process as we watch his poetics in action.

As we consider Neihardt's revising transcript and memory into draft, a schematic such as that in Figure 4.1 can help us reference the location of some key elements of text appearing in the 1931 transcripts Enid Neihardt made of her stenographic notes and will help us understand the placement of those elements in the 1931 manuscript drafted by John Neihardt immediately following the family's return to Branson, Missouri. John Neihardt clearly used the typed transcript of Enid's stenographic notes extensively. As Enid's reminiscence, dated March 19, 1932, says: "I took down in shorthand all the material Daddy acquired while there, which was voluminous. Black Elk's son, Ben Black Elk, translated into English, as his father, Black Elk, and others spoke in Sioux. I remember being concerned at whether or not my notes would get 'cold,' but they didn't" (c3716 f464).

Of course, substantial overlap exists between these sections of notes, and much material found in one place in the steno notes or their transcripts is distributed across the text of *Black Elk Speaks* as it is needed or where it would make the most sense. For example, a note on "Tablet Two-A," "Black Elk's Youth," says "See Wounded Knee book for the rest of the horse dance etc. Then return here" (c3716 f403).

Figure 4.1 Chart showing location of key parts of Black Elk Speaks *in collection folders. Courtesy, the John G. Neihardt Papers, c. 1858–1974, Western Historical Manuscript Collection, Columbia, Missouri; the John G. Neihardt Trust.*

1931 Manuscript	*1931 Transcript*
PRAYER ORIGIN OF PIPE f249 pp. 2–7	PRAYER ORIGIN OF PIPE f412 pp. 1–13
YOUTH TO FIRST VISION f250 pp. 8–28	YOUTH TO FIRST VISION f413
THE GREAT VISION f251 pp. 29–52 f252 pp. 52a–73	THE GREAT VISION f414
THE BUTCHERING AT WOUNDED KNEE f274 pp. 353–368	GHOST DANCE AND WOUNDED KNEE f420
AFTERMATH f275 pp. 369–379	
EPILOGUE f275 pp. 380–385	

Neihardt's sensitivity to his material appears in his reshaping, condensation, clarification of scenes, and poetic techniques. These qualities are prominent in several episodes: the offering of the pipe, Red Cloud's speech at the Stronghold (from the Wounded Knee material), the group conversation of "Fire Thunder Speaks" and its subsequent presentation of Black Elk's first vision, the account of Wounded Knee, and the book's postscript. These are examined next. Transcript and manuscript sections including them appear after this discussion, with my annotations.

THE TRANSCRIPT PAGES COVERING THE ORIGIN OF THE PIPE CONTAIN MUCH other material not used in the order it appeared. Their relationship to the manuscript of *Black Elk Speaks* indicates the excellence of Neihardt's editing. In transcript this section begins with the story of the Calf Pipe Woman bringing the sacred pipe to the Lakota, follows with a brief digression on the spirit-keeping ceremony, returns to the story of the Calf Pipe Woman, then digresses (using a third-person reference to Black Elk: "Black Elk thinks . . .") about the Indian relationship to animals. All this appears on pages 1–3 of Enid's typescript! Pages 4–5 of the typescript contain a glossary of terms that recur in different spots in *Black Elk Speaks*: names for the months, lunar phases, weather phenomena (3–5). A discussion of Lakota star knowledge (5) includes details explaining traveling by night. The sixth page (numbered page 1) begins Standing Bear's introduction of the traditional prayer known to him and Black Elk; the seventh page (numbered page 2) continues the prayer's rendition but interrupts it with a note about the value and sacred properties of the cottonwood tree mentioned in the prayer. After the note an offering invocation and song are recorded (2–3); the prayer resumes at the bottom of page 3. Here the transcripts do not make clear distinctions about which speaker is the source of particular parts of the text.

Next comes a large diagram by Standing Bear of the Custer battle, with annotations by John Neihardt. An unpaginated leaf contains a glossary of terms (such as *Oh-ohna-gazhee,* used late in *Black Elk Speaks*) and lists reminders—"Bulletin No. 61, Bureau of American Ethnology," for example. The next sheet contains a description of Crazy Horse (parts of which are used in the discussion of Crazy Horse in *Black Elk Speaks,* 84–87). The last two pages of the sequence (actually pages 12 and 13) contain fragmented notes about the "kill talks" made at one of the dances in which the Neihardts participated (see Figure 4.2). Although it is fascinating ethnography, this disjointed and compressed section of the transcripts lacks appeal as a literary work for any reading public Neihardt must reach.

Perusing these thirteen pages gives us a sense of how much information was coming at the Neihardts and of the great speed at which it emerged, but reading the corresponding manuscript of *Black Elk Speaks* as it carefully unfolds makes us aware of Neihardt's choices in presentation. The Custer material surfaces much later in *Black Elk Speaks,* for example, as do the many terms and allusions to events. But at the beginning Neihardt focuses on the pipe and the prayer, two issues central to a reader's understanding of Black Elk's outlook. Drawing upon experiences and material from his first encounter with Black Elk and from the later interviews and making the speaker's voice personal again, Neihardt directs the reader to those important points (see Figure 4.3).

Following such direction, pages 3 and 4 of the draft establish the theme of synecdoche begun in the opening of *Black Elk Speaks,* in which we learn that this book is not a conventional autobiography but rather an image of a people, a life, and a view of the universe. The pipe is also a reflection of the entire Lakota cosmos and its interrelationships. The pipe is presented as a synecdoche beginning with the passage "before we smoke it, you must see how it is made, + what it means" (3). The ribbons are the four quarters with their associations; the directional powers are enfolded into One, represented by the eagle feather (3–4). Neihardt strikes out the intellectualizing words *such* and *like* in this description, opting not for simile but for direct equivalence in "Is not the sky a father + the earth a mother" and in substituting "the thoughts that should rise high as eagles do" for "such thoughts . . . ," which is what was first written (4). Neihardt intensifies the image of humanity nursing at the breast of Mother Earth by replacing "little children" with "babies," a warmer image and a truer one (4).

Resisting a wasichu impulse to rush through events, Neihardt closes his extended synecdoche and inserts the material beginning on page 4a, which is derived from the stenographic transcripts and tells the story of the Calf Pipe Woman. Neihardt wants a reverent, poetic diction but not stilted phrasing; that is why he replaces "Then a foolish one among the scouts had bad thoughts + spoke bad words" with "Then one of the scouts, being foolish, had bad thoughts + spoke them" (4a). This revised choice has a smoother cadence and avoids pompous repetition. A similar revision occurs on page 5a, when "the man who was very much afraid went quickly and told the people, who did at once as they were told." The preliminary phrasing, apparent through the strikeovers, is "the man who was very much afraid went quickly and told the people, who were very much excited" (4a)—again, a rhetorical balance that seems stilted. But when repetition counts, when it is central to the artifact itself, Neihardt retains it. For example, he does not alter the translation of the Calf Pipe Woman's song as it appears on pages 1–2 of the transcript:

> With visible breath I am walking.
> A voice I am sending as I walk.
> In a sacred manner I am walking.
> With visible tracks I am walking.
> In a sacred manner I am walking. (c3716 f412; c3716 f249)

Finally, employing transition by concept and returning to the lighting of the pipe as he resumes page 4, Neihardt induces the reader to connect "visible breath" with the smoke (4–5).

Page 5 links the discussion of the pipe to the offering prayer (as it is described in the transcripts). Here we see Neihardt considering other language—"I raise my," "Raising the," "Giving the"—but returning to the central word from the transcript, "offering": "Offering the mouthpiece first of all to the One above—so—I send a voice" (5). Lest an uninformed readership misunderstand the concept of "power," Neihardt twice replaces it with "strength" on page 6 of the manuscript.

RED CLOUD'S SPEECH AT THE STRONGHOLD EXEMPLIFIES NEIHARDT'S ROLE IN organizing information for the reader when the sources are confusing. Earlier we observed that Neihardt solidifies the digressive transcriptions to give the reader a sharp perception of the four ascents Black Elk is to know. Neihardt employs the same strategy when condensing other material in the transcripts. For example, c3716 f420, page 149, reproduced in Figure 4.8, reports two speeches with similar content made at the Stronghold when Afraid-of-His-Horses and Red Cloud urge peace despite the holdouts' desire for revenge. Red Cloud is reported to have said, "Boys, this is a hard winter. If it were in the summer we would keep on fighting; but, boys, we cannot go on fighting, because the winter is hard on us, so we should make peace and I'll see that nobody will be hurt."

Privately, according to the transcripts, Afraid-of-His-Horses tells Black Elk, Good Thunder, Kicking Bear, and Short Bull:

> Relatives, if this were in summer time it would not be so hard. If this were winter, my people at Pine Ridge would have joined you and we would have had to fight to a finish, and I don't want mine and your people to make us kill each other among ourselves. I don't care how many the soldiers are, without the Indian scouts they cannot fight and the army will be helpless. So, relatives, if this were in the summer we would have joined you and had it to a finish. But this is winter and it is hard on our children especially, so let us go back and make peace.

Neihardt combines the two overlapping speeches into

> Our party wanted to go out and fight anyway, but Red Cloud made a speech to us something like this: "Brothers, this is a very hard winter. The women and children are starving and freezing. If this were summer, I would say to keep on fighting to the end. But we cannot do this. We must think of the women and children and that it is very bad for them. So we must make peace, and I will see that nobody is hurt by the soldiers." (Bison edition 269–270; also c3716 f275, 378)

The abrupt material attributed to Red Cloud in the transcripts and the disjointed speech credited to Afraid-of-His-Horses in the transcripts have been combined, their best qualities distilled. The phrase "women and children" echoes the tragedy of Wounded Knee that has just occurred (262) and continues the theme both in Black Elk's telling and Neihardt's retelling that the continuing generations are more important than the individual; the large pattern overshadows the transient details. Throughout *Black Elk Speaks* the writer strives for clarity, structure, and cadence so that the reader will understand. The decisions made are not arbitrary but instead are the work of a collaborator intent on conveying the essence of Black Elk's message.

DRAMA AND CHORUS FUNCTION AS ANOTHER KEY STRATEGY OF PRESENTATION. Yet the transcripts discussing Black Elk's "Youth and First Vision" indicate that the polyvocal element in the telling of his story is not an arbitrary creation of Neihardt but rather a natural consequence of events. At the beginning of the transcript a list of the participants in the discussion appears: Standing Bear, Black Elk, Fire Thunder, and Holy Black Tail Deer. Had Neihardt wanted to enhance some latent classical choric quality of this material (noticed by Bataille 140), he might have retained the list of participants in his final text. If Neihardt were unduly influenced by Latin literature or writers in the "accepted" Euro-American tradition, he might even have labeled the list "Dramatis Personae." Instead he allows the reader to see the discussions unfold naturally, enhancing them with detail when necessary to clarify items for a general readership and compressing other speeches that divert the reader's attention from main points. Notice Figure 4.4, "Fire Thunder Speaks," pages 2–4 in the transcript; and Figure 4.5, "Fire Thunder Speaks," pages 15–19 in Neihardt's manuscript. Neihardt weaves together the abruptly stated material of the transcription, repositioning clauses and using compound sentences, as in this example.

> From page 2 of the transcript
> I was 16 years old at this time. We were camped on Tongue River. A man by the name of Big Road was the chief of our band at this time. Red Cloud was of course over all of us.
>
> From page 15 of Neihardt's manuscript
> I was 16 years old when this happened and after the big council on the Powder we had moved over to the Tongue river where we were camping at the mouth of Peno Creek. There were many of us there. Red Cloud was over all of us, but the chief of our band was Big Road.

Here the abrupt transcript reacquires the coherence of a speech by an actual character through joining concepts with coordinate conjunctions, eliminating redundancy, and adding contextualizing detail necessary to establish the scene; the reader needs to know where everyone was.

Such a strategy of clarifying the background or scene emerges as we study the development of the manuscript section discussing Black Elk's first vision.[2] Figure 4.6 depicts its page in the transcript—a typed summary numbered page 1, although not first in the sequence recorded. Figure 4.7 reproduces the material as integrated into *Black Elk Speaks*—pages 27–28 of f250. Both accounts contain the thunderstorm, the desire to shoot birds with a newly made bow and arrows, the two messengers calling Black Elk and turning into geese, and the kingbird telling Black Elk that the clouds were "one-sided" and that a voice was summoning him. The detail and sequencing of the manuscript improve the flow of events, however, by explaining context to the reader. Specific description of the storm is clearer in the manuscript: at the beginning a thunderstorm is building; next the clouds look at Black Elk as the action unfolds; finally, when the messengers veer toward the west, changing into geese, the storm begins.

Neihardt intensifies the natural backdrop from which a supernatural event emerges, creating a dramatic tension mirroring the psyche of the young, naive Black Elk—for earlier in this section of the transcripts Black Elk interjects amid the reminiscences of the other men "When I was four years old, I played a little here and there and while playing I would hear a voice now and then, but I did not catch on to it very well then" (f413, 7). The manuscript sums up the young Black Elk's internal quandary with the remark "I did not tell this vision to anyone. I liked to think about it, but I was afraid to tell it" (28). The potential of energy inherent in the thunderstorm has been internalized in the youthful Black Elk, where it will brew again; in addition, the apparently "natural" and "supernatural" are united in the perception and very being of Black Elk, with consequences to emerge later. Such forecasting acts as a link to future events in the book, including its ending; the reader has been primed to anticipate what will come while being taught that Black Elk's worldview contains no dualistic division of phenomena—communication flows between all parts of a spiritually interconnected universe in which nature is itself a character.

Neihardt's respect and understanding promote the artful conveying of this unity. But the magnitude of the challenge Neihardt faced was great, and had it not been for his empathy, the book he produced would have failed. It would have either bordered on clinical, nonliterary ethnography or dissolved into the saccharine unctuousness of many other early-twentieth-century productions, including one that narrates a vision. Consider *The Indians' Book: Songs and Legends of the American Indians* by Natalie Curtis (2d ed., 1923), which records cultural artifacts but embeds those elements in a progressivist matrix that ironically freezes them in time and renders their telling suspect.

Contained within the text is "Short Bull's Narrative," the testament of the former Ghost Dance leader. His account is prefaced with a note by Curtis, explaining:

> The white reader should bear in mind that this is the narrative of a seer. As is usual with Indians, the language is often figurative. In the English rendering, the attempt has been made to reflect the rhythmic dignity and simplicity of the Dakota. The narrated visit to the spirit-camp was probably a vision, or was made in a trance. To the Indian, such a vision is as real as a waking event. The visit to the other camp was a reality. (45)

In mediating between a "white reader" and a Native American speaker, Curtis not only intrudes on the telling and imposes Euro-American dualism upon it, but her tone is patronizing. And Curtis adheres to another Eurocentrism, the "Idea of Progress" or "social evolution." Seemingly a part of Short Bull's narrative, following it in the same font, is this passage:

> With clasped hands stood the Indian narrator and the white recorder, and then the white friend spoke:
>
> "I leave you with this word: Be of good heart. Even though the old days are gone, never to come again, still be of good heart. A better day will dawn for you and your people. The old days will never be again, even as a man will never again be a child. Those days were the happy childhood of your race. Manhood brings sorrow and sorrow wisdom. . . . In the land where the sun rises the Indians have friends. Not westward, but eastward seek the coming of the light." (47)

This speech of the "recorder" is, curiously, told in the same prose style as Short Bull's narrative, using unwarranted repetition and intrusive imagery and thereby calling into question the veracity of the telling itself, which is of similar construction. For example, a reference either to government paternalism or to Christianity replacing other beliefs lurks behind the "progressive" image ending this passage, which admonishes Short Bull to turn from the "west," the home of Wovoka, and face the east—either the American East, the seat of federal legislation, or the cartographic East, the place of origin of Christianity. Had Neihardt been profoundly influenced by the doctrines of dualism and social evolution that motivated Curtis to poeticize her discourse with Short Bull, a very different *Black Elk Speaks* would have emerged, particularly in the closing section on Wounded Knee.[3]

A STARK CONTRAST WITH CURTIS'S MISAPPLIED AND UNDIFFERENTIATED POETICIZing appears when we analyze Neihardt's treatment of Wounded Knee. The transcripts reflect stenographic material taken down at the site of the Wounded Knee Massacre but obviously only recorded while stationary, not while Black Elk, Ben, and the Neihardts walked about the location. The transcripts are, as usual, choppy. Now John Neihardt, as he states in the preface to *Black Elk Speaks*, had obtained the "facts" of history before coming to Pine Ridge but needed the emotional understanding that contact with Black Elk could bring. That is, Neihardt at that point possessed the ideas but not the poetry to explicate the tragedy, to pull its diverse threads together. Studying excerpts from the transcript covering Wounded Knee (Figure 4.8), from the corresponding manuscript (Figure 4.9), and from the 1988 Bison text of *Black Elk Speaks* will help us understand Neihardt's role in endowing the facts with the poetic impact he had gathered from his time with Black Elk.

Neihardt puts Black Elk's skirmish with the soldiers first and *then* tells the story of the massacre as Black Elk gives it. This reversing of order allows the chapter to end with the scene of the aftermath: cold, lifeless, and somber. Nature, as we have observed, provides a continual backdrop for and commentary on events in *Black Elk Speaks*. We have moved from the vibrant world of the changing seasons that surrounds traditional Lakota life to the dead world of ice and snow, as the victims and all they have stood for seem to have perished. But not so fast. Remember that Black Elk and others save relatives, including babies, as mentioned in the manuscript and text. The Lakota, including the new generation, will survive.

This is not the "end of the trail." Had Neihardt been of Curtis's mind, he would have incorporated resurrection imagery or paternalistic effluvium at this point. Neihardt does neither. He provides and intensifies descriptions of the landscape that his readers need and turns this description into a poetic statement at the end of the section. The final text begins with short sentences and culminates in a lengthy compound construction that reflects the sight of the long, twisting gulch full of bodies:

> It was a good winter day when all this happened. The sun was shining. But after the soldiers marched away from their dirty work, a heavy snow began to fall. The wind came up in the night. There was a big blizzard, and it grew very cold. The snow drifted deep in the crooked gulch, and it was one long grave of butchered women and children and babies, who had never done any harm and were only trying to run away. (262)

This shift from day to night and from brightness to deathly cold occurs at the end of chapter 24 in *Black Elk Speaks.* Night, metaphorically, has settled in. But remember Neihardt's metaphor of the looped lines of history and Black Elk's view of history as cycles, as stated in the beginning of *The Sacred Pipe* (Brown xix). This is not a permanent night. Chapter 25 chronicles the beginning of painful recovery and opens with the rescued babies; life goes on.

This condensation of Black Elk's experience, gathered from the totality of his telling, seems the product of effortless speech or fluid writing, but in fact pages 367 and 368 of Neihardt's manuscript show the difficulty with which the poetic expression of ideas emerged. Crossed-out passages, represented here in parentheses and brackets, show the gradual focusing of the concept; underlining represents Neihardt's insertions; bracketed hyphens depict unreadable scratch-outs.

> It was a good winter day when [that] all this happened. The sun was shining. But after the soldiers marched away from their dirty work a heavy snow began to fall [+] The wind came up [-] in the night. [-] [-] There was a big blizzard + [Three days afterward the people who came to find (look) (about) (for) the relatives] it grew very cold. The snow drifted deep in [The snow was deep, and under it] [The drifts were deep along the] the crooked gulch, and it was one long grave of [-] butchered women + children + babies who had never done any harm + were only trying to run away.

The deleted passages are prose; the final passages are poetry, a poetic crystallization of the essence of the slaughter. "Women and children and babies who" even scans as a sequence of dactyls. Such faithful literary development of the factual is the kind of writing to which Michael Castro refers when he notes that the added sections "extend" the original rather than originate something and that the "extension" is derived from "a hard-earned mutual understanding and trust" (90). Here, confronting the abyss and desolation, the consciousnesses of Neihardt and Black Elk merge in the truth of art.

AESTHETIC AND SPIRITUAL CONSISTENCY UNIFIES THE BOOK AS AN ARTISTIC AND a religious statement. Art and spirit converge, in fact, in the book's final part. The last section of Neihardt's manuscript is the "Author's Postscript" in which Neihardt narrates the trip to Harney Peak and Black Elk's prayer there (Figure 4.10). Corroborative detail appears in Hilda Neihardt's *Black Elk and Flaming Rainbow,* pages 90–95 and 127–129; pages 127–129 reproduce a transcript of a tape in which Ben Black Elk and John Neihardt reminisce about the event. A March 8, 1956, copy of this tape, produced by KOMU television, is in the Western Historical Manuscript Collection, c3716 vc4, and a videotape of the original is also at the John G. Neihardt Center, Bancroft, Nebraska. It is not just that John Neihardt wanted to deflect depressiveness at the end of *Black Elk Speaks* by recounting the trip up Harney and the prayer at the top. Rather, this episode is artistically and spiritually consistent with the entire book, constituting a validation of Black Elk as holy man and of his message as holy while itself performing the function of prophecy.

First, in both the spiritual and physical topography of the text, the journey to and prayer at Harney Peak is an ascent, like others in the text: a spiritual quest made not without trepidation and difficulty. Ben Black Elk remembered

> That while we was going up—he was old, you know—and he wanted to go up, and he was in a rush. I asked him to sit down and said, "Why, father, are you in a rush?" And he said, "Well, son, you probably know what I told you about my vision, and you probably know now about the tree—the tree of life." And he said, "That's where I saw the whole works. Everybody was in unity under the Great Spirit." (H. Neihardt 127)

Ben Black Elk continued, reminiscing about the validation of Black Elk by the Powers:

> Now, he said, "There's going to be something happen up there *today*. See, that tree has withered; it's all withered. But if there is a little root that is living, something is going to happen. And if I and my vision is true," he said, "the thunder beings will answer my prayers." (H. Neihardt 127)

Neihardt and Ben Black Elk then recall that out of a clear sky the clouds arrived, and it rained, as Neihardt said, "about five minutes. And we could see seventy-five miles everyplace—and it was *clear*" (H. Neihardt 128). Neihardt said later that he believed, other than this rain in the middle of the drought, "it did not rain all summer." Neihardt did not understand this rain to be "coincidence" (c3716 ac53). Rather, the validation of Black Elk included a message that the tree was not dead, that it would revive. Neihardt interprets part of the prophecy as coming true when he writes in the 1971 preface to *Black Elk*

Speaks that "the old prophet's wish that I bring his message to the world is actually being fulfilled" (1972 ed. xiii). But in 1931 the book had to win acceptance from skeptical readers of the dominant culture. Reading the manuscript draft of the "Postscript" to *Black Elk Speaks* reveals Neihardt employing poetic strategies to deliver the conclusion's prophetic message (see Figure 4.10).

At the outset of the postscript the narrative setting is Cuny Table, overlooking the dead world that is symbolized by the Badlands and that reflects the seeming annihilation of the sacred hoop; page 379 of the manuscript has just told us that there seems to be "no center any longer, + the sacred tree is dead" (Neihardt's summary at the close of the preceding chapter; c3716 f275). But again, not so fast. Out of apparent annihilation emerges the promise implicit in the events at Harney Peak. From Cuny Table, looking across at the desolate landscape, Black Elk and his group can see the visionary center of the world, Harney Peak, standing "black above the far sky-rim" (Figure 4.10, 380). Neihardt began this passage with the phrase "On the far sky rim" but replaced that agentless construction with a clause depicting Black Elk pointing at the peak. For Black Elk initiates the quest that ends the book:

> There, when I was young, the spirits took me in my vision to the center of the earth [world to show to] and showed me all the good things in the sacred hoop of the world. I [want to go] wish I could stand up there in the flesh before I die, for there is something I [must] want to say to the Six Grandfathers. (380)

Hiking toward the summit, Black Elk tells Ben that "the Thunder Beings of the West should hear me when I send a voice, + there should be at least [a little rain + some thunder] a little thunder and a little rain" (381); here Neihardt uses parallelism to reinforce the speech. Then Neihardt the narrator steps back from the scene, back from the text itself, and addresses the reader directly. Perhaps he had in mind the frustrating cynicism, materialism, and limited empiricism of the dominant culture that he had combated in years of poems, essays, and reviews, for his first choice of words—"20th century," "our progressive age," "amusing coincidence," "In a progressive age, notably proficient"—seethes with an irony Neihardt decided to control in the final version of the text:

> What happened is, of course, related to Wasichu readers as being merely a more or less striking coincidence. It was a bright and cloudless day, and after we had reached the summit the sky was perfectly

> clear. It was a season of drouth, one of the worst in the memory of the old men. The sky remained clear until about the conclusion of the ceremony. (1988 Bison ed. 271–272)

Here the understatement itself carries the burden of irony and the word "Wasichu" encapsulates all the frustrating aspects of the dominant culture.

The manuscript version of the prayer Black Elk then gives contains few passages that were rewritten and comprises an unbroken, conceptual unity. But then gently interposing in the final moments of the prayer is this passage:

> [Here]
>
> We who listened, [-] now noted that thin clouds had gathered [above] about us. A scant [chill] chill rain was falling + there was low muttering thunder without lightning. [Raising his voice] With tears running down his cheeks, the old man raised his voice to a thin high wail, + chanted. (384–385)

The published text retains the selected wording except for its "A scant chill rain began to fall" and its addition of a comma after "low" (1988 Bison ed. 274).

The final petition of the prayer then comes, and a line below it in manuscript shows that Neihardt thought of ending the book right there. A lesser writer might have done so, or a writer believing in the end of the Lakota journey. But both artistically and spiritually that ending, although it provides strong closure, is unsatisfactory. In part it is unsatisfactory *because* it provides strong closure. It could imply that, rain or not, Black Elk's world and belief system are finished, the outworn product of a past that has been overtaken by the progressive present. Yet everything in *Black Elk Speaks* and in Neihardt's personal makeup militates against that point of view.

SO THE MANUSCRIPT PROCEEDS, ADDING ADDITIONAL DETAIL, SHOWING—EVEN as we saw in Black Elk's first vision—the universe and Black Elk becoming one. Black Elk, attired ceremonially and made pitiable so the Grandfathers will help him, weeps; it rains as the Grandfathers validate his power and the truth of his vision; and then "In a little while" the sky clears again (385) as the light reappears. We have moved from the dark-night aftermath of Wounded Knee through tears to a promise of renewal. And after the rain has passed, the world will be greener as the cycle continues.

NOTES

1. I use the 1988 Bison edition of *Black Elk Speaks* throughout this discussion, since it has been the most widely cited version in recent commentary. All page numbers reference this edition.

Of relevance to studying the primary materials is the 1995 Modern Language Association "Statement on the Significance of Primary Records," which urges that such artifacts be preserved for use. Neihardt's original papers and manuscripts reveal minute particulars not readily noticed in scanned or photostatic copies, which is why original texts are important to the scholar.

2. Author and professor N. Scott Momaday provides an excellent analysis of Neihardt's account of Black Elk's first vision, seeing in it an exemplar of the oral tradition in storytelling. See Momaday's "To Save a Great Vision," 34.

3. Curiously, some critics of *Black Elk Speaks* seem themselves influenced by the Eurocentric concepts of dualism and social evolution, as Dale Stover indicates in "Eurocentrism and Native Americans."

THE ART OF TRANSFORMATION—FROM TRANSCRIPT TO MANUSCRIPT

This section presents images of John Neihardt's notes and draft pages, allowing us to study his art at work. The original documents are in the Western Historical Manuscript Collection, 23 Ellis Library, University of Missouri, Columbia, Missouri. They are used with permission from that collection and from the John G. Neihardt Trust. My notes accompanying these figures explore the relationship of transcript, manuscript, and finished book.

In providing notes to these figures, I employ the following abbreviations:

T = transcript(s)

M = Neihardt's handwritten manuscript that became *Black Elk Speaks*

BES = 1988 University of Nebraska Press Bison edition of *Black Elk Speaks*, which reproduces the original 1932 text, although not all illustrations

Page numbers, when necessary, follow the abbreviations.

These notes complement discussions in other parts of this book covering development of style, adaptation of tangled or choppy raw material to a reader-friendly narrative, and issues of continuity or organization. The transcripts preserve artifacts of the original interviews that are inconsistent or are oral/poetic—such as abrupt shifts of theme, pronoun, or speaker—not always noted in the pages and requiring memorial reconstruction later. Also, elliptical statements and sudden initial appearances of recondite information assumed to be known suggest a range of discussion far wider than that partially recorded in the transcripts. Not only was memory required to turn the interviews into a draft; the manuscript reveals that Neihardt worked hard to provide proportion, since extended digression and its opposite—extreme, elliptical compression—both features of oral communication, are adjusted for a smooth-flowing text sustaining reader interest.

In addition, certain aspects of the transcripts that DeMallie at times removed from his presentation for the general reader's benefit (*Sixth* xxv–xxvi) are nevertheless important, especially as they impact discussions of Neihardt's supposed "poeticizing" of the raw material through the use of archaic diction, the prevalence of run-on sentences, the verse-style utterances standing as paragraphs, and the effect gained by inverting subject and object. *Thee* and *thy* as translations of second-person personal pronouns, the run-on sentence, the irregular paragraphing in associational bursts of expression or in verselike rhythm, and the inverted sentence are all features of the transcripts' material.

SUBJECT LIST OF FIGURES 4.2–4.10

BEGINNINGS AND INVOCATIONS: PIPE AND PRAYER

Figure 4.2 (T): c3716 f412. This material covers the pipe, the prayer, vocabulary, and context.

Figure 4.3 (M): c3716 f249. Pages 3 onward integrate the pipe and the prayer in Neihardt's manuscript.

EARLY CONFLICT: FIRE THUNDER SPEAKS

Figure 4.4 (T): c3716 f413, 1–4. Pages 2–4 contain the transcript of "Fire Thunder Speaks."

Figure 4.5 (M): c3716 f250. Pages 15–19 depict "Fire Thunder Speaks" in manuscript.

THE FIRST VISION

Figure 4.6 (T): c3716 f413. The last page in the folder, although numbered "1," is a summary of Black Elk's first vision in the transcripts.

Figure 4.7 (M): c3716 f250. Pages 27 and 28 contain the manuscript description of the first vision.

WOUNDED KNEE

Figure 4.8 (T): c3716 f420. Pages 139–150 of the transcripts discuss Wounded Knee and its aftermath.

Figure 4.9 (M): c3716 f274. Pages 353–360 and 365–368 of the manuscript discuss Wounded Knee and its aftermath.

THE ENDING OF *BLACK ELK SPEAKS* IN MANUSCRIPT

Figure 4.10 (M): c3716 f275. Death moves to rebirth.

BEGINNINGS AND INVOCATIONS: PIPE AND PRAYER NOTES TO TRANSCRIPT, FIGURE 4.2

Origins of Peace Pipe

Although several versions of the story exist, T reinforces the concept that the scout with untoward thoughts was evil, adding, "That is what happened to him for being bad"; this is not Neihardt's alleged crypto-Puritanism at work, and Neihardt deletes the repeated moralizing. Compare BES 3–4, which ends with the image of the skeleton covered with worms, using "foolish" twice in the telling:

> And the foolish one went; but just as he stood before her, there was a white cloud that came and covered them. And the beautiful young woman came out of the cloud, and when it blew away the foolish man was a skeleton covered with worms. [Omits "That is what happened to him for being bad"].

T also uses "thy nation" twice; BES 4 uses "the nation," editing out a construction some regard as "biblical."

T shows that the Calf Pipe Woman is seen carrying something, which turns out to be the pipe; BES 4 connects the "something" with the "pipe." T contains lore about the pipe deleted or subsumed in BES; BES deletes the second story of the buffalo changing into a human but retains the connection T makes between the Indian and the buffalo in the text of BES 9.

Months of the year/lunar phases/weather/star lore. T provides these terms used throughout BES, as in BES 138, "so cold the sun made himself fires."

Prayer to go with vision. T shows Standing Bear introducing prayer. Prayer's "thee" is changed to "you" in BES 5 (and in DeMallie, *Sixth* 286). BES condenses T section and its parenthetical digression on the Flowering Tree (which image pervades all of BES) and retains the ideas of tenderness, emergence from the ground, and hopes for a prosperous nation. Rest of T is very close to BES 5–6.

Sketch of Custer fight. Used in BES 105–130.

List of terms. Used throughout BES.

Crazy Horse. BES 84–87 uses detail in T.

Dance notes. BES 266–267 uses material in T notes of Black Elk's kill talk describing Black Elk's being wounded.

Wounded Knee Massacre. BES 256–260 contains some of T material.

Origination of peace pipe.

The Indians were in camp and they had a meeting to send scouts out to kill buffalo. They (Scouts) were on top of a hill and as they looked to the north in the distance something was appearing. They were going on, but they wanted to find out what it was and they kept looking and finally it came closer; then they found out it was a woman. Then one of the men said: "That is a woman coming." One of them had bad thoughts of her and one of them said: "This is a sacred woman, throw all bad thots aside." She came up the hill where they were. She was very beautiful, her long hair hanging down and she had on a beautiful buckskin coat. She put down what she was carrying and covered it up with sage. She knew what they had in their minds. She said: "Probably you do not know me, but if you want to do as you think, come." So the one said to the other, "That is what I told you, but you wouldn't listen to me." So the man (scout) went and just as he faced her, there was a cloud that came and covered them. The beautiful woman walked out of the cloud and stood there. Then the cloud blew off and the man was nothing but a skeleton with worms eating on it. That is what happened to him for being bad. She turned to the other one and said, "You shall go home and tell thy nation that I am coming. Therefore in the center of thy nation they shall build a big teepee and there I will come." So this man left at once and he was very scared, for his friend was a skeleton. He told the tribe what had happened and they all got excited and right away they prepared a place for her to come. They built a teepee right in the center and she was now in it. She put what she was carrying facing the East. All the people gathered right there. She sang a song as she entered the teepee:

"With visible breath I am walking.
A voice I am sending as I walk.
In a sacred manner I am walking.

Figure 4.2 c3716 f412 This material covers the pipe, the prayer, vocabulary, and context. It contains information about the Custer battle, a description of Crazy Horse, and notes about one of the dances. Black Elk's prayer is introduced by Standing Bear, who also draws the map of the Custer fight. Courtesy, the John G. Neihardt Papers, c. 1858–1974, Western Historical Manuscript Collection, Columbia, Missouri; the John G. Neihardt Trust.

-2-

With visible tracks I am walking.
In a sacred manner I am walking."

Then she presented the pipe to the chief. It was an ordinary pipe but there was a calf carved in one side and there were twelve eagle feathers tied on with a grass that never breaks. She said: "Behold this, for you shall multiply with this and a good nation thou shalt be. You shall get nothing but good from this pipe, so I want it to be in the hands of a good man and the bood shall have the privilege of seeing it, but the bad shall not have the privilege of seeing it." This pipe is still in the possession of the Sioux. The first man who kept it was a man by the name of High Hollow Horn. The pipe is handed down from son to son.

She taught them to "keep spirits" and if a man's son dies, the man keeps a piece of his hair. This woman was really a white buffalo. Thus the respect for the white buffalo. She told them that when there was no food they should offer this pipe to the Great Spirit and they would know from this pipe when they were going to have trouble. The pipe gets long at certain times and this means hard times. When it gets short the times are good. After she went back she sang another song. As she went out of the teepee everyone saw a white buffalo kicking up his hind legs and leaving in a hurry snorting as it went.

"Some hunters went out and got a buffalo and it was in the spring of the year when the calves are in the somb yet. They got the insides out and found a calf in it and cut the womb open and to their surprize it was a human in there. It looked more like an old woman. The hair was pure white. All the men gathered there and saw it. This actually happened about 80 years ago. It was too long ago for any white man to have been here and so it was a real miracle. Black Elk thinks the Indian has been an animal changed into a human. According to that he says if we were animals the fact that the white men are killing off animals he says perhaps when the wild animal s are all gone that the

2

-3-

Indians will also be all gone.

*****

Months of the Year.

The Moon of the frost in the teepee--January

The Moon of the Dark Red Calf--Feb.

The Moon of the Snowblind--Mar.

The Moon of the Red Grass Appearing--April

The Moon when the Ponies Shed--May

The Moon of the blooming turnip)
The moon of making fat) June

The Moon of Red Cherries--July

The Moon of Black Cherries--August

The Moon of the Black Calf) --Sept.
The Moon when the Calf Grows Hair)

The Moon of the Changing Seasons--October

The Moon of the Falling Leaves--November

The Moon of Popping Trees--December

*****

Phases of the Moon

The appearing of the moon--new moon

The round moon--full moon

When the bitten moon is delayed

The time of the moon bitten off

The little left of the moon--nearly dark

(most storms come at this time)

The time when the moon is dark.

Weather

Sun dogs--Sun making himself fires

In the winter time the sun gets cold and makes them start fires.According to these phases the Indians know what type of storm is coming. (blizzards, etc.)

-2-

The first star noticed is the morning star. (daybreak star). In travel-ling by night they go by the seven stars (the big dipper--the man carrying) The star right west of the big dipper is "Comes Against." (coming toward the man carries.)
North star is called "Sitting With the Little One". (there used to be a little star beside it, but it is gone now, apparently)
Wagon travellers when asked about the distance say it is one camp, etc. from where they are to a certain place (by the stars).
If you go horseback, they call it one bedding.

****

Travelling by night they go by the Big Dipper (Man Carrier). Handle is in the west in the evening and when they are going out they figure so much from the handle toward the south and they allow so much space. A long time ago a big chief got wounded and so someone carried him home and everyone went to meet him and that is why they called the one next "Comes Against". All Indians know what the meaning of the stars are and he'll study these stars carefully.

*****

Prayer to go with Vision

The Indians put everything aside and pray with body and soul. Standing Bear talks:

"When I was 20 years old I heard this prayer. This prayer has been used before Black Elk was ever born. They call upon the Great Spirit.- andxthexfirstxwordsxtheyxwillxsayxarexx (hold pipe with the stem towards the heavens). In the old history of our people there are seven teepees (7 stars--7 teepees.) and from this time these prayers have originated. We had this prayer from the seven teepees of our people from whence our wisdom comes. (as far back as we can remember.) The first thing to do in making an offering is this: "A voice we will send to the Great Spirits." The prayer:

"He he he hey. (4 times)

Grandfather, the Great Spirit You have been always, and before thee no one has been. There is no other one to pray to but you. You, Yourself, everything that You see, everything has been made by you. The star nations all over the universe you have finished. The four quarters of the earth you have finished. The day, and in that day everything you have made. On earth everything you have done. Grandfather, Great Spirit, lean close to the earth, so you may hear the voice I send. A nation we shall make; without difficulties we shall make it. Towards where the sun goes down, behold me. The thunder beings behold me. Where the giant lives there is power with the buffaloes, so I heard, behold me. To where the sun shines continually with the elks, behold me. To where you always face a man with power, behold me. (each time the pipe is pointed to the direction about which they are speaking.) To the depths of the heavens, so I heard, an eagle with power, behold me. To Mother Earth, it is said, (pointing to earth with pipe) you are the only Mother that has shown mercy to thy children.

(Now, the prayer to all of these places. One must make a vow that he will make an offering to the Great Spirit and that he is going to talk

-2-

to the Great Spirit through this hole in the pipe. Holds the pipe up and makes offering.)

"Behold me, the four quarters of the earth, relative-like I am. Give me power to see and the strength to walk the soft earth, relative-like I have been. Give me the eyes of power and the strength of knowledge so I may be like unto thee. With thy strength I may face the winds. In facing the winds, may you behold me. May I have the power of the winds.

"Oh Great Spirit, Great Spirit, my Grandfather, may my people be likened unto the flowering stick. Thy stick of sticks, tree of trees, forest of forests, tree of trees of the earth, trees of all kinds of the earth. Oh, Flowering Tree, here on earth trees are like unto thee; thy trees of all kinds are like unto thee, but yet they have chosen thee. Oh, Tree, you are mild, you are likened unto the One above. My nation shall depend on Thee. My nation on Thee shall bloom.

(The cottonwood is mild, and like other trees, it has beauty and it could grow anywhere and bloom, even in the Badlands. This tree is used for sundances, the sacred pole, and they use this form of prayer in these sundances. When they get so far in the prayer, they burn a sweet grass which has a beautiful fragrance.)

Offering

"To the Great Spirit's Day; to the center of that day I will go and make an offering." ThisxIxburnxasxanxofferingxbeholdxit

Songs at the offering.

"This I burn as an offering; behold it.
A sacred praise I will make. (repeat this verse twice)
The nation may you behold it.

"The path of the night moon will be my robe.
The day of the sun promised me a robe. (meaning that everything works in the daytime and that when it gets dark it is like a robe coming over the heavens in the path of the moon. At night men lie down and in that robe

Put the sun's song when B. E. sees it rising after this vision, when he is walking toward home with the eagle ... this

-3-

of night most of the Indians get their power.)(sun talking as it comes up)

"With visible face I am appearing.
In a sacred manner I am appearing.
For the greening earth a pleasantness I make.
With a visible face I am appearing.
Your center of the nation's hoop a pleasantness I make.

"With visible face I am appearing.
Your earth on it the four-leggeds, I have made them walk.

"With visible face I am appearing.
My day, I have made it sacred."

****

Prayer continued from page two at center

"All over the earth faces of all living things are all alike. Mother Earth has turned these faces out of the earth with tenderness. Oh, Great Spirit, behold them, all these faces with children in their hands without difficulty they shall walk facing the wind, walking on the Good Road towards the day of quiet. Great Spirit, mercy may you have on us (winter) that without difficulty may we walk the Good Road. Great Spirit, this is my prayer, hear me. The voice I have sent may be unworthy; yet with earnestness I have sent the voice. With final words once again I say, hear me. It is finished."

****

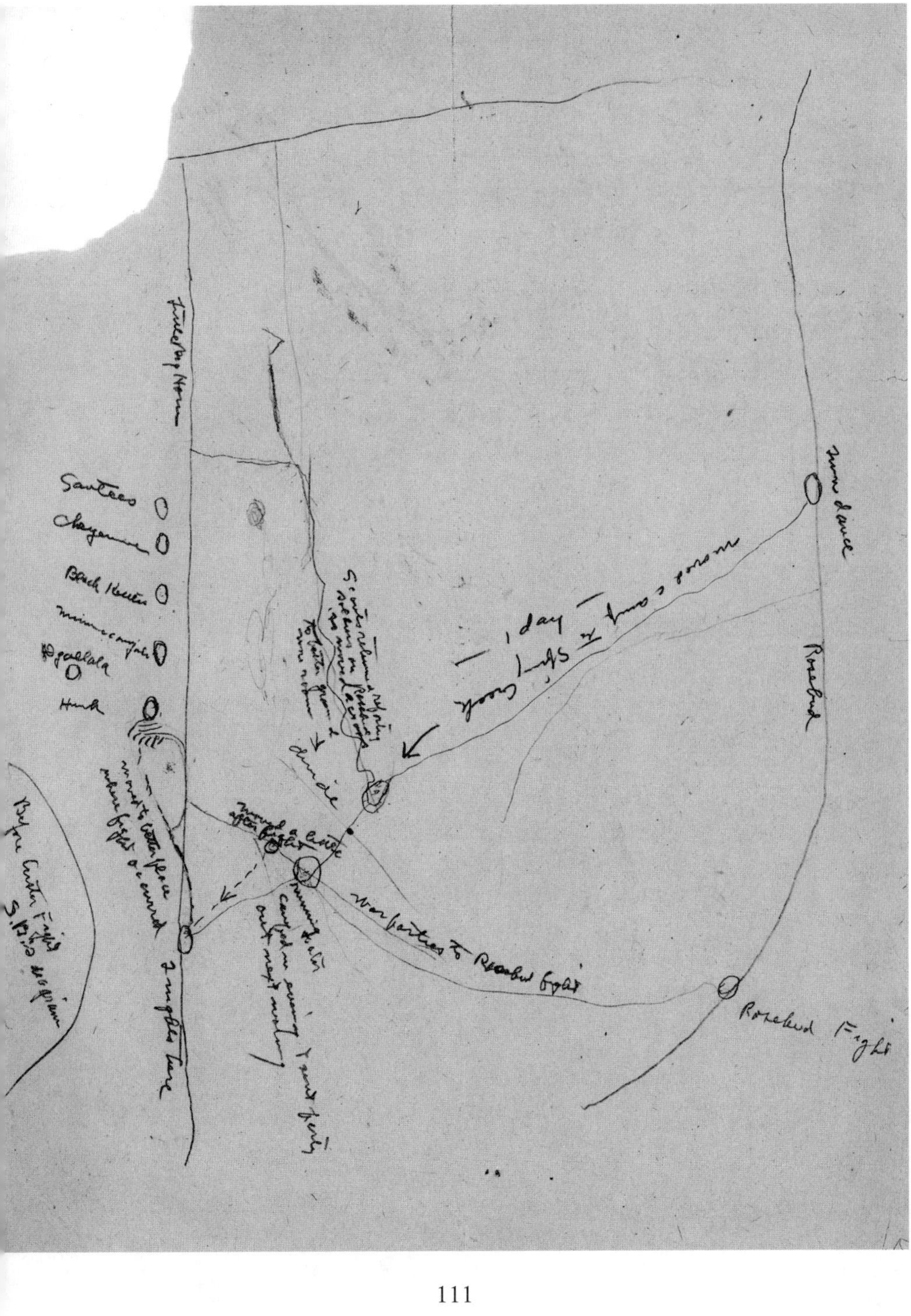
Santees
Rosebud
Rosebud Fight
1 day
War parties to Rosebud fight
Sun dance

Oh-ohna-gazhee -- sheltering place or stronghold.

Mukasitche -- bad earth or bad lands.

wasitcu -- refers to white men. Word of doubtful origin.

eyapi kage (gaga) (word maker) -- lyric poet.

han(g) balogala ga (chanter of words) -- epic poet.

Bulletin No. 61, Bureau of American Ethnology

Teton Sioux M̄usic by Frances Densmore (1918)

Pāhŭská gŏsōt(h)āb -- rubbing out of Custer.

Crazy Horse

This is not the one I mean. There was a more circumstantial account of him his character & feats of daring. Told of his fight with Crow & saving his brother.

Never was excited. Sociable in the teepee, but at war he was not at all sociable. He never had a good horse in his life. Horses couldn't go far with him for some reason. He was small and slender. Warriers think that the stone he carried with him had something to do with this. They think he had a vision about a rock and that he was as heavy as a rock. That's why no horse could pack him. He got wounded once when he was fourteen or fifteen years old, but ever since that time he was never wounded and was in a great many battles too. At Crazy's Horse's deathbed he said nothing except "Hey, hey, hey." (regret) He had killed nothing and was going to die. He was wounded by his own tribe.

*****

Pāhuskā gōs-ō-thāb -- rubbing out of Custer

Heyo'ka Ka'ga (fool impersonation)

Save this.

Dance Notes

Standing Bear made the first kill talk about his part in the fight on the Greasy Grass.

"We were in camp on the Greasy Grass when something happened. The soldiers were coming. I went to get my pony. It was a gray pony. Then the Indians charged. The bullets were raining. It was so smoky and dusty we could see nothing. Then suddenly I met one of the soldiers face to face and I pulled my pistol out and shot him."

Black Tail Deer's Kill Talk

"There was a man lying there amidst the bullets and I saved him. Afterward I ran my horse up against a bank and they retreated and I tried to get on top of a bank and some men pushed me over and I got scalps of the man. Then I returned. I saved two of my friends and then I scalped the enemy and when I got home the people said: "We knew you were going to do this, because you are brave." This happened when I was about fifteen years old. At this present time, a fifteen-year-old boy couldn't do this, but when I was that age, boys were men at this age."

B. T. D.'s another deed.

"About twelve years old at that time and there was a fight between the Crows and Sioux, and then they had quite a skirmish. The Sioux were camped and the Crows were upon them before theyknew it. I was out looking for horses. There was a blind man in camp and I went and rescued him from among the bullets. The people said about this: "We knew you were going to do it."

****

Song sung while Black Elk was dancing his dance:

"With great difficulty they are bringing him. (meaning that he is wounded) Black Elk the Great--with great difficulty they are brinīging him."

Black Elk's Kill Talk 13

-2-

Wounded Knee Massacre

"The Ogalalas were camped somehwere I dont know; but up the Wounded Knee Creek there was something going on so I went up on my pony. I got up on top the hill and it was terrible! Soldiers were standing there mowing the women and children down! So I decided that I must defend my people some way and I just went over. I depended on my vision and so I went down and showed the soldiers what power I had and the bullets were raining and again I came within three hundred yards of them and wasn't shot. Soon we made a retreat. I did all I could do to defend my people. It was hopeless. So I decided to take it just as it was. It was a butchering and I cried because I couldn't defend my people in time."

(After the talk Black Elk was required to give away something to the singers. He gave them $1.00)

*****

BEGINNINGS AND INVOCATIONS: PIPE AND PRAYER
NOTES TO MANUSCRIPT, FIGURE 4.3

The Offering of the Pipe

Neihardt brings the central teachings of the pipe and the prayer to the foreground of BES, since they are the starting points for understanding Black Elk and his message. Pages 4 and 4a in M show that originally Neihardt considered a linear approach in which Black Elk's explanation of the pipe was immediately followed by the offering of the pipe. Neihardt then splices page 4a in M, the story of the Calf Pipe Woman, in between the preliminary teaching about the pipe and its offering. This provides the context for understanding the pipe and also reflects oral discourse; as the pipe is prepared, the teller reveals its sacred context.

Neihardt has provided this initial focus for another reason, too: he must convey Black Elk's teachings to an audience largely familiar only with crude, stereotyped depictions of alleged "savage" behavior. One of the goals of BES, as in the Duhamel pageants and *The Sacred Pipe*, is to teach the rest of the world that Lakota culture is complex and spiritual and that its view of the universe and the human position in that universe is highly articulated and moral. When BES presents Lakota spirituality, it combats reams of propaganda concealing in its jargon the dominant culture's ethnocentric self-justification. When BES does talk about warfare, it is in the context of a people's self-defense, the fight for the right to live and worship freely. In this sense, too, BES constitutes not just an exposition but a question asked of the dominant culture that supposedly values these same things.

Figure 4.3 c3716 f249 Pages 3 onward integrate the pipe and the prayer in Neihardt's manuscript. Courtesy, the John G. Neihardt Papers, c. 1858–1974, Western Historical Manuscript Collection, Columbia, Missouri; the John G. Neihardt Trust.

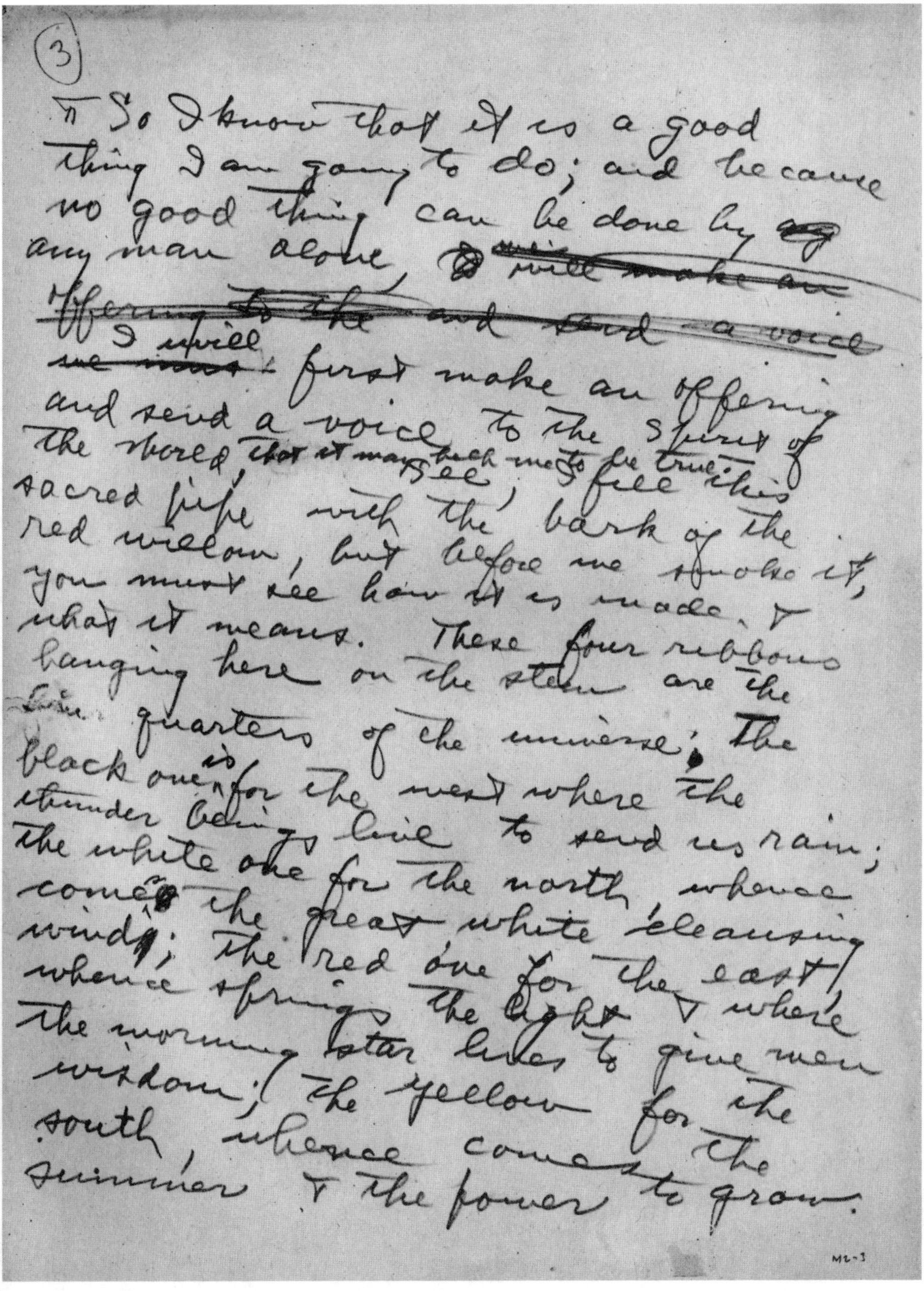
(3)

¶ So I know that it is a good thing I am going to do; and because no good thing can be done by ~~any~~ any man alone, ~~I will make an offering to the and send a voice~~ ~~we must~~ I will first make an offering and send a voice to the Spirit of the world, ~~that it may help me to be true.~~ See, I fill this sacred pipe with the bark of the red willow, but before we smoke it, you must see how it is made & what it means. These four ribbons hanging here on the stem are the ~~four~~ quarters of the universe. The black one is for the west where the thunder beings live to send us rain; the white one for the north whence comes the great white cleansing wind; the red one for the east whence springs the light & where the morning star lives to give men wisdom; the yellow for the south, whence comes the summer & the power to grow.

ML-3

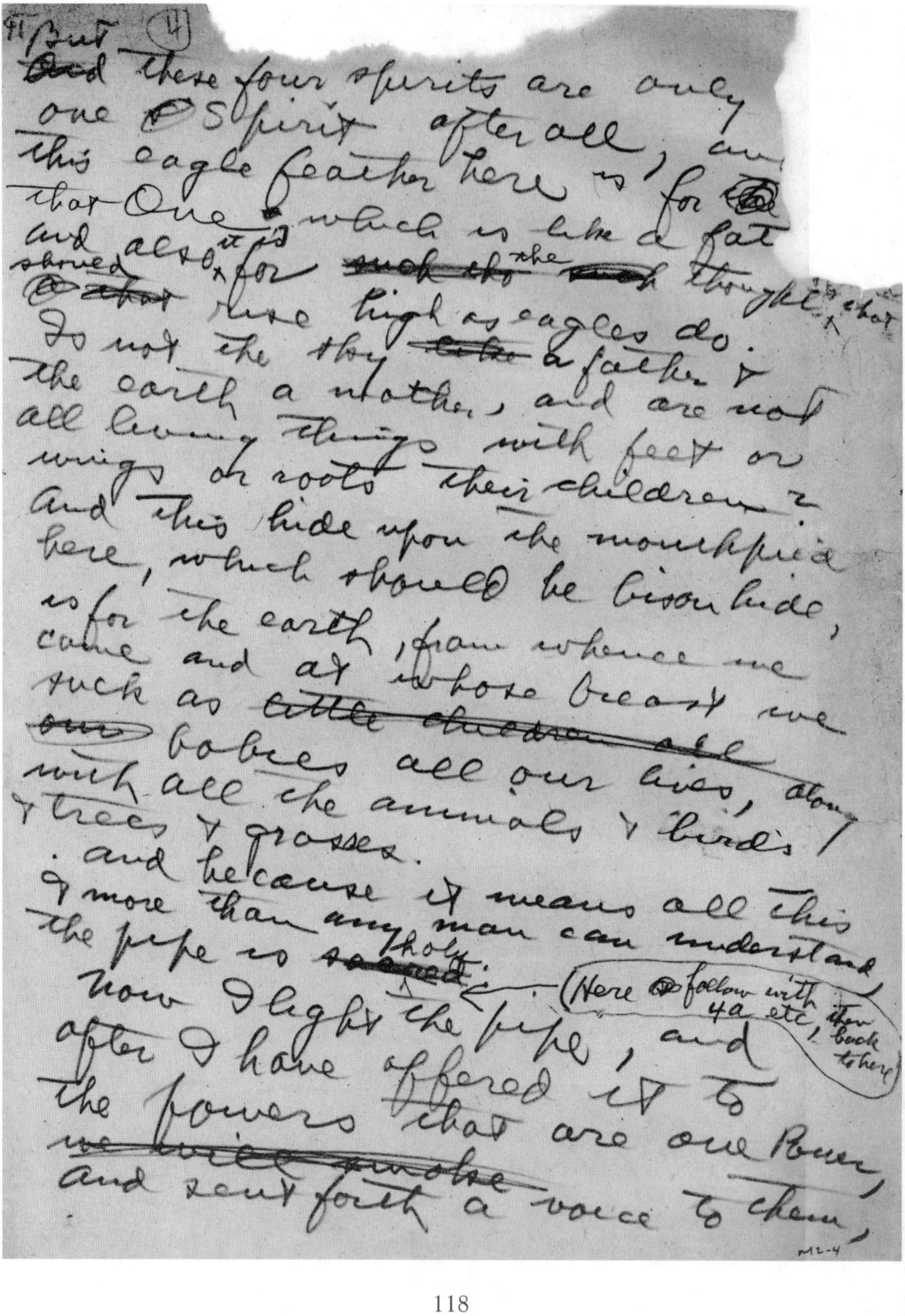

¶ But (4)
~~And~~ these four spirits are only
one Spirit after all, and
this eagle feather here is for
that One, which is like a father
and also it is for the thoughts that
rise high as eagles do.
Do not the sky ~~like~~ a father &
the earth a mother, and are not
all living things with feet or
wings or roots their children?
And this hide upon the mouthpiece
here, which should be bison hide,
is for the earth, from whence we
came and at whose breast we
suck as ~~little children all~~ babies all our lives, along
with all the animals & birds &
trees & grasses.
And because it means all this
& more than any man can understand
the pipe is ~~sacred~~ holy.
Now I light the pipe, and (Here follow with 4a etc, then back to here)
after I have offered it to
the powers that are one Power,
~~we will smoke~~
and send forth a voice to them,

M2-4

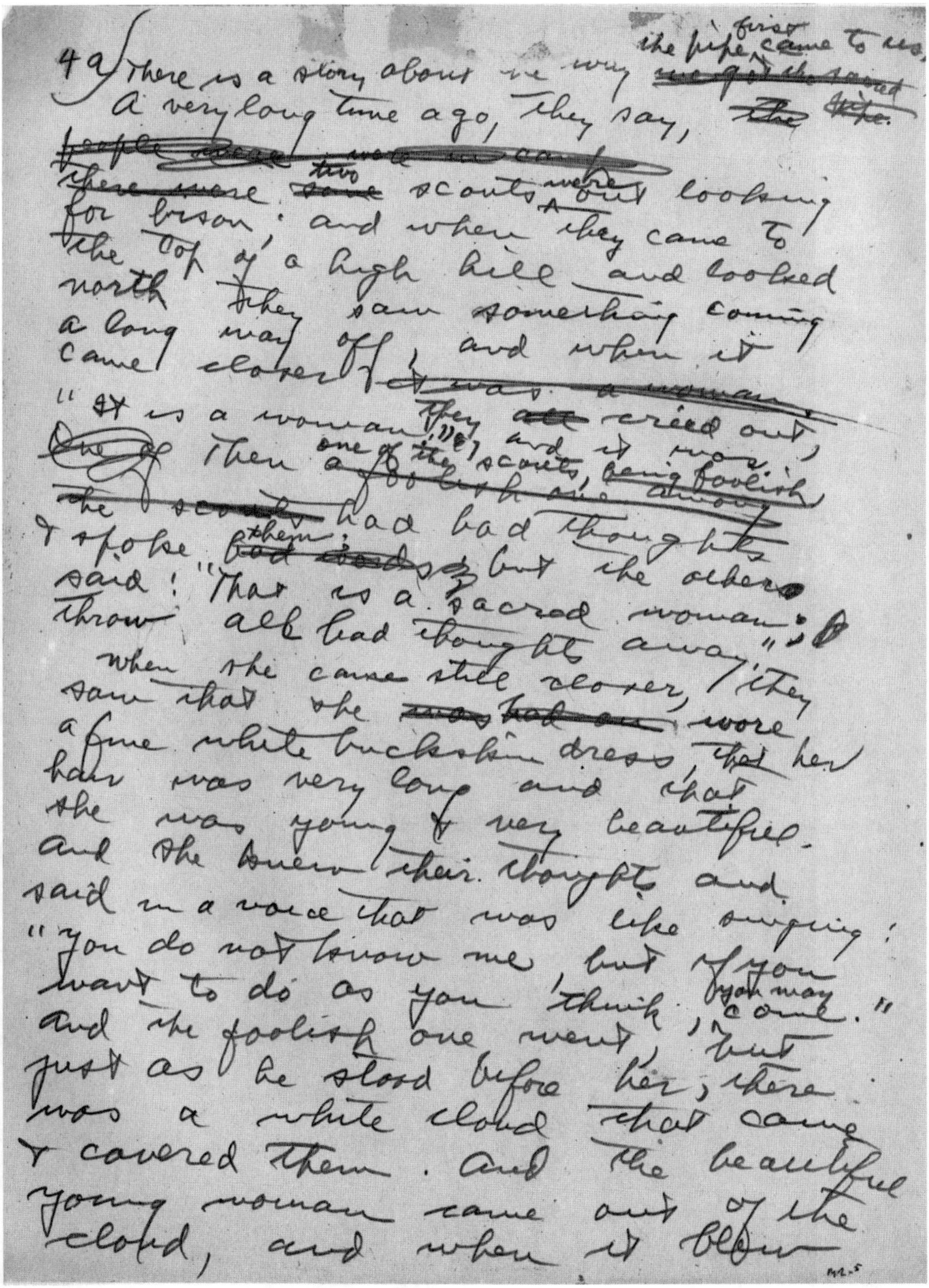

4a) There is a story about the way the pipe first came to us.
A very long time ago, they say, two scouts were out looking for bison; and when they came to the top of a high hill and looked north, they saw something coming a long way off, and when it came closer, "It is a woman," they cried out, and it was. Then one of the scouts, being foolish, had bad thoughts & spoke them; but the other said: "That is a sacred woman; throw all bad thoughts away."
When she came still closer, they saw that she wore a fine white buckskin dress, that her hair was very long and that she was young & very beautiful. And she knew their thoughts and said in a voice that was like singing: "You do not know me, but if you want to do as you think, you may come." And the foolish one went, but just as he stood before her, there was a white cloud that came & covered them. And the beautiful young woman came out of the cloud, and when it blew

5a

away the foolish man was a skeleton
~~and the worms~~ covered with worms.
Then the woman spoke to the one
who was not foolish: "You shall
go home & tell your ~~nation~~ people that
I am coming & that a big tepee
shall be built for me in the
center of the nation." And the
man who was very much afraid
went quickly and told the
people, ~~and they were very much excited~~ who
did at once as they were told;
& there around the big ~~teep~~ tepee
they waited for the sacred woman
and after a while she came,
very beautiful & singing, and
as she went into the tepee this
is what she sang:

"With visible breath I am walking.
A voice I am sending as I walk.
In a sacred manner I am walking.
With visible tracks I am walking.
In a sacred manner I am walking."

and as she sang ~~a white cloud~~
~~came~~ there came from her
mouth a white cloud that was sweet
to smell.

M2-6

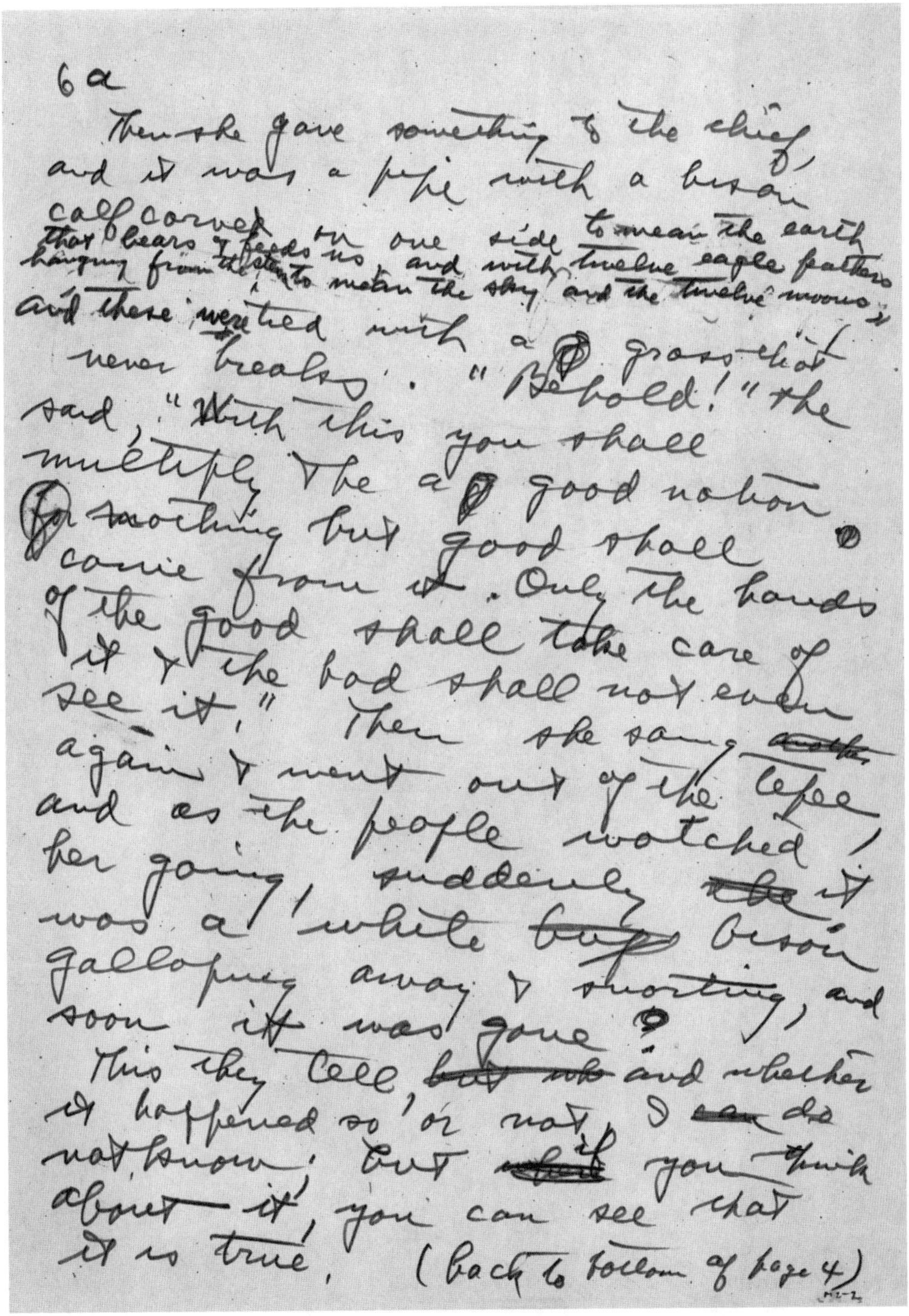

6a

Then she gave something to the chief, and it was a pipe with a bison calf carved on one side to mean the earth that bears & feeds us, and with twelve eagle feathers hanging from the stem to mean the sky and the twelve moons, and these were tied with a grass that never breaks. "Behold!" she said, "With this you shall multiply & be a good nation. Nothing but good shall come from it. Only the hands of the good shall take care of it & the bad shall not even see it." Then she sang ~~another~~ again & went out of the tepee and as the people watched her going, suddenly ~~the~~ it was a white ~~buff~~ bison galloping away & snorting, and soon it was gone.

This they tell, ~~but who~~ and whether it happened so or not, I ~~can~~ do not know; but if you think about it, you can see that it is true.

(back to bottom of page 4)

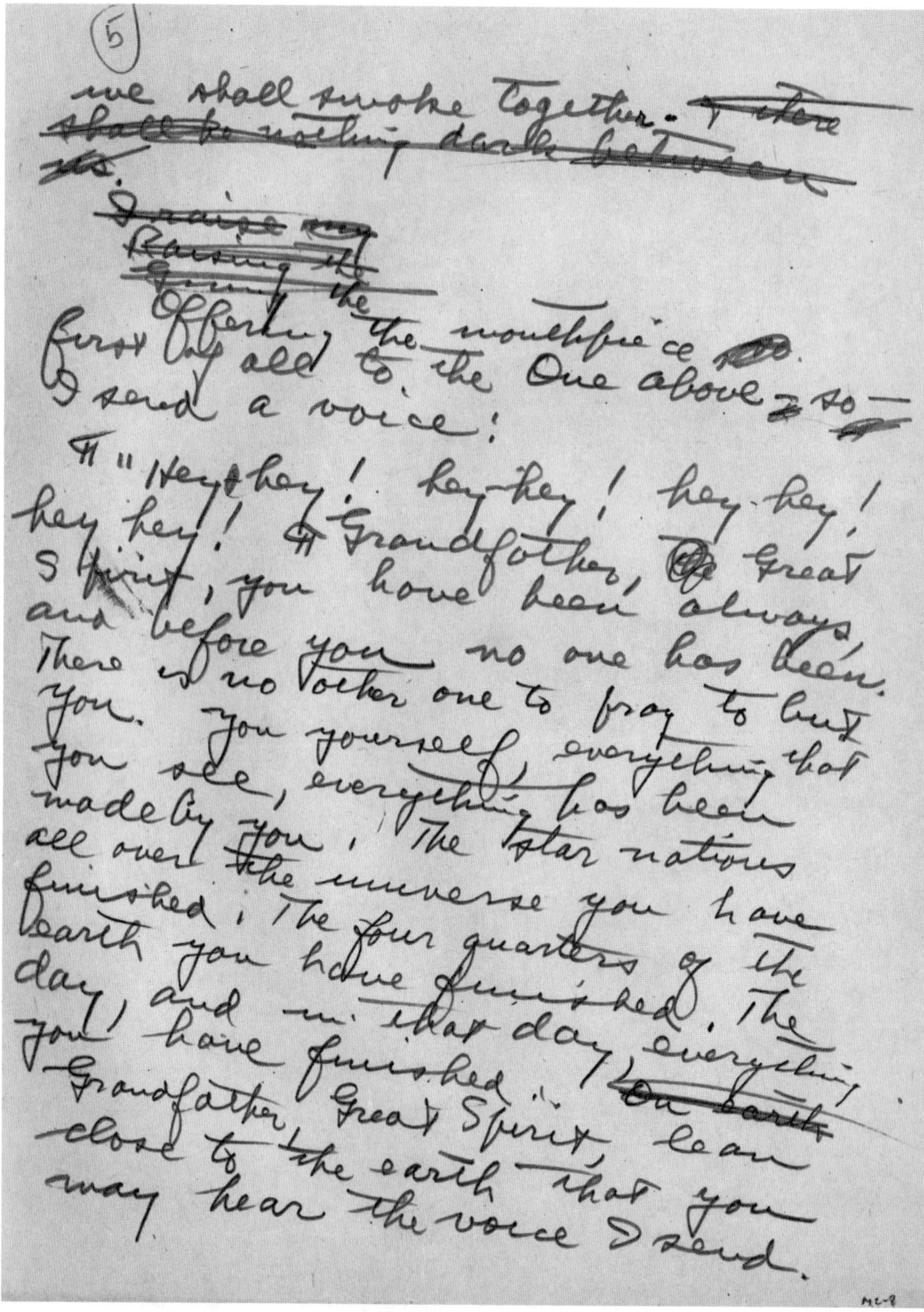
(5)
we shall smoke together. ~~There shall be nothing dark between us.~~
~~I raise my~~
~~Raising it~~
~~Turning the~~
Offering the mouthpiece
first of all to the One above—so—
I send a voice:
¶ "Hey-hey! hey-hey! hey-hey!
hey-hey! ¶ Grandfather, Great
Spirit, you have been always,
and before you no one has been.
There is no other one to pray to but
you. You yourself, everything that
you see, everything has been
made by you. The star nations
all over the universe you have
finished. The four quarters of the
earth you have finished. The
day, and in that day, everything
you have finished. ~~On earth~~
Grandfather, Great Spirit, lean
close to the earth that you
may hear the voice I send.
M2-8

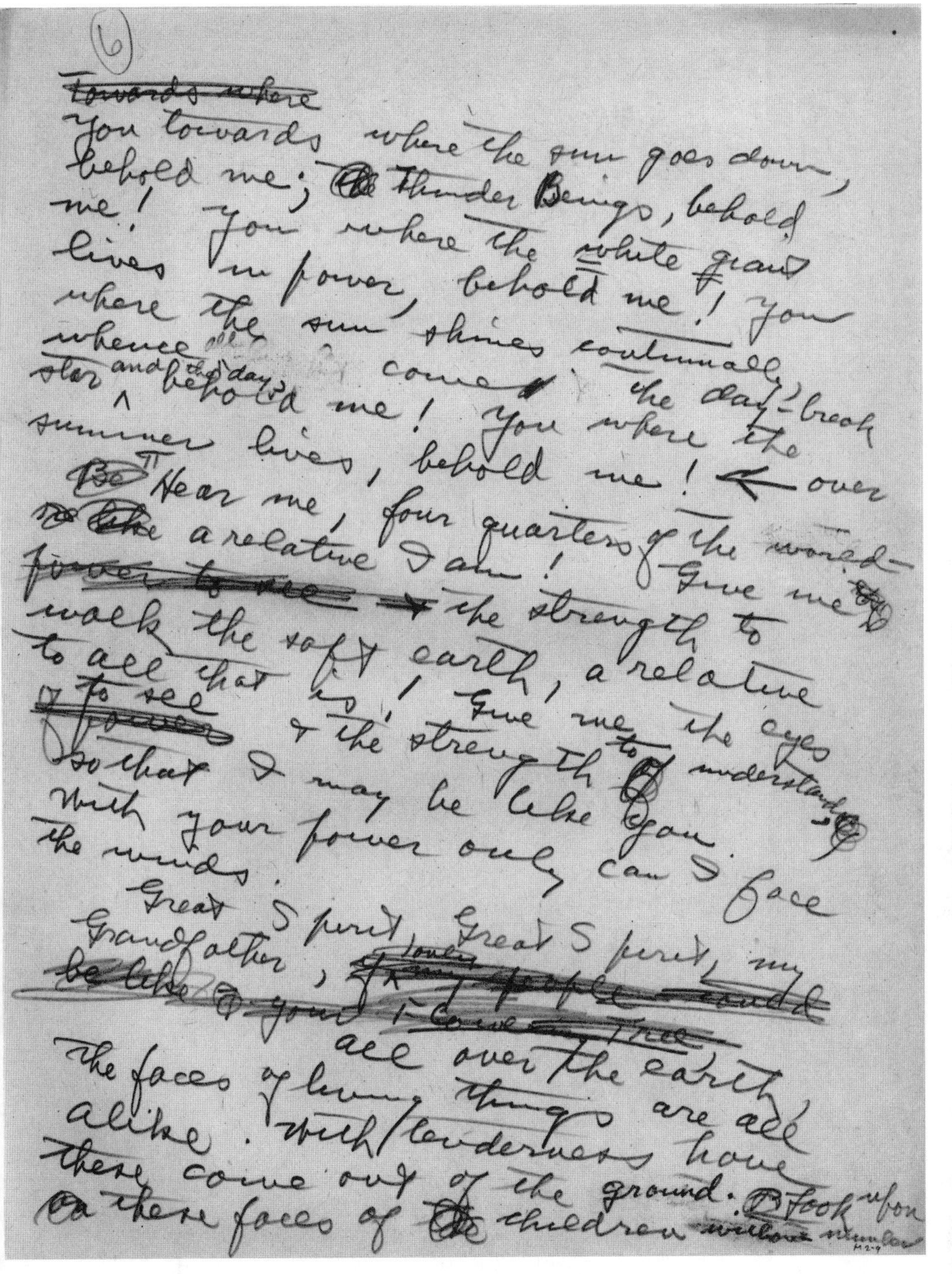

(6)

~~Towards where~~
You towards where the sun goes down,
behold me; Thunder Beings, behold
me! You where the white giant
lives in power, behold me! You
where the sun shines continually,
whence all come the day-break
star and the day, behold me! You where the
summer lives, behold me! ← over
Hear me, four quarters of the world—
a relative I am! Give me
~~power to me~~ → the strength to
walk the soft earth, a relative
to all that is! Give me the eyes
to see & the strength to understand
so that I may be like you.
With your power only can I face
the winds.

Great Spirit, Great Spirit, my
Grandfather, ~~be like your people could~~
~~... give ...~~
all over the earth
the faces of living things are all
alike. With tenderness have
these come out of the ground. Look upon
these faces of children without number

You, in the depths of the heavens, an eagle of power, behold! ~~me!~~ and you, Mother Earth, the only mother, you who have shown mercy to your children!

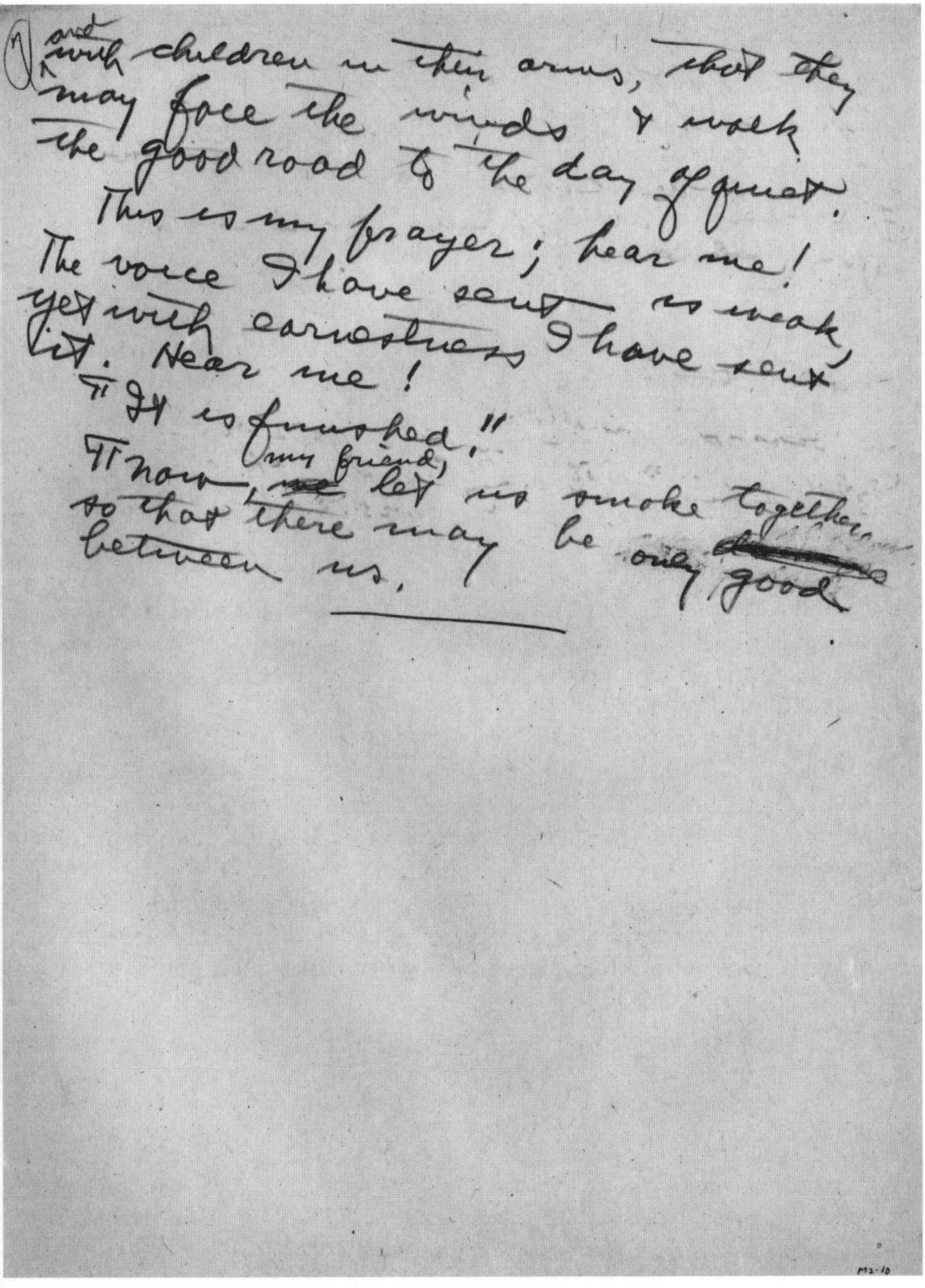
7 ~~with~~ and children in their arms, that they may face the winds & walk the good road to the day of quiet.

This is my prayer; hear me! The voice I have sent is weak, yet with earnestness I have sent it. Hear me!

¶ "It is finished!"

¶ Now, my friend, ~~we~~ let us smoke together so that there may be only good between us.

M2-10

EARLY CONFLICT: FIRE THUNDER SPEAKS
NOTES TO TRANSCRIPT, FIGURE 4.4

Preliminary Material

T lists speakers and some preliminary information, indicating (as does BES 7–19) that this is a record of a group discussion.

Black Elk's Story

BES 7 adds the name of the senior Black Elk's mother. BES and T both use the traditional style of locating personal events in time next to social events (for instance, the father of Black Elk dying at the time of Big Foot's massacre).

BES 8–9 uses material on the definition of wasichu derived elsewhere from T, "Youth," where the term is explained to him by his grandfather.

Fire Thunder Speaks

BES 11–13 adds context so the reader will know where the action takes place. BES also combines sentences so compound and other constructions smooth out the delivery, rendered choppily in T. Some differences in diction occur: T has "locusts" for BES 12's "grasshoppers." The words "white men" in T are cast back into the original "Wasichu" in BES 12 but are given an English plural ending so readers will understand the term. T has Fire Thunder's own group not killing the dog, but BES 13 adds that others "did shoot." BES 13 clarifies the nature of the wound suffered by Black Elk's father, stated earlier in this section of T.

Black Elk Continues

BES 13 adds the common admonishment that if a child is not well behaved, the whites will take him (see Lame Deer and Erdoes 27: "But when I was real bad, Grandma would say, '*Wasicun anigni kte*'—'the white man will come and take you to his home'—and that scared me all right. Wasicun were for real." And see Fools Crow's comments in a similar vein in Mails 41).

T provides the songs used in Creeping's curing of snow blindness; the distracting account of his gun conjuring has been deleted from BES 14.

Figure 4.4 c3716 f413 Pages 1–4. Pages 2–4 contain the transcript of "Fire Thunder Speaks." Courtesy, the John G. Neihardt Papers, c. 1858–1974, Western Historical Manuscript Collection, Columbia, Missouri; the John G. Neihardt Trust.

Standing Bear - Mato Naji - 72
Black Elk - Heraka Sapa - 72 69
Fire Thunder - Wankinyan Pieta - 82
Holy Black Tail Deer - Sinta Sapa Wakan -74

Black Elk

I was born on Little Powder River in 1863 the winter when the four Crows were killed. (Tongue River)

Standing Bear

I was born on Tongue River in the winter when the children died of coughing. (1859)

Fire Thunder

I was born at the mouth of Beaver Creek in Wyoming during the year when the Indians died of cramps. (1849)

Holy Black Tail Deer

I was born in the western Black Hills on the Wyoming side on Bear Creek in the year when Yellow Blanket was killed. (1854) (Yellow Blanket was a Crow Indian, who was scouting for a war party and they chased him and killed him.)

BLACK ELK'S STORY

To begin with I am the fourth of the name Black Elk. My father was a medicine man and is brother to several medicine men. My father was cousin to Crazy Horse's father. (Sioux Medicine man--Wapiapi--fixing up.) My grandfather was killed by Ponees. My mother's name was White Cow Sees. I remember my grandmother on my mother's side--her name was Plenty Eagle Feathers. My mother's father's name was Refuse-To-Go. At this time my grandmother and grandfather on my father's side died. I was three years old when my father was in battle of the Fetterman fight--he got his right leg broken.

-2-

Just about the year of the Big Foot Massacre, my father died and was buried out in these hills in 1889.

Fire Thunder Speaks

I was 16 years old at this time. We were camped on Tongue River. A man by the name of Big Road was the chief of our band at this time. Red Cloud was of course over all of us. We decided to go on a war path, several different bands all taking part on horseback. We were out to fight anything, but particularly were we after the soldiers. We started out, camping twice from Tongue River the same day. We were going towards the Piney Creek Fort. We had some out to attack the fort. Sent ten men ahead to try to coax them out of the Fort and then we were going to hide there nearby. There is a hill here near and this band of ours divided into two parts and stood on either side of this hill. We waited there for an hour or so and heard a shot soon. We knew then that the soldiers were coming. This happened right on the north side of Piney Creek. I was on the west side of the hill. The riders were coaxing the soldiers back. Some got off their horses, leading them pretending they were worn out. The Indians came first down hill and the soldiers following firing on the running Indians all the time. My weapons were six-shooters and bows and arrows, which I had traded for. As the Indians got down the hill, got to a little flat, the soldiers in between them began to holler. I was riding a sorrel horse, and just as I was about to get on my sorrel, the soldiers stopped and began to fight the Indians back up the hill. I hung on to my sorrel. As they charged I pulled out my six-shooter and began killing them. There were lots of bullets and lots of arrows--like locusts. The

-3-

soldiers did not kill all the Indians that were killed, as the Indians killed each other as well as the soldiers. I saw them shot through the arms and legs. They charged up the hill, losing men as they went. There were only a few left. There was no place to hide, so they got on the hill and surrounded them. As they charged up the hill some of the soldiers let go of their horses and the Indians tried to capture some of the horses. I tried to catch a horse, but I thought it was a good day to die so I just went ahead fighting. I wasn't after horses--I was after white men. Just as I was going up the hill I saw there were seven horses left, so I just caught one of them, as it came right by me. We were told to crawl inch by inch onto the soldiers, so I got off my horse. When we came closer someone hollered: "Let's go; this is a good day to die. If we don't someone is going to die today, and at home our women are hungry". Then they all hollered "Hoka Hi!" Then we all jumped up and went for them. I was pretty quick on my feet and was first to get there. I killed five or six of these soldiers myself--three with my six-shooter and three with arrows. Some of the soldiers that we were among now were dead and some of them were alive. They all got up and fought hard. There were none of them left at the end of the fight. The only living thing was a dog. We didn't kill the dog because he looked too sweet. After this fight was over, we picked up our wounded and started back to the Tongue and just left the dead lying there. It was pretty cold weather to bury anything--the ground was frozen solid. We did bury a few by just turning them over in the hollow ground. There was a terribly big blizzard that night and we lost most of our wounded going home, and most of the

-4-

wounded died when they did get home. This was the same time when Black Elk's father was wounded.

Black Elk continues

I was at this time not allowed to play outside. At this same winter they broke camp. They went somewhere, but I was too young to remember just exactly where. During this winter everyone got snowblind. They couldn't see anything. There was only one who wasn't snowblind, so he led the rest. This was in March and we were moving west. Holy Black Tail Deer was nine years old then at the same camp. We were trying to find elk, and I remember that we moved camp after this and there was a big famine and we started out for meat. My uncle went with us hunting, and they finally brought meat back. We were hunting all over after the rest of our band which had broken camp a little before. We roamed all over and I was the lookout sitting in a travois, my mother on a horse. We went to a creek and camped here and the men went out hunting, bringing back meat. One day in camp a medicine man by the name of Creeping cam around curing snowblinds. He would put snow before the eyes and blow on the back of the head and this blew dirt out of their eyes and they were thus cured. He was curing people all day long. This medicine man had a way of loading a gun just once and singing this sacred song of his and the gun would go off each time he sang the song regardless of the fact that there seemingly could be no loading in the gun. Here are the words of the song:

"Who is this that you face the dragon fly?
They are the people I belong to.

2nd song

Boys, face me, like butterfly I am, Imyself."

EARLY CONFLICT: FIRE THUNDER SPEAKS
NOTES TO MANUSCRIPT, FIGURE 4.5

Introductory Section

Page 15 of M locates the time precisely using the terminology learned in T (see Figure 4.2).

Fire Thunder Speaks

Pages 15–19 of M clarify the description of the topographical context of the fight; the reader must be able to visualize the geography and terrain.

Page 19 of M shows Neihardt following T and using language that will resonate later in BES—at the Wounded Knee site, for example: "Dead men + horses + wounded Indians were scattered all the way up the hill, and their blood was frozen, for a storm had come up + it was very cold + getting colder all the time" (see BES 13 for the same passage, and notice its parallel in BES 260, 262). Again this section shows Neihardt taking the choppy transcription and casting it back into living language. He forgoes short, abrupt statements; the presence of "and" unifies the speech and provides the effect of someone recollecting more and more information as he talks—another example of writing made to reenact telling.

Figure 4.5 (overleaf) c3716 f250 Pages 15–19, depicting "Fire Thunder Speaks" in manuscript. Courtesy, the John G. Neihardt Papers, c. 1858–1974, Western Historical Manuscript Collection, Columbia, Missouri; the John G. Neihardt Trust.

(13)

~~And it was in the time of the popping trees~~

¶ And it was about when the bitter moon was delayed (last quarter) in the time of the popping trees when the hundred were rubbed out. My friend, Fire Thunder here, who is older than I, was in that fight and he can tell you how it was.

Fire Thunder Speaks:

I was 16 years old when this happened and ~~we~~ after the big council on the Powder we had moved over to the Tongue river where we were camping at the mouth of Peno Creek. There were many of us there. Red Cloud was over all of us, but the chief of our band was Big Road. We started out on horseback just about sunrise, riding up the creek toward the soldiers' town on the Piney, for we were going to attack it. The sun was about half way up when we ~~came to~~ stopped at the place where the Wasichu's road ~~crossed the creek at the bottom of a long ridge~~ came down a steep, narrow ridge & crossed

(16)

the creek. It was a good place to fight, and we sent some men ahead to coax the soldiers out. While they were gone, ~~we divided into two~~ parts & hid in the gullies on both sides of the ridge and waited. After a long while we heard a shot up over the hill, & we knew the soldiers were coming. So we held ~~our~~ the noses of our ponies ~~so~~ that they ~~could~~ might not whinny at the soldiers' horses. I was on the west side of the ridge. Soon we saw our men coming back, & some of them were walking & leading their ~~horses~~ horses, ~~as though they were worn out, so that the soldiers would~~ so that the soldiers would think they were worn out. Then the ~~people~~ men we had sent ahead came running down the ~~hill between us~~ road between us & the soldiers ~~followed~~ on horseback followed shooting. When they came to the flat at the ~~bottom~~ of the hill, the fighting began all at once.

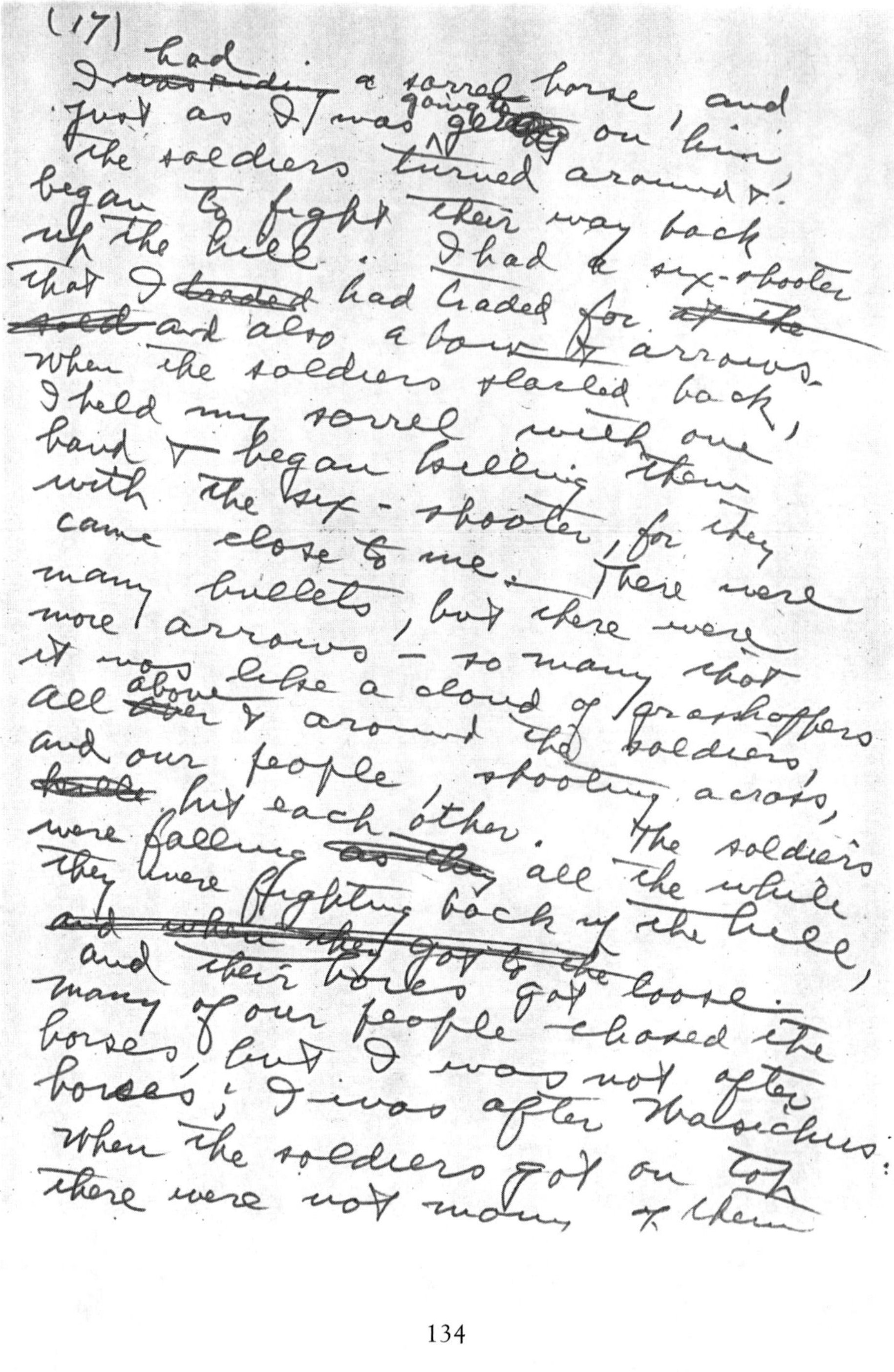

(17)
~~I was riding~~ had a sorrel horse, and
just as I was ~~getting~~ going to get on him
the soldiers turned around &
began to fight their way back
up the hill. I had a six-shooter
that I ~~traded~~ had traded for ~~at the~~
~~sold~~ and also a bow & arrows.
When the soldiers started back,
I held my sorrel with one
hand & began killing them
with the six-shooter, for they
came close to me. There were
many bullets, but there were
more arrows—so many that
it was like a cloud of grasshoppers
all ~~over~~ above & around the soldiers,
and our people, shooting across,
~~hit~~ hit each other. The soldiers
were falling ~~as they~~ all the while
they were fighting back up the hill,
~~and when they got to the~~
and their horses got loose.
Many of our people chased the
horses, but I was not after
horses; I was after Wasichus.
When the soldiers got on top
there were not many of them

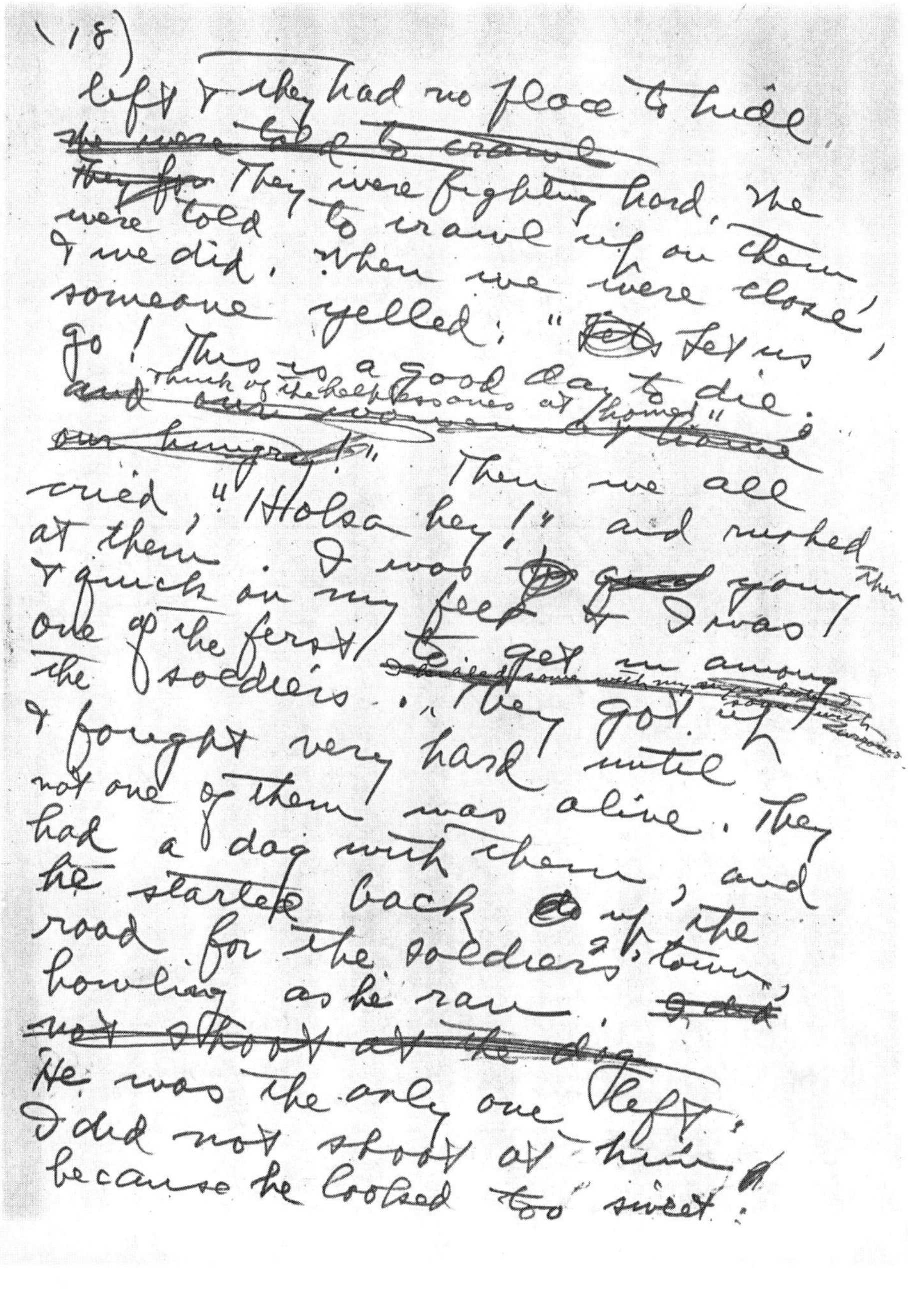

(18)
left & they had no place to hide.
~~we were told to crawl~~
~~They fir~~ They were fighting hard. We
were told to crawl up on them
& we did. When we were close,
someone yelled: "~~Let~~ Let us
go! ~~This is a good day to die.~~
~~and our women~~ Think of the helpless ones at home!"
~~our hungry!~~" Then we all
cried, "Hoka hey!" and rushed
at them. I was ~~so good~~ young then
& quick on my feet & I was
one of the first to get in among
the soldiers. ~~I killed some with my...~~ They got up
& fought very hard until
not one of them was alive. They
had a dog with them, and
he started back ~~to~~ up the
road for the soldiers' town,
howling as he ran. ~~I did~~
~~not shoot at the dog~~
He was the only one left.
I did not shoot at him
because he looked too sweet!

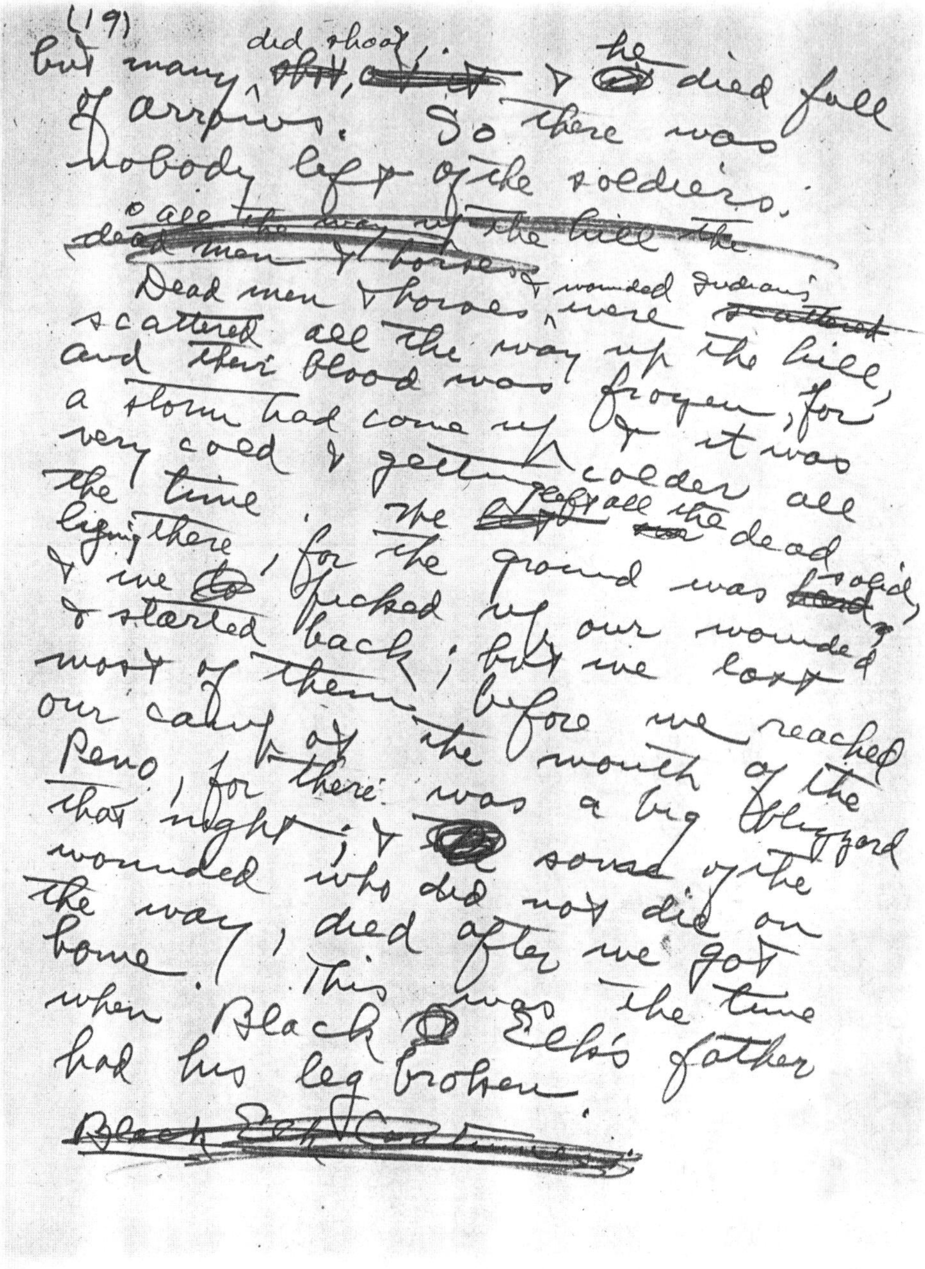

(19)
but many did shoot, & he died full of arrows. So there was nobody left of the soldiers.

~~all the way up the hill the dead men & horses~~

Dead men & horses & wounded Indians were scattered all the way up the hill and their blood was frozen, for a storm had come up & it was very cold & getting colder all the time. We left all the dead lying there, for the ground was solid, & we picked up our wounded & started back; but we lost most of them before we reached our camp at the mouth of the Peno, for there was a big blizzard that night; & some of the wounded who did not die on the way, died after we got home. This was the time when Black Elk's father had his leg broken.

~~Black Elk Continues:~~

THE FIRST VISION
NOTES TO TRANSCRIPT, FIGURE 4.6, AND MANUSCRIPT, FIGURE 4.7

Black Elk's First Vision

T material is used in BES 18–19; M 27–28. T has "father" for BES 18's "Grandfather"; M shows that Neihardt at first wrote "father," following the transcript, but corrected it to "grandfather."

M and BES show the building of the thunderstorm, culminating in its occurrence, as more than a backdrop for the vision; the storm is an expression of the Thunder Beings signaling Black Elk and a demonstration that nature and the spiritual are fused. T has the ingredients of M and BES but is abrupt in delivery. BES uses the transliterated names for north and west, which T translates simply into "north" and "west." T describes the vision as lasting "twenty minutes," not present in M or BES 19 but replaced with a closing sentence showing Black Elk's naïveté, previously indicated in T, as discussed in my text.

DeMallie points out that the name of the kingbird in the accounts is, in Lakota, a wordplay on "one-sided," or "unordinary, sacred" (*Sixth* 109)—yet another indication of how what readers from the dominant culture call the natural, supernatural, and cerebral realms are united in Black Elk's perception and in the account of this episode. Probably because of the need to emphasize this unity, Neihardt deleted the reference to wasichu chronometry that appears in the transcript but deflects reader attention.

Figure 4.6 (overleaf) c3716 f413 The last page in the folder, although numbered "1," is a summary of Black Elk's first vision in the transcripts. Courtesy, the John G. Neihardt Papers, c. 1858–1974, Western Historical Manuscript Collection, Columbia, Missouri; the John G. Neihardt Trust.

1

BLACK ELK'S FIRST VISION

The first time I rode a horse I was five years old and my father made me some bows and arrows. This was in the Spring. I was out in the woods trying to get a bird and just as I was going into the woods, there was a thunder storm coming and I heard a voice over there. This was not a dream--it actually happened. I saw two men coming out of a cloud with spears. As I was looking up to that, there was a kingbird sitting there and these two men were coming toward me sining the sacred song and that bird told me to listen to the two men. The kingbird said: "The clouds all over are one-sided, a voice is calling you". I looked up and the two men were coming down singing:

"Behold him, a sacred voice is calling you.
All over the sky a sacred voice is calling you."

I stood gazing at them and they were coming from the north; then they started towards the west and were geese.

This vision lasted about twenty minutes.

******

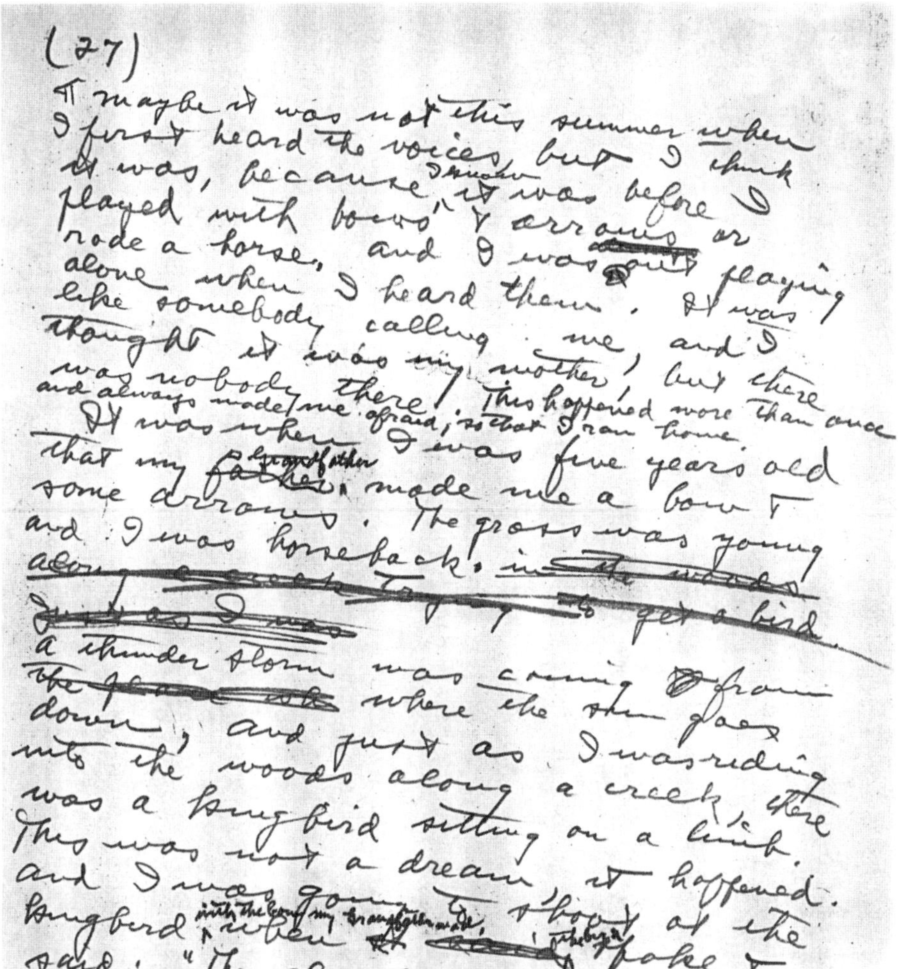

(27)
¶ maybe it was not this summer when
I first heard the voices, but I think
it was, because I think it was before I
played with bows & arrows or
rode a horse, and I was out playing
alone when I heard them. It was
like somebody calling me, and I
thought it was my mother, but there
was nobody there. This happened more than once
and always made me afraid, so that I ran home.
It was when I was five years old
that my grandfather made me a bow &
some arrows. The grass was young
and I was horseback.
a thunder storm was coming from
where the sun goes
down, and just as I was riding
into the woods along a creek, there
was a kingbird sitting on a limb.
This was not a dream, it happened.
and I was going to shoot at the
kingbird with the bow my grandfather made, when the kingbird spoke &
said: "The clouds all over are
one-sided". Perhaps it meant that
all the clouds were looking at
me. And then it said: "Listen!
a voice is calling you!"

Figure 4.7 c3716 f250 Pages 27 and 28: the manuscript description of the first vision. Courtesy, the John G. Neihardt Papers, c. 1858–1974, Western Historical Manuscript Collection, Columbia, Missouri; the John G. Neihardt Trust.

—28—

Then I looked up at the clouds, and ~~two~~ men were coming there, headfirst like arrows slanting down; and as they came they sang a sacred song ~~that~~ and the thunder was like drumming. I will sing it for you. The song and the drumming were like this:

"Behold, a sacred voice is calling you;
All over the sky a sacred voice is calling."

~~I stood looking at them~~

I sat there gazing at them, and they were coming from the place where the giant lives (north). ~~Then~~ But when they were very close to me, they wheeled about toward where the sun goes down, & suddenly they were geese. ~~and~~ Then they were gone, and ~~then~~ the rain came with a big wind & a roaring.

I did not tell this vision to anyone. I liked to think about it, but I was afraid to tell it.

WOUNDED KNEE
NOTES TO TRANSCRIPT, FIGURE 4.8, THE GHOST DANCE AND WOUNDED KNEE
NOTES TO MANUSCRIPT, FIGURE 4.9, WOUNDED KNEE

The Ghost Dance

This excerpt from T picks up at the approximate location of BES 249, paragraph 4, and continues to the top of BES 250.

T 139 records Black Elk visiting the Brules, their returning with him, and Black Elk's speech to them. See BES 249–252. DeMallie (*Sixth* 266) notices that Black Elk's imagery and that of Short Bull are very close, even though Black Elk is not generally discussed as a Ghost Dance leader.

The transcript indicates that Black Elk "became the most important ghost dancer" (T 139) and that, when the holdouts in the Stronghold surrendered, Black Elk was one of four men selected to lead them in a procession to the agency (T 149–150). BES does not emphasize these personal aspects (see BES 250, 270), in keeping with the book's focus on the universal as set forth in its "thesis statement," BES 1–2. Both T and BES do depict the pressure of need Black Elk's people exerted on him in those terrible times.

Wounded Knee

BES 255–256 and M 353–354 reflect T 143–144; before the massacre Black Elk, having felt something bad would happen, cannot sleep and walks around the camp. The next morning he hears firing, and a man riding back from Pine Ridge warns him that people are being shot. Without a gun, Black Elk goes to the site attired in sacred regalia, first alone and then accompanied by others. He has doubts about "the Wanekia religion" (BES 264) or "this Messiah business" (T 144), unsure whether to fight. Neihardt defers explicitly mentioning the doubts until after Black Elk sees the holocaust, where the early doubts contrast with the feelings provoked by the slaughter of Black Elk's people: "After what I had seen over there, I wanted revenge; I wanted to kill" (BES 264). T reveals a further pressure, since Black Elk tells us that the opinion of others drove him on toward the location of the massacre (144). M, BES, and T record the major incidents of the return to the deserted camp, the skirmish with the soldiers, the wounding of Black Elk and his being saved by Protector, and the flight to the Stronghold.

M 368 contains Neihardt's writing and rewriting of the ending episode of the Wounded Knee massacre, paring away inessential language and building short clauses up to the ending compound sentence.

Neihardt deletes the section of T in which Black Elk's invocation of the Grandfathers is followed by a seemingly affirmative thunderstorm in favor of showing us Black Elk's power at the end of the book; BES compresses the desire for revenge and the resistance to that desire into a paragraph on page 269 that precedes Red Cloud's speech. BES 270 conveys Black Elk's frustration and regret expressed in T 149: it is now impossible to fight—with weapons—for the dream.

Figure 4.8 c3716 f420 Pages 139–150 of the transcripts, discussing Wounded Knee and its aftermath. Courtesy, the John G. Neihardt Papers, c. 1858–1974, Western Historical Manuscript Collection, Columbia, Missouri; the John G. Neihardt Trust.

and this might have been where I made my great mistake.
(Black Elk was considered the chief ghost dancer. Might hear that B. E. had made it, but he did not, only he had so much power that he became the most important ghost dancer.)
I was the leader in every dance. Soon I had developed so much power that even if I would stand in the center of the circle and wave this red stick that the people would fall into swoons without dancing and see their visions. The Brulees had wanted me to come because they thot they might get some power from me. I took a special trip over there for this purpose. I made six shirts and six dresses for them. I was over there four days and we were dancing every day. I told the Brulees what I had seen in my vision of the Promised Land. I told them everything that I had told the Ogalalas. In the center of the sacred tree and on either side were the six dressed in sacred clothes. Everyone raised their right hands towards the west and I recited that prayer and waved the sacred stick. Then they all began to cry and some of them began to have their visions before the beginning of the dance even. After the dance I stood right in the middle by the tree and talked to the people making this speech concerning the Messiah (Wanekia--make live) Son of the Great Spirit. In olden times way back the sacred men would make an offering to the Great Spirit saying: "Great Spirit, our grandfather, mercy may you have on us and make us live.")
I returned from the Brulees to the Ogalalas with lots of things to bring home with me. Before I left I heard that there were soldiers here at Pine Ridge already. When I left the Brulees all followed me. It seemed that I just drew them along with me. I knew that they were depending on me, so they just followed me. Still my people were dancing right below Manderson on the Wounded Knee. There was a big camp here. Next morning it was reported that the soldiers were coming over here, so we broke camp and started west across the country to Grass Creek. We broke camp there and moved from here to White Grass where we set up camp.
Over at Medicine Root Creek the largest part of the Brulees were

camping. Some chiefs cam e over from Pine Ridge to White Grass Creek north of Pine Ridge--Fire Thunder, Red Wound and Young American Horse. These men brot a message in behalf of the soldiers that this matter of the ghost dance should be looked into, that there should be rulings over it, but they did not mean to take the dance away from us. We moved camp from White Clay Creek and we moved nearer to Pine Ridge and camped here. We had a meeting over this ghost dance, but I did not attend it. I knew that Good Thunder and Kicking Bear were at the meeting. There were many soldiers there now. We were dancing nearly every day and I heard that this is what the agent said to the people:

He had made a ruling that we should dance three days every month and at the rest of the time we should go out and make a living of some kind for themselves. This was all he said to them. (McLaughlin) When these men brot the news back, we were all satisfied without and we agreed to do it. While I was sitting in a teepee with Good Thunder a policeman came over from Pine Ridge. He said: "I was not ordered to come, but I came over anyway just for an errand for the good of you and Good Thunder. He said I have heard that you two will be arrested and also Kicking Bear. Of course I did not want to flee and I was going to take it as it came. If it was the will of the Great Spirit it was all right with me. The Brulees were coming and Good Thunder suggest d that we go out and meet them. So we saddled up that evening and started out. We came thru WhiteHorse Creek and followed it down to the mouth of Wounded Knee. We followed this creek down about six miles below Manderson. There was a big camp of Brulees here. Early in the morning the crier announced that we would have a meeting with the Brulees. When the people got together this is what I told them: "My relatives, there is a certain thing that we have done. From that certain sacred thing we have done, we have had visions. In our visions that we have seen and we have also heard that our relatives that have gone before us are actually in the Promised Land and that we are also going there. They are with the wanekia. So therfore the Wasicsu if they want to they may fight us, and

-141

if they fight us, if we are going to we will win; so have in your minds a strong desire and take courage. We must depend upon the departed ones who are in the Promised Land that's coming and who are with the cenkekec wanekia. We should remember this. Because in the first place our grandfather has set the two-leggeds on earth with the power of where the sun goes down (meaning that the two-leggeds have the thunderbeings' power.)."

Some more Brulees came over soon after this time from the Porcupine and Medicine Root Creeks. From Wounded Knee camp, we followed the Wounded Knee down towards White River. That same evening of the day that I had talked, my mother was overxxxx there at the camp. We moved camp again to Red Hawk's place. When we camped here, some of the Ogalalas turned back. A black robe priest dame here and some of them turned back with him. Later this priest was stabbed at the Big Foot Massacre. From here we moved camp to plage called High Pockets place southwest of Kuny Table in the Badlands. Then again some chiefs came from Pine Ridge with many people.

Note--(Kuny Table is called by the Sioux as the Top of the Badlands.)

American Horse and Fast Thunder came over to where I was and askedme to put this ghost dance aside quietly (in other words, stop it) Just then Kicking Bear and Good Thunder and Big Road came in. xxxxxx I knew there was trouble now, so I consented to do this. Then we moved camp, as the chiefs had come after us. The Brulees interfered and kept us from moving, as they did not want us to go. The soldiers band of the Brulees tried to stop us and we tried to go anyway and they hit us and many of us were hit. We had quite a little struggle here and Good Thunder, Kicking Bear and others were trying to quiet them down. Somehow they induced Kicking Bear to go back to the Brulees, althogh he was going to go with us. Then we left them peacably. Then we camped on White River. We started and moved north of Ogalala to White Clay Creek. Some of the Brulees wentwith some of the Ogalalas, but more of them stayed in the camp at Kuny Table. Later, the Brulees and Ogalalas who stayed back went to the Onagazhee (place of shelter) on the top of the Badlands. We moved camp to Cheyenne Creek north of Pine Ridge. Most of the Ogalalsa were camping

BLACK ELK SPEAKS Transcription

page 142 Missing

-143-

behind the soldiers on the south. Yellow Bird and the white officer were wrestling with this gun and they had rolled down together on the floor and were wrestling with it. Dog Chief was right there where they took the guns and was standing right by these men while wrestling. This man was a friend of Black Elk's and he saw the whole thing. Big Foot was the first Indian that was killed by an officer before the guns began. They had carried Big Foot over to where the guns were being given up and immediately after the shot of Yellow Shirt the official shot Big Foot. Yellow Bird went into a teepee nearby and killed lots of them probably before he died. The Indians all ran to the stacks of guns and got their guns during a lull while the soldiers were loading again. A soldier ran up to tear the teepee away to get at Yellow Bird, but the latter shot at them as they came up and killed them. They fired at the teepee and the soldiers' guns set it afire and he died in there. The night before this I wasoverin the Camp at Pine Ridge and I couldn't sleep. When I saw the soldiers going out it seemed that I knew there would be trouble. I was walking around all night until daylight. After my meal early that morning I got my horse and while I was out I heard shooting over to the east—I heard wagon guns going off. This was a little distance from the camp and when I heard this gun I felt it right in my body, so I went out and drove the horses back to the damp forI knew there was trouble. Just as I got back with the horses there was a man who returned from Pine Ridge and had come back because he had heard this: He said: "Hey, hey, Son, the people that are coming are fired upon, I know it." I took my buckskin and saddled up. I had no gun. The only thing I had was the sacred red stick. I put on my sacred shirt. Thiswas a shirt I had made to be worn by no one but myself, which had a spotted eagle outstretched on the back of it, a star on the left shoulder, the rainbow diagnally across the breast from the left shoulder downward towards the hip. I made another rainbow around the neck, xxxxxxxx like a necklace with a star at the bottom. At the shoulder, elbows andwrists were eagle feathers. And over the whole shirt I had red streaks of lightning. This was a bullet-proof shirt. I painted my face red. I had another eagle

(Thes)

feather thrust through my hair at the top of my head. Of course I was going out by myself, and I could see that there were someyoung men following me. The first two men who followed me were Loves War and Iron White Man. I asked them where they were going and they said they were just going over to see where the firing was. I told them that I was going there xxx to fight for my people's rights and if they wanted to they could come along. So they went with me and Ixpmx about this time some more men older came. I just thot it over and thot I should not fight. I doubted about this Messiah business and therefore it seemed that I should not fight for it, but anyway I was going because I had already decided to. If I xxxxxx turned back the people would think it funny, so I just decided to go anyway. There were now over 20 of us going. As we neared there there was a horseback coming towards us. He said: "hey, hey, hey, they have murdered them." Just then right before us I could see a troop of soldiers coming down a canyon. They stopped their horses and asked me what to do, so we decided we'd fxxx first see what we could do and then we'd do it. We started out and at the head of the gulch we went along the creek and got on the top of the hill at the head of the Gulch now called Battle Creek.

(Proceeded with his account of Wounded Knee previously taken.)

After the battle after we went back on the north side of Pine Ridge where the hospital now is and as we were standing here the soldiers at Pine Ridge shot at us. We went back because we thot there was peace back home. The Indians fled from our camp at Pine Ridge and there wasnno one at home. The camp we left in the morning had been deserted. We were pretty hungry so we peeked in from teepee to teppee and we saw something cooked txxx to eat, and so we had something real to eat. Thiswas Red Crow and myself alone. As we were feasting there about three feet apart we heard some shots and just then the bullet went right between us and thru dust over our plates. We kept on eating anyway and had our fill and we got on our horses and went the way the people had fled. Probably if I had been killed there I would have had papa in my mouth. The people fled downstream (White Clay) and we followed them down. It was now dark. We followed them up all night and finally we found their camp below the streamwhich is east of Ogalala. The people had no teepees, they were just sitting by their fires. They had fled without their teepees. I went among them and I heard my mother singing a death song for me. I followed the voice and found her in a little loghouse which they had found and moved inot. Mother was very glad to see me, as she thot I had died over there. Of course, I did not sl ep the night before and I had fought all day and then there was a war party that went out, but I did not go as I was very tired and wanted to sleep that night. Some of the Brulees and Ogalalas were gathered here now. I gotup at daybreak the next morning. This morning more war parties went out to Pine Ridge to fight. A man by the name of He Crow and I went xftex east of the White Clay Creek staying as far from it as possible, because we could see all over the country from here and we could see just where the trouble was all the time. This war party had met the soldiers right where the Mission is today and we could hear the cannon go off here. We proceeded towards this. We went to the White Clay Creek and crossed it, xxxthxxxxxekk.w following the creek up on the west side and we could now hear the gun shots plainly. We then proceeded west following the ridge to where the fight was going on. Right from this ridge we could see that the Indians were on either side of the creek and were pumping at the soldiers who were coming down the creek between the Indians. ~~Aftex~~ As we looked down we saw a little ravine and across this was a big hill and we went down the ravine and got on the big hill. The men were fighting right here. They sent a voice to me saying: "Black Elk, this day is the xxghtx kind in which to do something great," so I said "How". I got off my horse and started putting dirt all over myself. I had a rifle and I proceeded up the hill and right below here the soldiers were firing and they told me not to go up, that they were pretty good riflemen there. I got on up the hill anyway and I was ~~xxx~~ in very close range of the enemy. Then I recalled my vision, the north where the geese were, then I outstretched my hands and made the goose sound. They pumped away at me from the creek then, but not a single bullet came near me--they couldn't hit me. As I went back down the hill again I heard them say: "They are gone." So I got on my horse and started down the north side of the hill and right there a buckskin rider went passed me, his name was Protector. He went past me xhrxughx to look at them and just then they fired so he came back again. I did not expect them to be so close and I went up there right away and they were about 100 yards from me and they began to shoot at me. I proceeded towards them anyway. If I had kept on I would not have gotten hit, probably, some of them started to flee towards the creek and I turned around and as I fled towards the hill I could hear the bullets hitting my clothes. Then something hit me on the belt on the right side. I reeled on my horse and rode on over the hill. I was riding my buckskin then. I should have kept on coming like that with my hands up. I was in fear and had forgotten my power. I had forgotten to make the goose sound there to keep my hands up. I doubted my power right there and I should have gone right on imitating the goose with my power and I would have been bullet proof. My doubt and my fear for the moment killed my power and during that moment I was shot. Protector ran up to me and grabbed me for I was falling off my horse. I said: "Let me go, I'll go over there. It is a good day to die so I'll go over there." He said: "No, nephew." Protector xxxxx tore his blanket up and rapt it around my wound. This kept my insides from falling out. Then Protector told me to go home and said: "You must not die today, you must live, for the people depend upon you." The soldiers were now retreating and the Indians were fighting harder. The Mission was there then and there were lots of Indians children in there. The Priests and Sisters were all over there praying. That building now has many shots in it. A man by the name of Little Soldier brot me back to the camp near the Stronghold. When I got back the people were on top the Stronghold. Old Hollow Horn was a bear medicine man and he came over to heal my wound. Of course he was a powerful medicine man and my wound began to heal and I was able to walk in about three days.

Here I heard that soldiers were coming now and I caught up my buckskin. My mother asked me not to go, but I went anyway. About 60 men of us started out on a Warpath east. We heard that the soldiers from battlefield were marching thru Wounded Knee to White River and were coming to the Stronghold. The soldiers were now at Black Feather's place. We Indians followed Grass creek down and got on the west side of the river on a hill and saw the soldiers down on White River. We got off our horses and we saw some Indians coming on the other side on the north. The Indians began to correll the wagons and were preparing themselves to fight. We proceeded down towards the Indians on the other side. They saw us and they fired on the soldiers because they took courage by seeing us coming. As we neared the Little Creek flowing into White River on the south side, right above was a little knoll--the soldiers across the creek--as we looked over the bank of the creek we saw some soldiers' horses coming to the water with harnesses on. I said: "Fire at them and I will go and get the horses." The Indians fired at the soldiers and I got the soldiers' horses and drove them southward. Then they saw me and began to pump on me. I got back with five horses and they killed two of otheir own horses. There was a little gulch there and I got away with five of their horses. When I got out of bullet range with the horses I caught the best horse--a bay horse with a ball-face--I turned mine loose and from there I drove the rest of them back. About this time there was a whole detatchment of cavalry coming up the river. I knew there were a lot of them, so I hurried with the horses. Just then I met a man running on foot without a horse. The Indians on the north side had retreated up the river. About that time they had come up to where I was. This man on foot was Red Willow. His horse had played out. He said: "Cousin, I am on foot." So I caught him a roan horse with a halter on dragging a rope--a soldier's horse. About that time the soldiers were very near us and you could see the bullets coming and the dust kicking up. Then ther was another man whose horse played out, so I caught him a brown horse and gave it to him. I was a wanekia just then, serving these two men by giving them horses. There was hard fighting now since the cavalrymen came up. The soldiers had come around and stopped the men in front. The soldiers werenot crack shots so several fellows got away. Two of the men got wounded but they got home alive even tho' they were badly wounded. One of them was Long Bear, but I don't remember the other one's name. After we got into the Badlands the soldiers xxxxxxd left us go so we came back to the Stronghold that night. The next morning I got up early and myself, One Side, Poor Buffalo and Brave Heart, we all started out east again and we came to where Manderson is at present. When we were there we could see the soldiers coming up the creek towards Manderson. They were cavalrymen coming back after that fight. On either side of them there were scouts and we had xxx gone on the other side of the hill on the west side of the store and hid there. I wanted to shoot, but the other three men didn't allow me to. I said: "Let's stay here and kill at least one." They said they would kill us if we did. We had quite an argument. So the three men led me away on my horse to stop me. We came up past this Sacred Butte up thru this little cut and went over to Grass Creek. There were a lot of cattle there, so we butchered three of them and took the meat back to the Stronghold on White Clay. As we were on top the Stronghold we could see Sioux xxxxxxxx xxxxxx hiding along the rocks guarding the Stronghold all night. They were guarding all around the camp. They asked us if the soldiers were coming and we told them that everything was all right now. That day that we had butchered there was a lieutenant and some scouts that came over there and they surrounded him and killed him. We thought that the scouts would probably report this and there would be a surprize attack so we were on guard all night and did not sleep any. The next day I went on the highest point and asked the people to gather there. The announcer announced it and the crowd came. This day I remembered my six grandfathers, altho I had completely forgotten my vision for a spell before this. I had some white paint with me, so I told them to bring their weapons that I might make them sacred. I put a little bit of white paint on every gun that they brot and when that was done everyone stood facing the west pointing their weapons towards the west. Then I thus sent a voice: "Hey-a-a-a-a (4 times) Grandfathers, the six grandfathers that I thus will recall to you today. Behold me! And also to the four quarters of the earth and its powers. Thus you have said if an enemy I should meet that I shold

-149-

recall thee. This you have said to me. Thus youhave xxixx set me in the center of the earth and have said that my people will be relative-like with the thunderbeings. Today my people are in despair so, six gran fathers, help me." About this time we could see a storm coming up (in Jan. in the middle of winter.) but the thunderbeings appeared with lightning and thunder. The people all raised their hands towards the thunderbeings and cried. The thunder-beings followed the White Clay up and went towards Pine Ridge. We were well prepared now and were going out again for revenge. Revenge is sweet. We got ready and just then Afraid-Of-His-Horses came over to make peace with Red Cloud who was in our bunch then. Miles had told Afraid-Of-His-Horses to come over and make peace. We had gathered there at this time. Red Cloud got up and made this speech: "Boys, this is a hard winter. If it were in the summer we would keep on fighting; but, boys, we cannot gxxx go on fighting, because the winter is hard on us, so we should make peace and I'll see that nobody will be hurt." After that meeting Afraid-Of-His-Horses wanted to talk to me, Good Thunder, Kicking Bear, Short Bull and we went over to a teepee and Afraid-Of-His-Horses began to speak:

"Relatives, if this were in summer time it would not be so hard. If this were winter, my people at Pine Ridge would have joined you and we would have had to fight to a finish, and I don't want mine and your peo le to make us kill each other among ourselves. I don't care how many the soldiers are, without the Indian scouts they cannot fight and the army will be helpless. So, relatives, if this were in the summer we would have joined you and had it to a finish. But this is winter andit is hard on our children especially, so let us go back and make peace."

We all agreed. I wanted revenge anyway. xhxxxthxxxx I knew that when those clouds had appeared the thunderbeings had talked to me. I did not want to have peace, but the people insisted so we broke camp the next day and went down from the Stronghold and camped several places and got to Pine Ridge where we camped on the northwest side. That day we were going to camp right in Pine Ridge. People gathered here—hundreds on horseback. Then Kicking Bear and High Hawk (Brulee) were among these young men who were going around among the young men. They came to me and made me stand at a certain place. They put another man by my side--his name was Lick-His-Lips. Another one was brot here named Red Willow and another man whom I do not know. These were supposed to be the great warriors and they told the people that we were commanders of the Indiand army and we were to take the lead. The men on foot were first, then the horsebacks followed. Then the wagons followed the horsebacks. We had started towards the office at Pine Ridge. We were now inside where the guards were and we could see soldiers all around. As we went down there, the soldiers that were coming stood in two bodies on either side of us and were ordered to present arms. We went right thru the middle of them. There were many soldiers there. We went thru Pine Ridge and went in front of the office, the officers saluted us. We went to a place on White Clay Creek and camped. The next day we were supposed to make peace. We made a law that anyone who should make trouble in the fort, ~~had been~~ should be arrested and tried and ~~xxxxxxxxxxx~~ if found guilty he should be punished.

*****

Two years later, I was married.

******

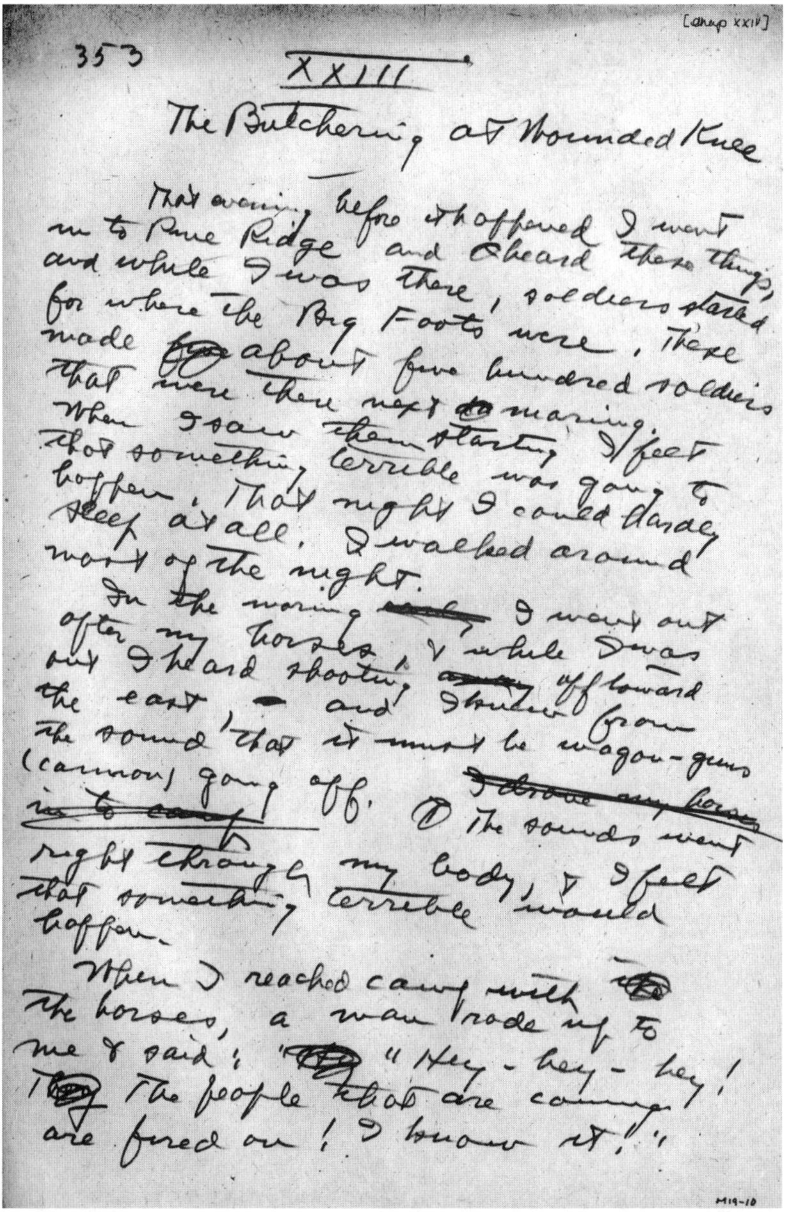
353 [chap XXIV]

XXIII

The Butchering at Wounded Knee

That evening before it happened I went in to Pine Ridge and heard these things, and while I was there, soldiers started for where the Big Foots were. These made about five hundred soldiers that were there next morning. When I saw them starting I felt that something terrible was going to happen. That night I could hardly sleep at all. I walked around most of the night.

In the morning ~~early~~ I went out after my horses, & while I was out I heard shooting ~~away~~ off toward the east, and I knew from the sound that it must be wagon-guns (cannon) going off. ~~I drove my horses in to camp.~~ The sounds went right through my body, & I felt that something terrible would happen.

When I reached camp with the horses, a man rode up to me & said: "Hey-hey-hey! The people that are coming are fired on! I know it!"

M19-10

Figure 4.9 c3716 f274 Pages 353–360 and 365–368 of the manuscript, discussing Wounded Knee and its aftermath. Courtesy, the John G. Neihardt Papers, c. 1858–1974, Western Historical Manuscript Collection, Columbia, Missouri; the John G. Neihardt Trust.

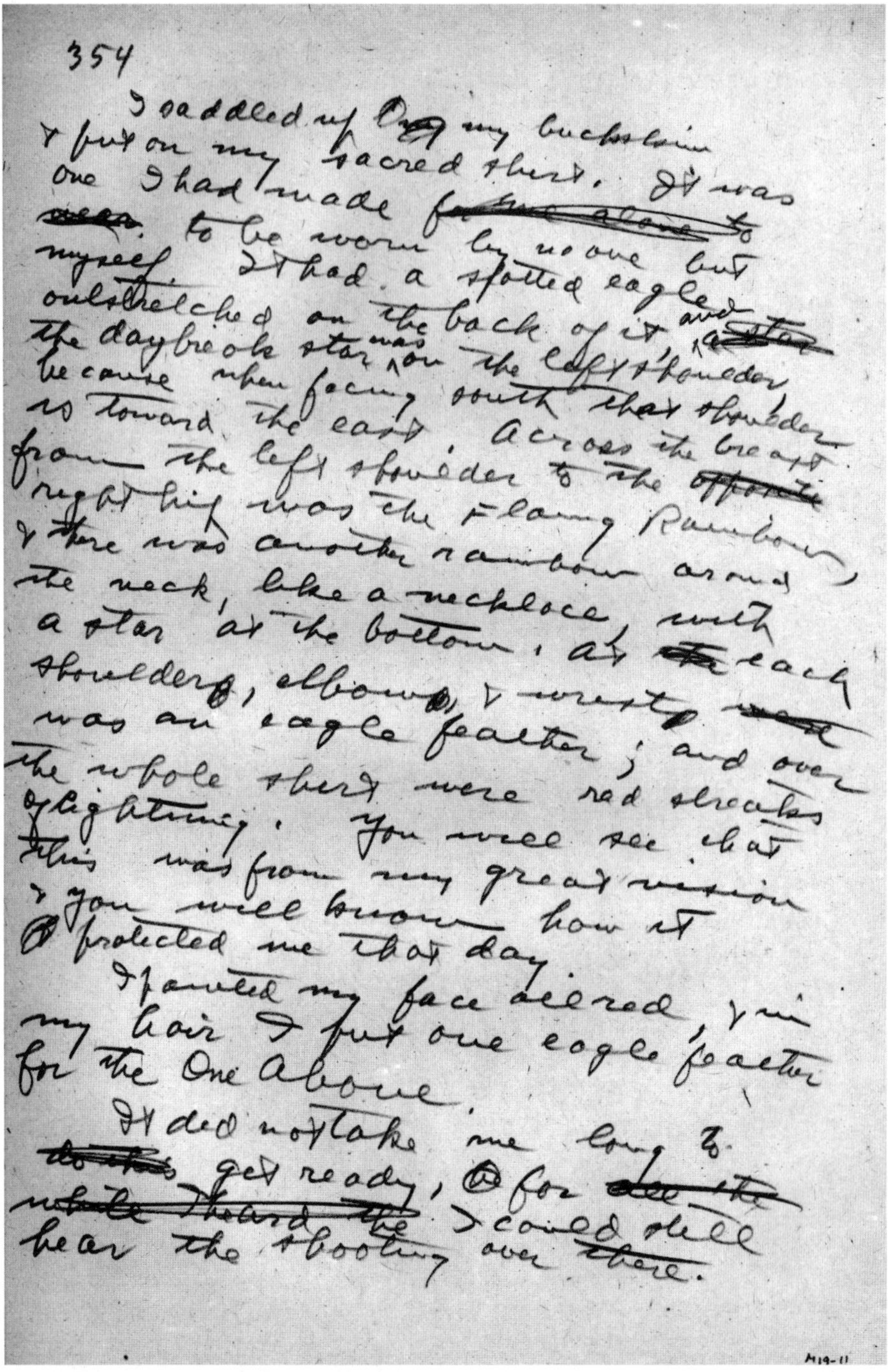

354

I saddled up ~~my~~ my buckskin & put on my sacred shirt. One I had made ~~for one alone to~~ It was ~~meant~~ to be worn by no one but myself. It had a spotted eagle outstretched on the back of it, and ~~a star~~ the daybreak star was on the left shoulder because when facing south that shoulder is toward the east. Across the breast from the left shoulder to the ~~opposite~~ right hip was the Flaming Rainbow & there was another rainbow around the neck, like a necklace, with a star at the bottom. At ~~the~~ each shoulder, elbow, & wrist ~~was~~ was an eagle feather; and over the whole shirt were red streaks of lightning. You will see that this was from my great vision & you will know how it protected me that day.

I painted my face all red, & in my hair I put one eagle feather for the One Above.

It did not take me long to ~~do this~~ get ready, for ~~all the while I heard the~~ I could still hear the shooting over there.

M19-11

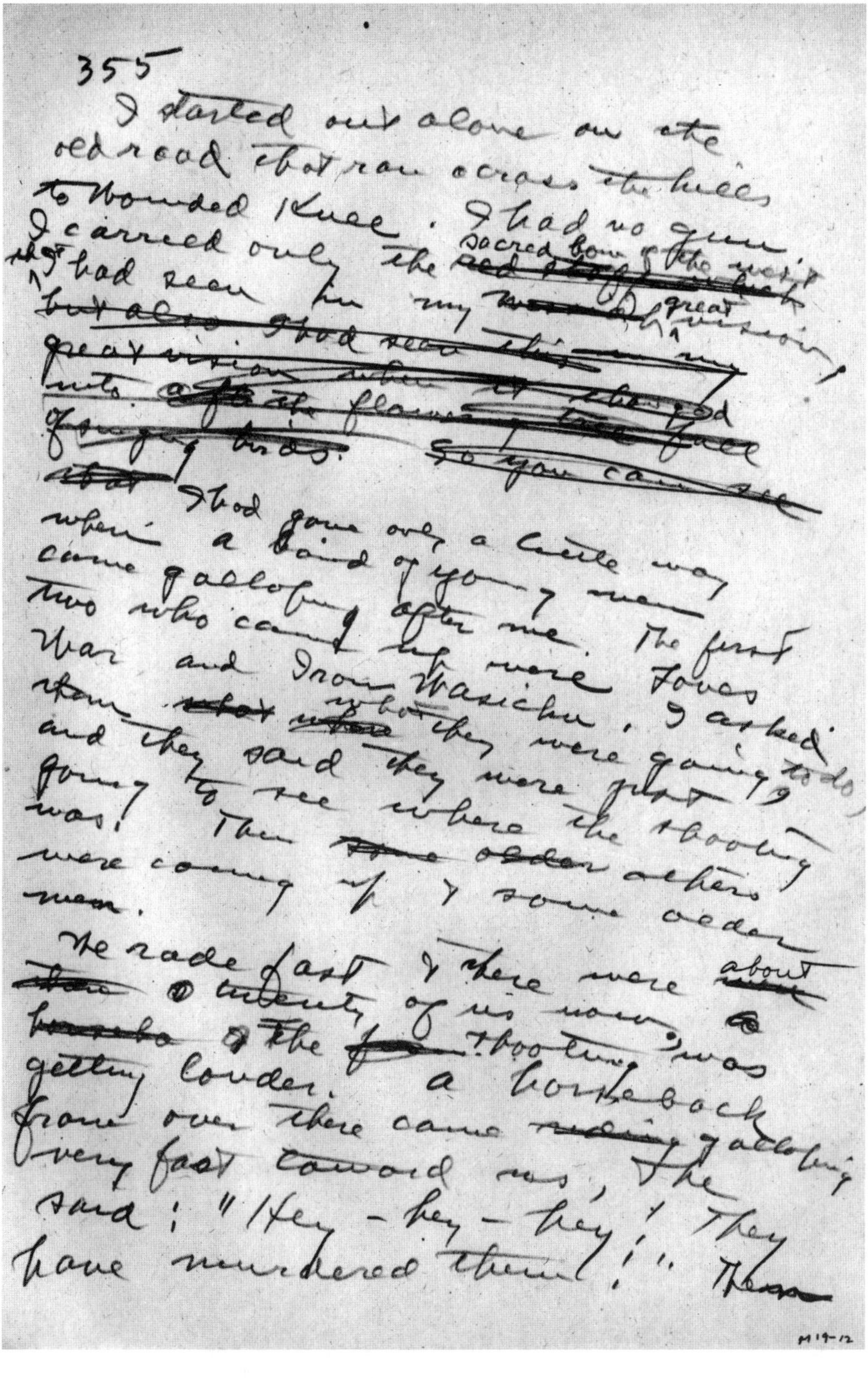

355

I ~~started~~ out alone on the old road that ran across the hills to Wounded Knee. I had no gun. I carried only the sacred bow of the west ~~red stuff which~~ that I had seen in my great vision. ~~but also I had seen this in my great vision when it changed into a flaming [illegible] full of singing birds. So you can see that~~

I had gone only a little way when a band of young men came galloping after me. The first two who came up were Loves War and Iron Wasichu. I asked them ~~what~~ ~~where~~ what they were going to do, and they said they were just going to see where the shooting was. Then ~~some older~~ others were coming up & some older men.

We rode fast & there were about ~~[illegible]~~ twenty of us now. ~~[illegible]~~ The ~~[illegible]~~ shooting was getting louder. A horseback from over there came ~~riding~~ galloping very fast toward us, & he said: "Hey-hey-hey! They have murdered them!" Then

M14-12

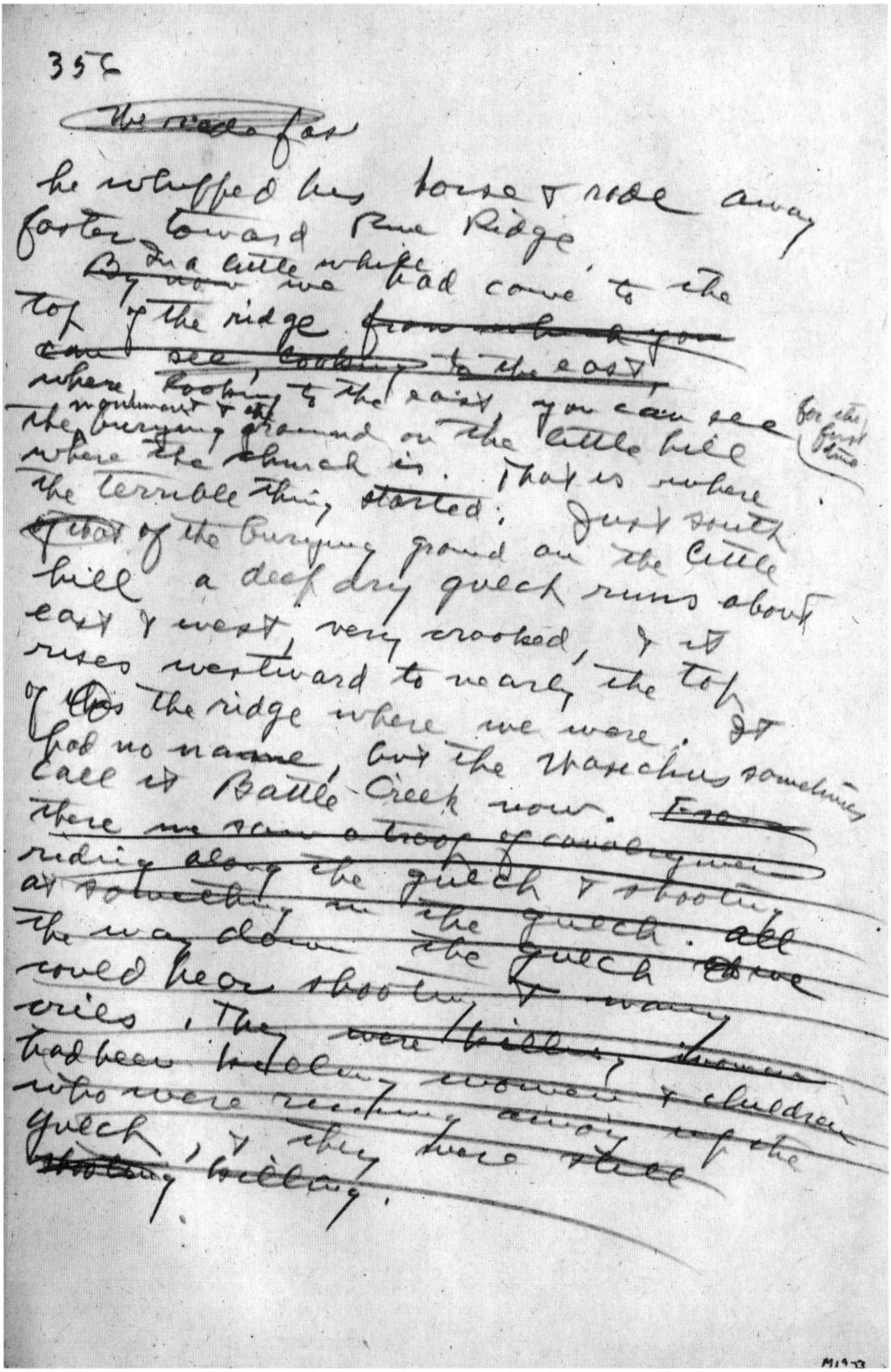
355

~~The rider~~ fast

he whipped his horse & rode away faster toward Pine Ridge.

~~By now~~ In a little while we had come to the top of the ridge ~~from where you can see looking to the east,~~ where, looking to the east, you can see for the first time the monument & the burying ground on the little hill where the church is. That is where the terrible thing ~~started~~. Just south ~~of that~~ of the burying ground on the little hill a deep dry gulch runs about east & west, very crooked, & it rises westward to nearly the top of ~~the~~ the ridge where we were. It had no name, but the Wasichus sometimes call it Battle Creek now. ~~From there we saw a troop of cavalrymen riding along the gulch & shooting at something in the gulch. All the way down the gulch we could hear shooting & women's cries. They were killing women~~ had been killing women & children who were running away up the gulch, & they were still ~~shooting~~ killing.

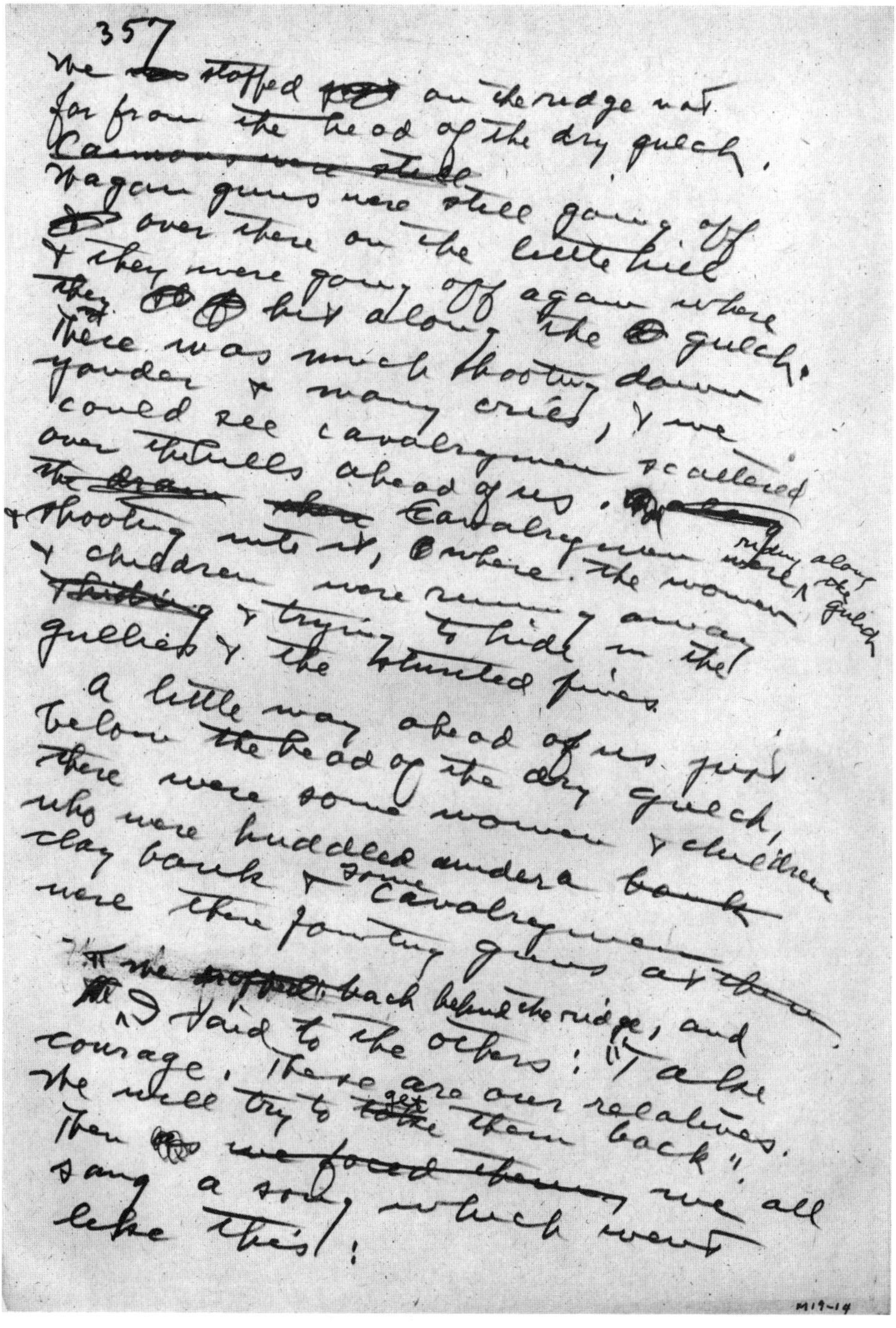
357
We stopped on the ridge not
far from ~~the~~ head of the dry gulch.
~~Cannons were still~~
Wagon guns were still going off
over there on the little hill
& they were going off again where
they hit along the gulch.
There was much shooting down
yonder & many cries, & we
could see cavalrymen scattered
over the hills ahead of us.
Cavalrymen were riding along the gulch
& shooting into it, where the women
& children were running away
& trying to hide in the
gullies & the stunted pines.
A little way ahead of us, just
below ~~the head of~~ the dry gulch,
there were some women & children
who were huddled under a ~~bank~~
clay bank & some cavalrymen
were there pointing guns at them.
~~We stopped~~ back behind the ridge, and
I said to the others: "Take
courage. These are our relatives.
We will try to ~~take~~ get them back".
Then ~~we faced them~~ we all
sang a song, which went
like this!

M19-14

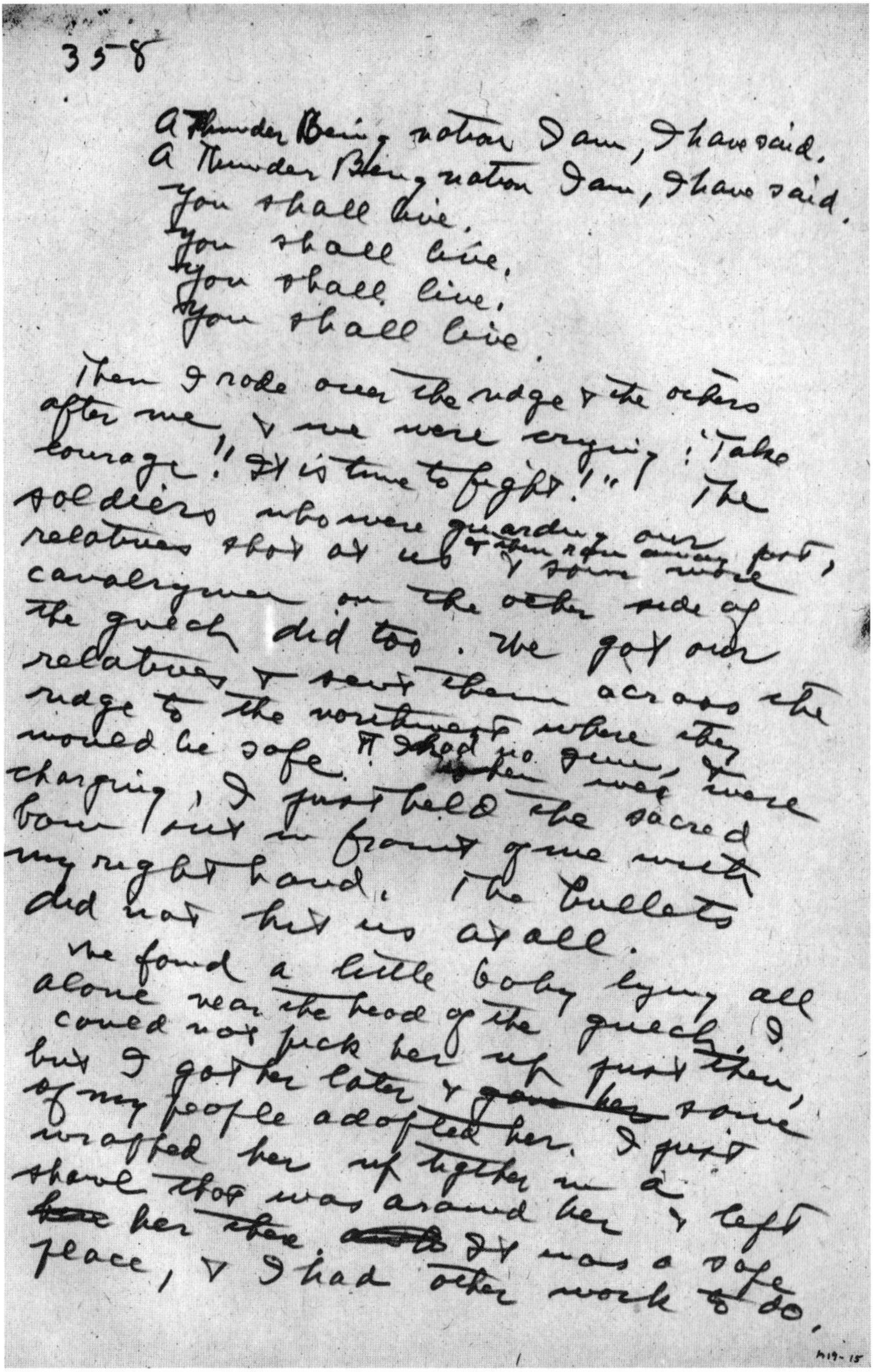

358

A Thunder Being nation I am, I have said.
A Thunder Being nation I am, I have said.
You shall live.
You shall live.
You shall live.
You shall live.

Then I rode over the ridge & the others after me, & we were crying: "Take courage! It is time to fight!" The soldiers who were guarding our relatives shot at us & then ran away fast, & some more cavalrymen on the other side of the gulch did too. We got our relatives & sent them across the ridge to the northwest where they would be safe. I had no gun, & when we were charging, I just held the sacred bow I sent in front of me with my right hand. The bullets did not hit us at all.

We found a little baby lying all alone near the head of the gulch. I could not pick her up just then, but I got her later & some of my people adopted her. I just wrapped her up tighter in a shawl that was around her & left her there. It was a safe place, & I had other work to do.

M19-15

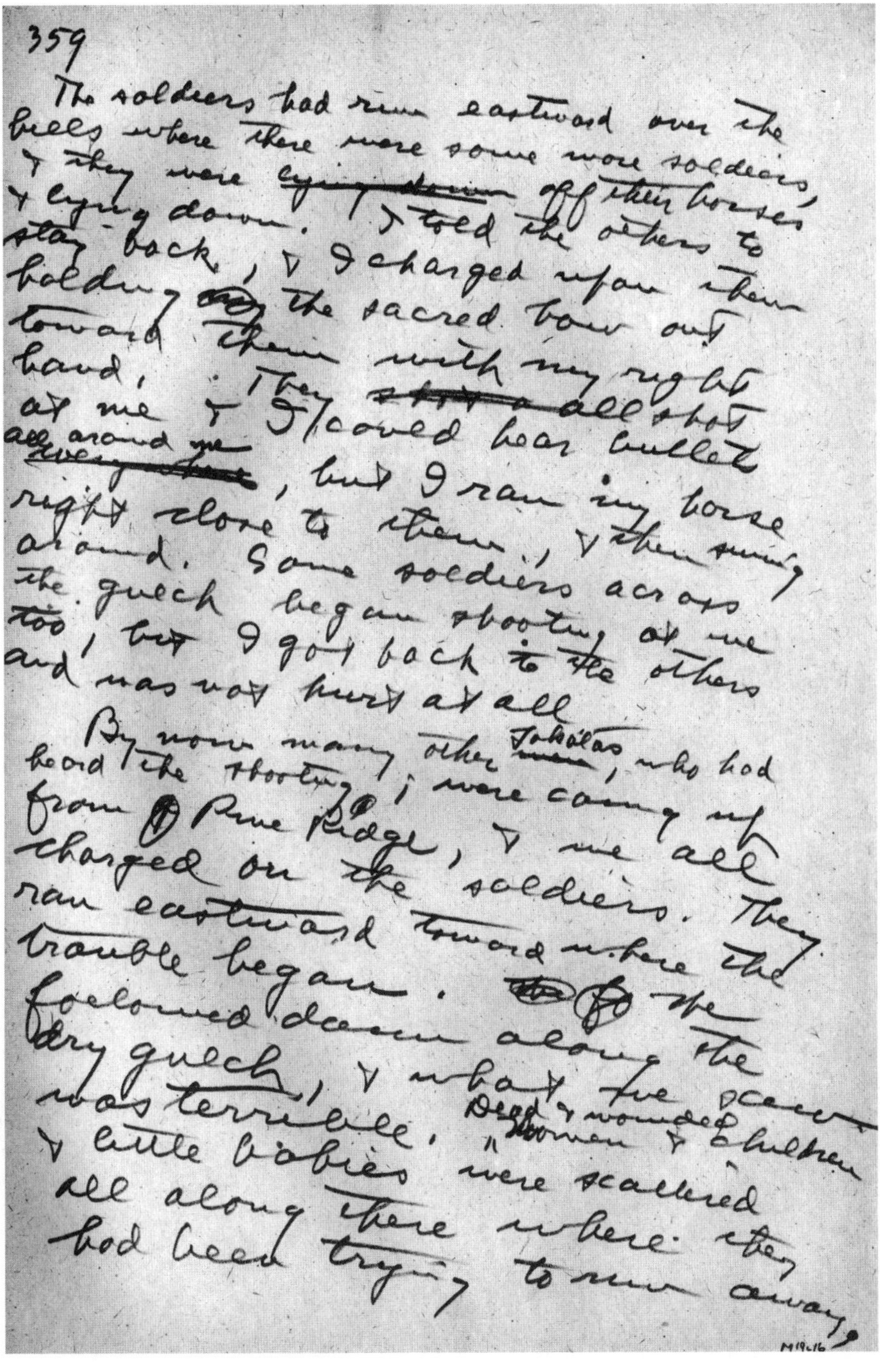

359

The soldiers had run eastward over the hills where there were some more soldiers, & they were ~~lying down~~ off their horses & lying down. I told the others to stay back, & I charged upon them holding ~~my~~ the sacred bow out toward them with my right hand. They ~~shot a~~ all shot at me & I could hear bullets all around me ~~everywhere~~, but I ran my horse right close to them, & then swung around. Some soldiers across the gulch began shooting at me too, but I got back to the others and was not hurt at all.

By now many other Lakotas ~~men~~, who had heard the shooting, were coming up from ~~P~~ Pine Ridge, & we all charged on the soldiers. They ran eastward toward where the trouble began. ~~We~~ So we followed down along the dry gulch, & what we saw was terrible. Dead & wounded women & children & little babies were scattered all along there where they had been trying to run away.

M19.16

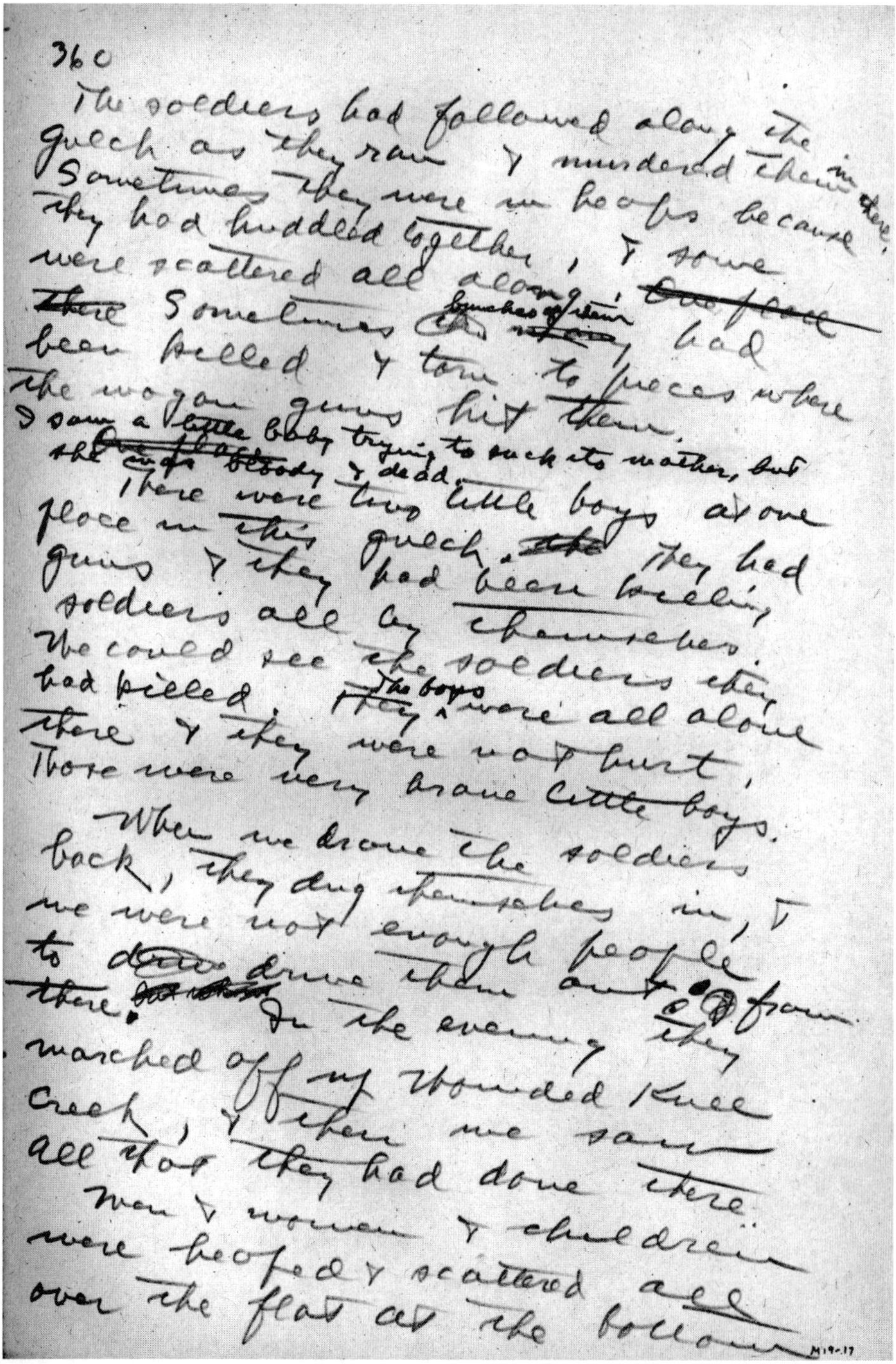

360
The soldiers had followed along the
gulch as they ran & murdered them in there.
Sometimes they were in heaps because
they had huddled together, & some
were scattered all along. ~~One place~~
~~there~~ Sometimes bunches of them ~~were~~ had
been killed & torn to pieces where
the wagon guns hit them.
I saw a ~~little~~ baby trying to suck its mother, but
she ~~One place~~ ~~was~~ bloody & dead.
There were two little boys at one
place in this gulch. ~~the~~ They had
guns & they had been killing
soldiers all by themselves.
We could see the soldiers they
had killed. ~~They~~ The boys were all alone
there & they were not hurt.
Those were very brave little boys.
When we drove the soldiers
back, they dug themselves in, &
we were not enough people
to ~~drive~~ drive them out ~~of~~ from
there. In the evening they
marched off up Wounded Knee
Creek, & then we saw
all that they had done there.
Men & women & children
were heaped & scattered all
over the flat at the bottom

M19-17

365

the little hill where the soldiers had their wagon guns, and westward up the dry gulch all the way to the high ridge, the ~~women & ch~~ dead women & children & babies were scattered.

When I saw this I wished that I had died too, but I was not sorry ~~about~~ for the women & children. It was better for them to be ~~dead~~ in the Other World, and I wanted to be there too. But ~~[illegible]~~ before I went there I wanted to have revenge. I thought there ~~would~~ might be a day & we ~~would have~~ should have revenge.

After the soldiers marched away, I heard from my friend Dog Chief how ~~who was right there,~~ ~~where~~ the trouble started. He was right there ~~at the tent~~ by Yellow Bird when it happened. This is the way it was.

In the morning the soldiers began to take all the guns away from the Big Foots, who were camped in the flat below the little hill where the monument & burying ground are now. The people had stacked most of their guns & even their knives by ~~the officers tent,~~

366

the tepee where Big Foot was lying sick. Soldiers were on the little hill & all around, & there were soldiers across the dry gulch to the south & over east along Wounded Knee Creek too. The people were nearly surrounded, & the wagon guns were pointing at them.

Some had not yet given up their guns, & so the soldiers were searching all the tepees, throwing things around & poking into everything. There was a man called Yellow Bird, (over) ~~& when an officer tried to take his gun, he would not let go.~~ He wrestled with the officer, & while they were wrestling, the gun went off & killed the officer. Wasichus ~~some~~ & some others have said he meant to do this, but Dog Chief was standing right there & he told me it was not so. As soon as the gun went off, ~~an officer~~ Dog Chief told me, an officer ~~who was~~ shot Big Foot ~~at once~~ & killed Big Foot who was lying sick inside the tepee.

Then suddenly nobody knew what was happening, except that ~~gun~~ the soldiers were all shooting & the wagon guns began going off right

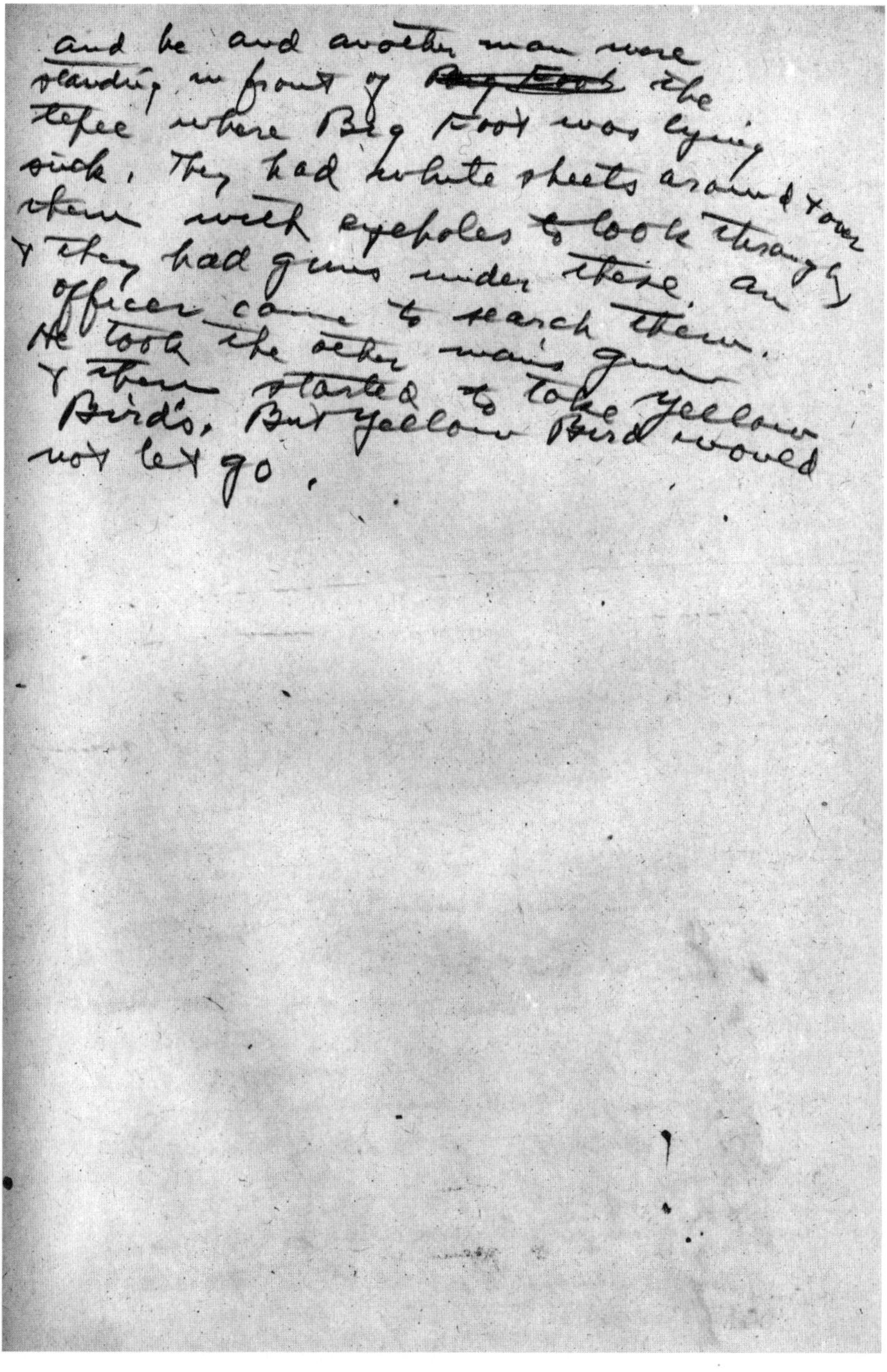

and he and another man were
standing in front of ~~Big Foot~~ the
tepee where Big Foot was lying
sick. They had white sheets around & over
them with eyeholes to look through
& they had guns under these. An
officer came to search them.
He took the other man's gun
& then started to take Yellow
Bird's. But Yellow Bird would
not let go.

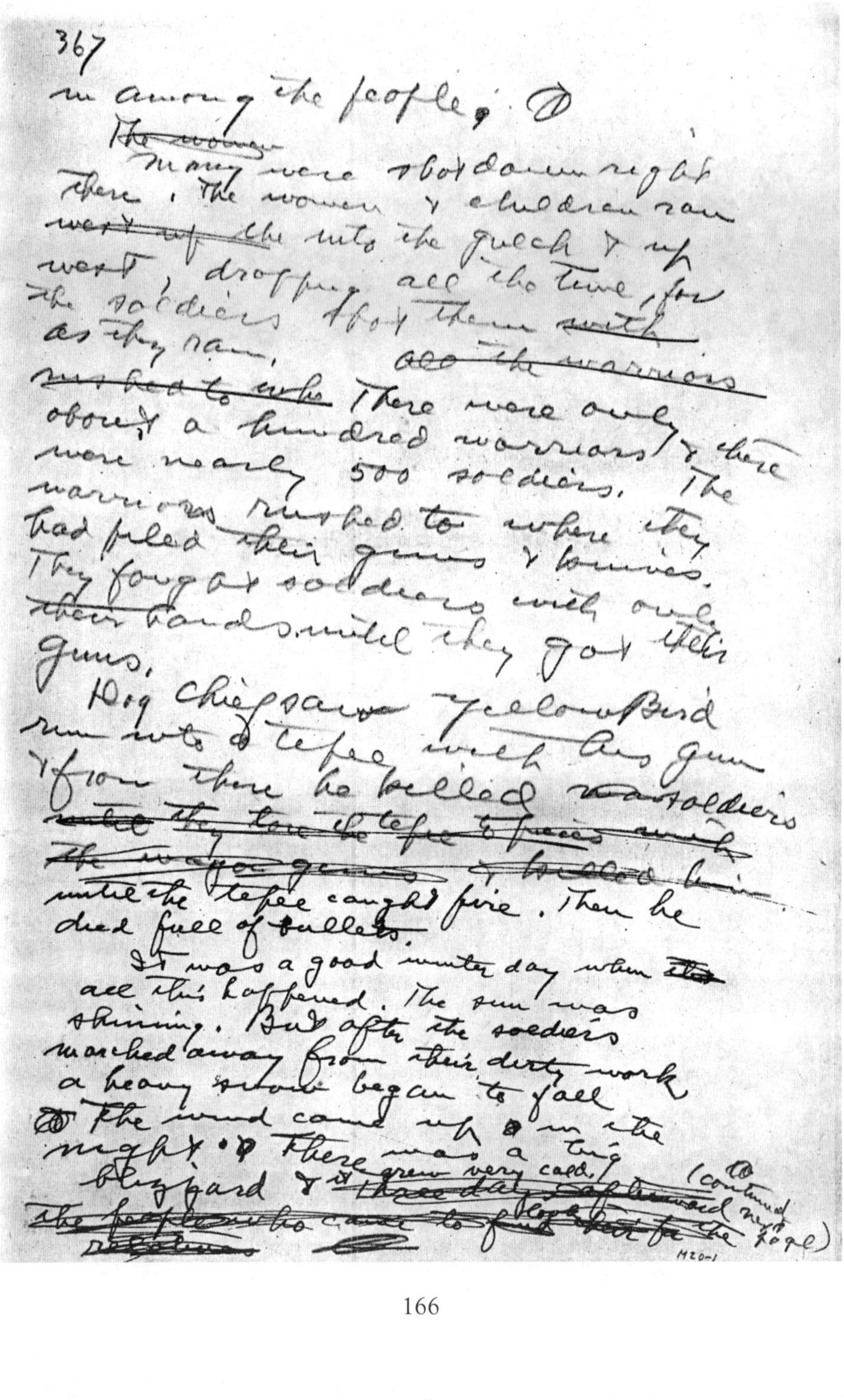
367
in among the people. ⓘ
~~The women~~
Many were shot down right
there. The women & children ran
~~west up the~~ into the gulch & up
west, dropping all the time, for
the soldiers shot them ~~with~~
as they ran. ~~All the warriors~~
~~rushed to whe~~ There were only
about a hundred warriors & there
were nearly 500 soldiers. The
warriors rushed to where they
had piled their guns & knives.
They fought soldiers with only
~~their~~ hands until they got their
guns.
Dog Chief saw Yellow Bird
run into a tepee with his gun
& from there he killed ~~many~~ soldiers
~~until they tore the tepee to pieces with~~
~~the wagon guns & killed him~~
until the tepee caught fire. Then he
died full of ~~bullets~~.
It was a good winter day when ~~the~~
all this happened. The sun was
shining. But after the soldiers
marched away from their dirty work
a heavy snow began to fall.
The wind came up in the
night. There was a big
blizzard & it grew very cold. ~~three days afterward~~ (continued to next
~~the people who came to~~ look for the ~~find their~~ page)
~~relatives~~
H20-1

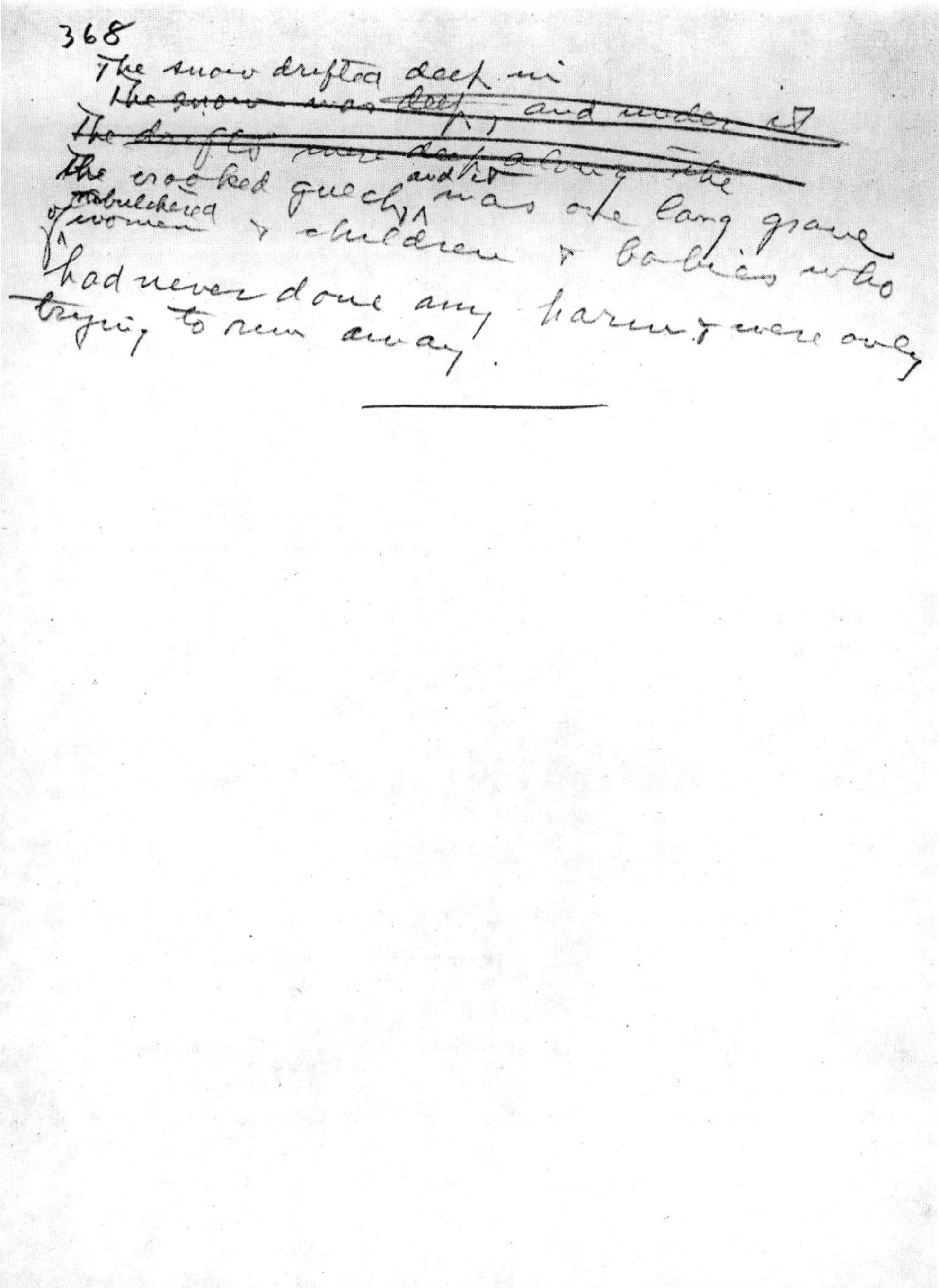
368
The snow drifted deep in
~~the snow was deep~~, and under it
~~The drifts were deep along the~~
the crooked gulch, and it was one long grave
of butchered women & children & babies who
had never done any harm & were only
trying to run away.

THE ENDING OF BLACK ELK SPEAKS IN MANUSCRIPT: FROM DEATH TO REBIRTH NOTES TO MANUSCRIPT, FIGURE 4.10

The Function of M 379

M 379, a passage Neihardt created using the imagery and tenor of Black Elk's telling, brings the reader to the lowest point in Black Elk's story or in the Lakota epic itself. From unity the people have passed into disunity and then into despair and total fragmentation, as previously discussed by Black Elk in describing the "ascents" he had been told he would see. And yet this nadir is a component of a cycle, as is nature, as are day and night, as is human life. Remember that both Neihardt and Black Elk thought in terms of such cycles—circles or loops—and that Black Elk's discussion of the Fourth Ascent prefigures a regeneration. In addition, the telling and ending of *Black Elk Speaks* take place not just within the context of nature but in integration with nature. One example of Neihardt's reinforcing this process is a division of the book paralleling a diurnal structure. Chapter 24 ends the cycle of Black Elk's narrative—the story of Black Elk from birth to Wounded Knee that the two collaborators agreed would be the substance of the book. Chapter 25 is "the end of the dream," the destruction of people and their ideals, and the aftermath of a hideous nightmare. The Postscript that follows, however, shows that, as in the diurnal cycle the book's structure simulates, this nadir is temporary. M 379, then, closes the old cycle and prepares for the new. It is also permeated in sorrow, thus connecting with Black Elk's lamenting described on M 383 and prefigured earlier in the book. M 379 both acts as coda to the narrative of birth through Wounded Knee, completing one downturn of the cycle, and introduces the forthcoming cycle.

The Postscript

The Postscript is a nonethnocentric, nonpatronizing version of hope: from bad times will come good. Contrast it with Curtis's recorded talk with Short Bull mentioned previously. The Postscript continues the theme of Black Elk communicating with the Six Grandfathers; indeed he is now old, resembling and identified with the Sixth Grandfather.

The Postscript is also both the narrative of a quest *and the representation of the physical enactment of such a seeking, which possesses the topography of a quest.* The reader familiar with this genre in Judaic, Christian, or Islamic literature will recognize a similarity in geographical description between Black Elk's ascent up Harney Peak and like accounts from other "religions of the book," which Black Elk's telling has now itself become. Excellent coverage of Judaic, Christian, and Islamic traditions in this regard appears in *Sacred Places and*

Profane Spaces, edited by Jamie Scott and Paul Simpson-Housley. In particular, Annemarie Schimmel's discussion in part of her chapter "Sacred Geography in Islam" (170–171) and Martha Himmelfarb's analysis of "Ezekiel's Temple Vision" (64–66) reveal interesting comparisons.

The Postscript begins with an overview of Nightmare or Despair. Not only is the hoop seemingly fragmented, but the party of Black Elk and Neihardt is stationed at the edge of the Badlands—the bad earth, the site of a world once destroyed by the gods, the twisted landscape of which contains the bones of monstrous creatures extinguished during that apocalypse. Black Elk looks across the desolate terrain and sees in the distance Harney Peak, the Center of the World in his great vision. As in Black Elk's first visionary experience, nature around him both is and tells the story. Here the landscape shows the story in its topography. On the other side of despair is the mount of vision, the center of the world. The landscape elicits Black Elk's recognition of what he must do, of the story he must live and live through:

> Pointing at Harney Peak that loomed black above the far sky rim, Black Elk said: "There, when I was young, the spirits took me in my vision to the center of the earth and showed me all the good things in the sacred hoop of the world. I wish I could stand up there in the flesh before I die, for there is something I want to say to the Six Grandfathers." (BES 271)

With Neihardt's help the journey is made, and the visionary party ascends the peak.

This journey reveals magical and spiritual implications emerging through nature. Black Elk tells Ben that some thunder and rain should come if his power is validated. And just as Black Elk's first vision was an intimation of his great revelation, so the view of the land from Cuny Table, over the Badlands and to the peak of vision itself, prefigures what follows. Neihardt teaches the dominant culture about such implications indirectly; these intimations and visionary outcomes are "not for" wasichu readers but really are for them, which is why Neihardt tones down the initially anger-laden irony—present in the draft—that damns modern culture for its inability to perceive the miraculous. Instead, "Wasichu readers" are shown "a more or less striking coincidence" (BES 271). In keeping with that understanding, the "apparent" reality seems to differ from the spiritual reality but actually does not. The experience at the top of Harney Peak shows that everything turns out to be interconnected, fused. At the end of the book as in the first vision, interior/exterior, natural/supernatural are not dichotomies but a unity melded in the world and in Black Elk himself.

M 382 shows us this. Black Elk begins his spiritual conversation in the customary sorrow and self-humbling prescribed for traditional lamenting, a deeply felt wound of the heart. M 383–384 depicts Black Elk standing by the spot where he saw the "hoop of the world" and the living tree that seem not to be. But remember M 381; what is apparent may simply be limited by perception. As Black Elk—attired as he appeared in his vision—prays for the healing of the hoop and the flowering of the tree, he describes these processes and evokes them. And as in his very first vision the cosmos manifests itself, uniting its features in Black Elk: the clouds build, the thunder rumbles. Black Elk and the world "rain" together—nature, Black Elk, and perception are one. When the vision has been validated, the sky clears, and a new stage in the cycle begins.

Figure 4.10 c3716 f275 The ending of Black Elk Speaks *in manuscript. Courtesy, the John G. Neihardt Papers, c. 1858–1974, Western Historical Manuscript Collection, Columbia, Missouri; the John G. Neihardt Trust.*

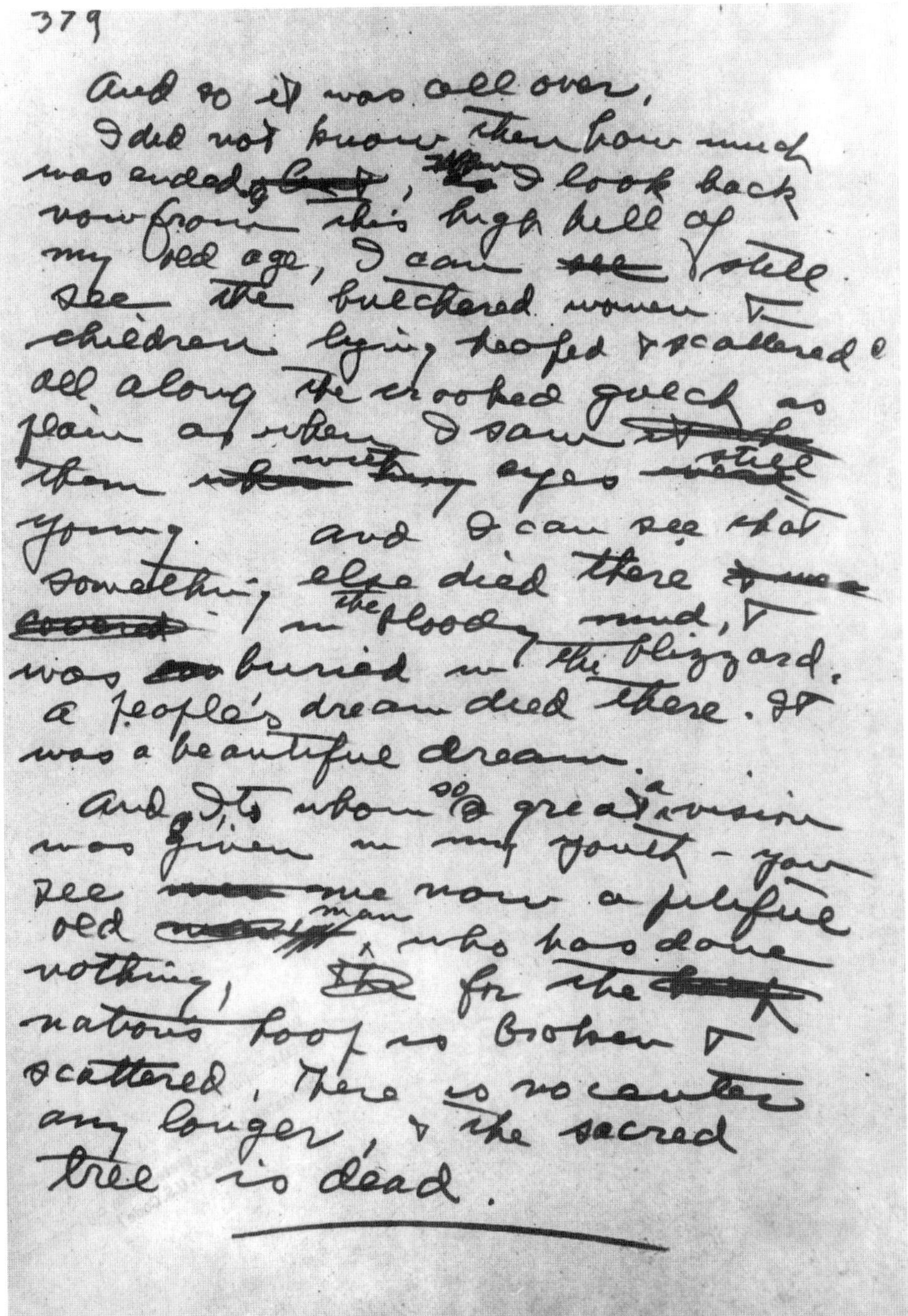

379

And so it was all over.
I did not know then how much was ended. ~~[illegible]~~ ~~[illegible]~~ I look back now from this high hill of my old age, I can ~~see~~ still see the butchered women & children lying heaped & scattered all along the crooked gulch as plain as when I saw ~~[illegible]~~ them with ~~[illegible]~~ eyes ~~[illegible]~~ still young. And I can see that something else died there ~~[illegible]~~ ~~[illegible]~~ in the bloody mud, & was ~~[illegible]~~ buried in the blizzard. A people's dream died there. It was a beautiful dream.
And I, to whom so a great vision was given in my youth—you see ~~[illegible]~~ me now a pitiful old ~~[illegible]~~ man who has done nothing, ~~[illegible]~~ for the ~~[illegible]~~ nation's hoop is broken & scattered. There is no center any longer, & the sacred tree is dead.

MBL-13

380

Postscript.

After the conclusion of ~~his~~ the narrative, Black Elk & our party were sitting ~~one day~~ at the north ~~end~~ edge of Cuny Table, looking off across the Badlands ("the beauty and the strangeness of the earth," as the old man expressed it). ~~On the far sky~~ So Pointing at Harney Peak that loomed black ~~against~~ above the far sky-rim, Black Elk said: "There, when I was young, the spirits took me in my vision to the center of the ~~world~~ earth and showed me all the good things in the sacred hoop of the world. I ~~wish to go~~ want to stand up there in the flesh before I die, for there is something I want to say to the Six Grandfathers."

So the trip to Harney Peak was arranged, & a few days later we were there. On the way up to the summit, Black

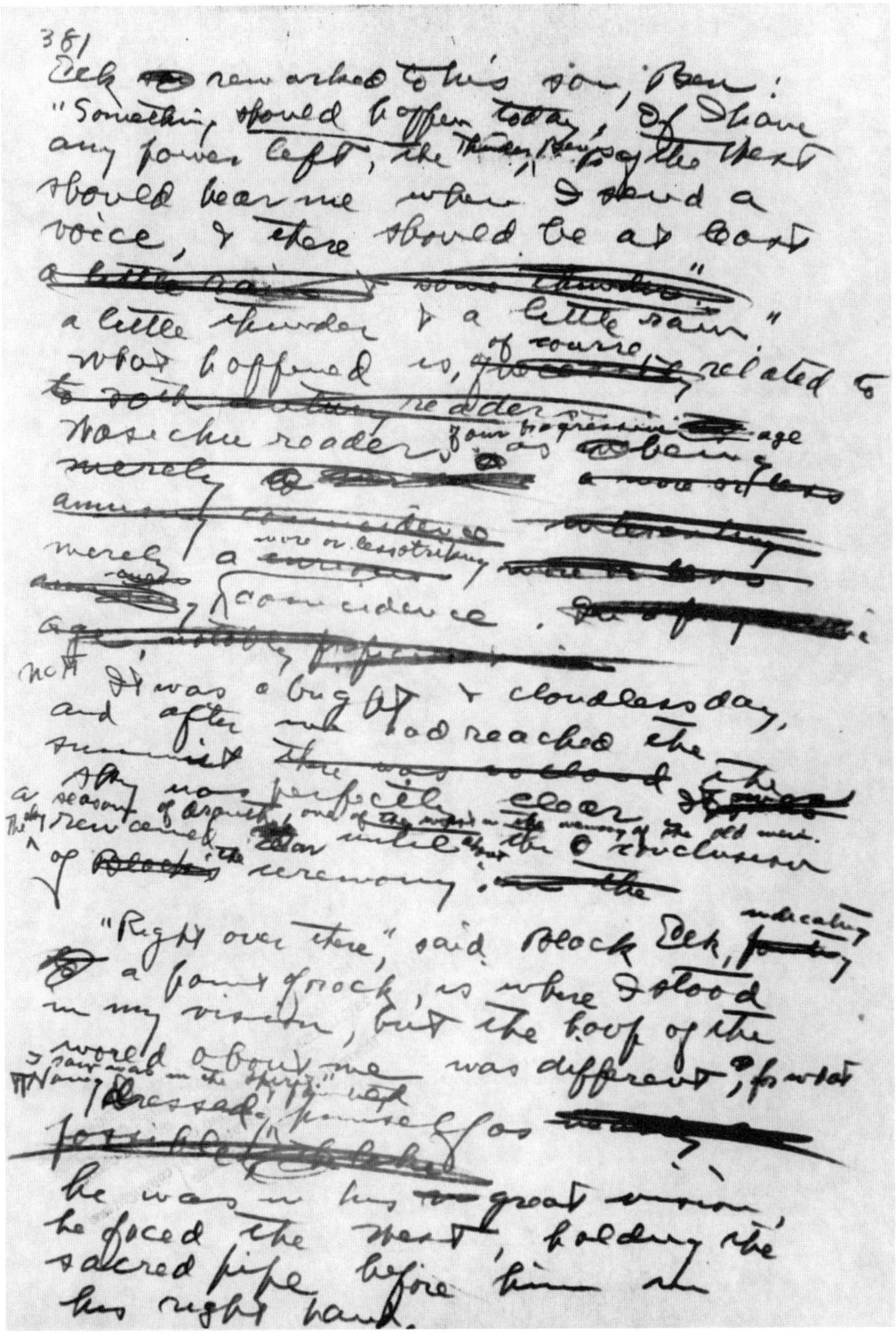

381
Elk remarked to his son, Ben:
"Something should happen today. If I have
any power left, the thunder beings of the west
should hear me when I send a
voice, & there should be at least
a little rain & some thunder."
a little thunder & a little rain."
What happened is, of course, related to
to both [illegible] readers
Wasichu reader, your progressive age as being
merely [illegible] a more or less
amusing coincidence [illegible] interesting
merely a more or less striking [illegible]
[illegible] coincidence. [illegible]
age, [illegible]
no ¶ It was a bright & cloudless day,
and after we had reached the
summit there was a cloud the
sky was perfectly clear. [illegible]
a season of drouth, one of the worst in the memory of the old men.
The sky remained clear until about the conclusion
of Black's the ceremony. [illegible]

"Right over there," said Black Elk, indicating
a point of rock, "is where I stood
in my vision, but the hoop of the
world about me was different, for what
I saw was in the spirit." [illegible]
Dressed himself as [illegible]
[illegible]
he was in his great vision,
he faced the west, holding the
sacred pipe before him in
his right hand.

–382–

Then he sent forth a voice; and a thin pathetic voice it seemed in that vast space around us:

"Hey-a-a-hey! Hey-a-a-hey! Hey-a-a-hey! Hey-a-a-hey!

Grandfather, Great Spirit, once more behold me on earth and lean to hear my feeble voice. You lived first, and you are older than all need, older than all prayer. All things belong to you — the two-leggeds, the four-leggeds, the wings of the air and all green things that live. You have set the powers of the Four Quarters to cross each other. The good road & the road of difficulties you have made to cross; and where they cross, the place is holy. Day in & day out, forever, you are the life of things.

Therefore I am sending a voice, Great Spirit, my Grandfather, forgetting nothing you have made, the stars of the universe & the grasses of the earth.

You have said to me, when I was still young & could hope, that in difficulty I should send a voice four times, once for each Quarter of the Earth, & you would hear me.

Today I send a voice for a people

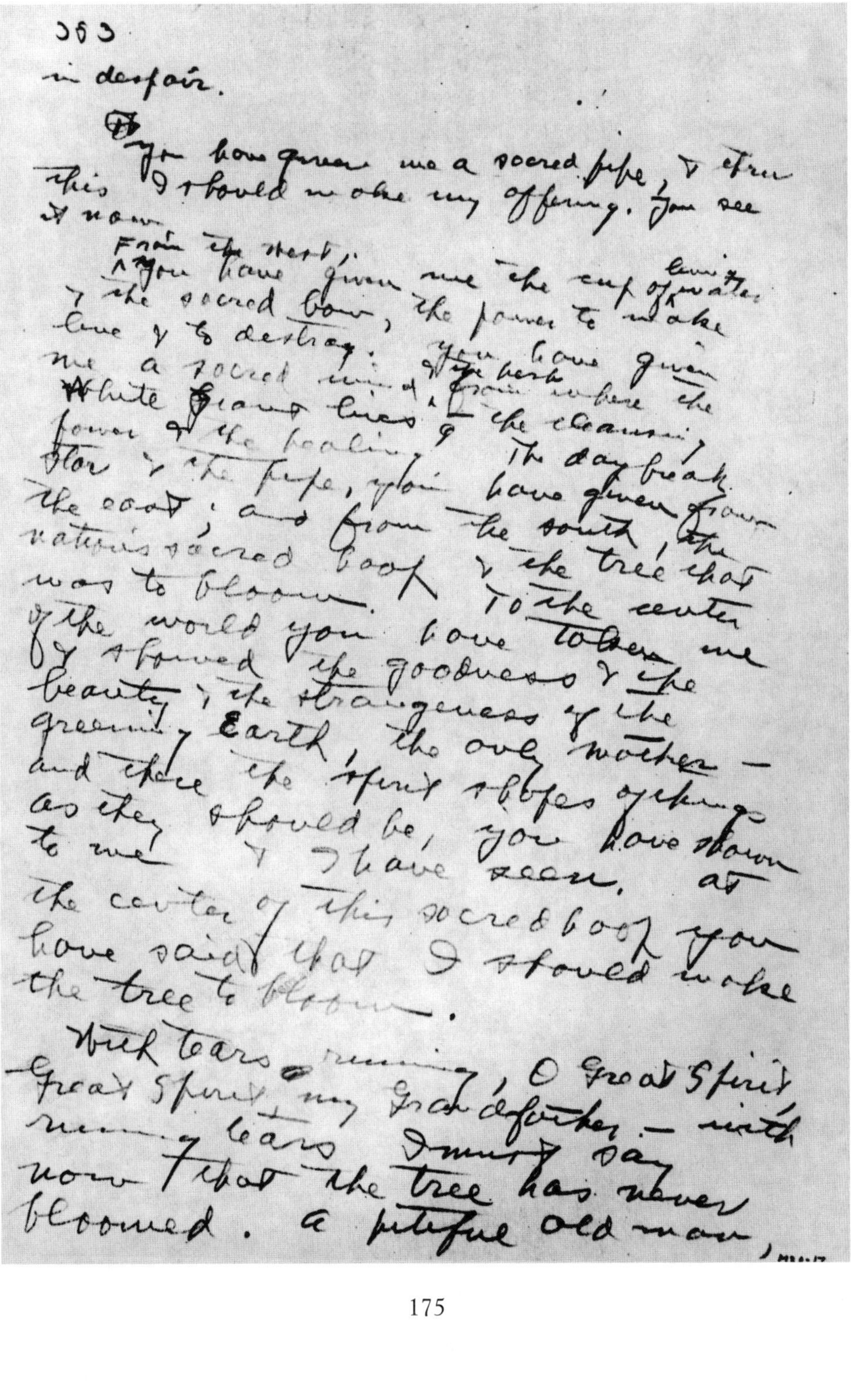
383
in despair.

You have given me a sacred pipe, & thru
this I should make my offering. You see
it now.
From the west,
You have given me the cup of living water
& the sacred bow, the power to make
live & to destroy. You have given
me a sacred wind & the herb
from where the
White Giant lives — the cleansing
power & the healing. The daybreak
star & the pipe, you have given from
the east; and from the south, the
nation's sacred hoop & the tree that
was to bloom. To the center
of the world you have taken me
& showed the goodness & the
beauty, & the strangeness of the
greening Earth, the only mother —
and there the spirit shapes of things
as they should be, you have shown
to me & I have seen. At
the center of this sacred hoop you
have said that I should make
the tree to bloom.

With tears running, O Great Spirit
Great Spirit, my Grandfather — with
running tears I must say
now that the tree has never
bloomed. A pitiful old man,

384

you see me ~~now~~ here, and I have fallen away & have done nothing. Here at the center of the world, ~~to the~~ ~~For~~ where you took me when I was young, & taught me, here, old; I stand, & the tree is withered, Grandfather, my Grandfather!

Again, & maybe the last time on this earth, I recall the great vision you sent me. ~~[illegible]~~ It may be that some little root of the sacred tree still lives. Nourish it then, that ~~it may grow, bearing many leaves with~~ it may leaf & bloom & fill with singing birds. Hear me, not for myself, but for my people; I am old. Hear me that they may once more go back into the sacred hoop & find the good Red Road, the shielding tree!"

~~Here~~

We who listened, now noted that thin clouds had gathered. ~~Above~~ about us. A scant chill rain was falling & there was low muttering thunder without lightning. ~~Raised his voice~~ With tears running down his cheeks, the old man raised his voice.

H20-18

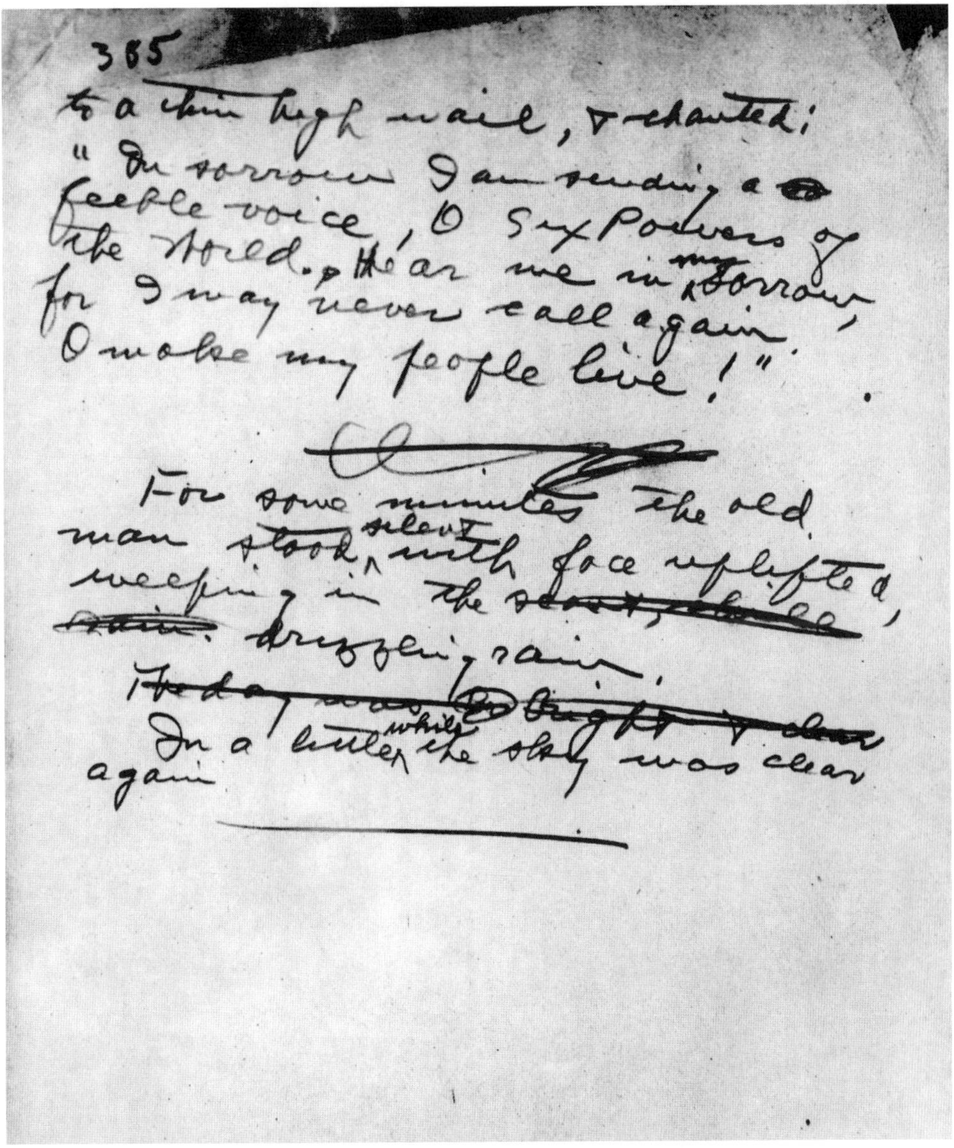

385

to a thin high wail, & chanted:
"In sorrow I am sending a feeble voice, O Six Powers of the World. Hear me in my sorrow, for I may never call again. O make my people live!"

For some ~~minutes~~ the old man ~~stood~~ silent, with face uplifted, weeping in the ~~[illegible]~~ drizzling rain.
~~The day was bright & clear~~
In a little while the sky was clear again.

5
SINCERESTFlattery

Surveying the literature of the American West, one will surely encounter styles shared by different authors who work with the same subject. This borrowing is inevitable because an established diction and syntax become, for the reading public, measures of authenticity when evaluating a new work. Not only is the mirroring of styles common in presenting Native American narrative, it has been acceptable practice in this genre. Consider as examples these quotes, both old and new and both from well-respected works. First, here is an expression used but not created by George Bird Grinnell in *The Fighting Cheyennes* (1915, reprinted 1995): "The soldiers toward the river backed away, and after that the fight did not last long enough to light a pipe" (341). This resembles a tag phrase in Paul Goble's children's story *Red Hawk's Account of Custer's Last Battle* (1969, reprinted 1992): "It was all over in the time it takes to light a pipe" (54). Second, here is an example, also from Grinnell, in which Brave Wolf repeats words for emphasis: "It was hard fighting;

very hard all the time. I have been in many hard fights, but I never saw such brave men" (340). Goble follows a similar strategy: "It was a hard struggle; very hard all the time. . . . I never saw such brave men" (*Red Hawk* 40).

When adapting from narratives that have become part of the mythic folklore of the West, it has been customary to cast stories in the language of those originals. But if such language itself is derived from a collaboration between two people from two cultures—one who narrates and one who writes in an idiom of American English reflecting the nuances of the teller—is there a point at which the idiom is uniquely their creation?

Because of Neihardt's skill in reproducing the qualities of an oral text, writers perusing *Black Elk Speaks* might get the notion that the book is a collection of verbatim transcriptions uttered as public knowledge and therefore subject to use without citation as public-domain material. Such assumptive thinking happens constantly, for example, in the commercial retelling and augmenting of folktales for children; certain authors decide that the tales do not require acknowledgment or that their variations on them are shielded by the tradition of which the tale is a part. Even illustrators of picture books sometimes copy each other. In fact, Betsy Hearne's response to this authorial practice in a *School Library Journal* article urges both the writer's specificity regarding sources and the librarian's sensitivity to the integrity of sources employed (22–27). Hearne is speaking of the particulars in children's literature, in which sources often migrate into new works without acknowledgment and sometimes get altered substantially in the process. The problem exists, however, with books for adults as well. Occasionally, it surfaces in an oblique way, appearing as an unwitting insult to either Black Elk or John Neihardt.

Take the anthology of Native American material *I Become Part of It: Sacred Dimensions in Native American Life* (1992). This excellent collection includes a two-page retelling, "White Buffalo Woman," attributed in the byline to the "Lakota" (204–205). All true. Other bylines elsewhere in the book contain names of authors, tellers, or retellers, however; this is part of the courtesy Hearne has urged. Yet only in the selection's endnote does information appear explaining that this telling is "From John G. Neihardt, *Black Elk Speaks*," the 1961 edition (280). Here only one of the collaborators receives partial credit, and the abbreviated title of the book does not communicate that this is a story "as told through." There is no intent to be discourteous, but this practice does encourage readers to consider that not only the universal story as archetype or myth but *the precise way in which the story is told* is in the public domain as "folklore."

For although much of the public may not know Neihardt directly, the unique style and strategies used in conveying his content—with their detailed attention to reconstructing eloquence and their carving away distractions so the archetypal stands clear—provide often-used models for emulation. Furthermore, Neihardt's effect on writers in his lineage does not just derive from the enduring, worldwide dissemination of *Black Elk Speaks*; his work as a teacher and mentor also has affected several successful authors. This phenomenon may continue indefinitely, since Neihardt still teaches on tape through the extension services of the University of Missouri.

On a large scale, this influence may be a sensitivity to the Western subject's archetypes, to the perception of life as constituting templates of events. For example, the spiritual and temporal roads, the mystic insight at the center of the universe, and life's remembrance from the high hill of old age are ancient concepts intensified and heightened in Neihardt's writing. Neihardt has left them to successive writers as part of his legacy, although general cross-cultural or archetypal aspects appearing in Neihardt's content are bound to recur from author to author anyway. We might recall some of these key images in *Black Elk Speaks* that have frequently appearing analogues in world religions and literature. Figure 5.1 relates and compares imagery in *Black Elk Speaks* to that noticed in other cultures by Mircea Eliade (10–460): the center of the world, the tree, the hoop, the healing herb, ascension, sacrifice, and the synecdochic, interconnected universe. Obviously, Neihardt and Black Elk did not originate these themes as manifested in *Black Elk Speaks*, but they did impart a certain flavor to them. I will soon explore how such generalities are presented with Neihardtian particularism in the work of other writers. Those who do not know Neihardt directly, then, may know him indirectly without being aware of him at all.

These concepts resonate with readers, who like the auditors of ancient epics can identify with their poetic crystallizations. *Black Elk Speaks* as book, or "testament," as N. Scott Momaday terms it (34), is not only pan-Indian but globally pancultural. We should not be surprised, then, if subsequent writing by other authors in the Neihardt "tradition" not only evokes such general imagery used by Neihardt and Black Elk but also imitates the specific techniques pioneered by Neihardt in a type of sincerest flattery. I shall examine four books that owe an enormous debt to *Black Elk Speaks*, regardless of whether they acknowledge that debt directly in academic citations.[1]

The four books have three authors, each working in a tradition of discourse established and popularized by *Black Elk Speaks*. The first author is an admirer and champion of Neihardt's work, perhaps overdoing literal emulation.

Figure 5.1 Main symbols in Eliade's Patterns in Comparative Religion *found in* Black Elk Speaks *(page references to Eliade).*

Symbol	*Location in Eliade*	*In* Black Elk Speaks
THE CENTER OF THE WORLD	Height as world-center, 111; anywhere is the center, 324; circle encompasses it, 370	Harney Peak—but anywhere is the center; Hoop of the World
HOOP	As mandala, 372; as a conduit from temporal to magic time, 392; describes a unity, 383	Contains all; is the intersection of time and timelessness; is mandala-like in its intersecting roads and colors; south to north is spiritual, timeless; east to west is the road of difficulties in time
TREE	Cosmos as tree, 265; Tree of Life, 265; axis of cosmos, 299; represents regeneration, 306	Flowering Tree in vision; Center Tree in Ghost Dance; Center Pole in Sun Dance
HEALING HERB	Sacred herb that heals, 298; plant of immortality, 294; vegetative health equals health of people, 306	Daybreak or four-rayed herb to heal the people
ASCENSION	Sacredness of height, 102; sacred passage, 102; associated with tree, 105; associated with ecstasy, vision, 108	Four ascents: note "stepped" quality in book and in transcripts; also, ascents (spiritual and physical) up Harney Peak
SACRIFICE	Holy person must perform everything in a ritual or sacrificial manner, 460	Lamenting for a vision, the Sun Dance, offerings, rituals
UNIVERSE AS INTER-CONNECTED, AS SYNECDOCHE	Religious objects' parts reflect parts of cosmos, 452; a force permeates the universe, 21; the force can be affected, 10	The life of one person reflects the Great Life of the People; the Pipe is a synecdoche; human action can affect the cosmos

The second, once a young protégé of Neihardt's, has established a certain distance while developing different novelistic interpretations of events in the West. The third, a producer of children's books, has done much to popularize Neihardt's mode of presentation, to the extent of emulating structural and visual components while bringing the tradition to a new, young audience.

OUR FIRST CASE MIGHT BE CALLED "HIS COUSIN'S VOICE: BLACK ELK, CRAZY Horse, and Mari Sandoz." As Sandoz scholar Helen Stauffer indicates, Mari Sandoz openly acknowledged her indebtedness to Neihardt, promoting *Black Elk Speaks* at a time when it was not widely known (2–3, 13). Sandoz cites

Neihardt in her notes to *Crazy Horse: The Strange Man of the Oglalas* (428). Stauffer believes much of the influence of *Black Elk Speaks* on *Crazy Horse* is indirect, having to do with attitudes Sandoz and Neihardt shared (10). But Stauffer describes several ways in which Neihardt's text directly influences *Crazy Horse* as well, both in idiom and plot. Stauffer notices that terms such as "wasichu," "walking on this new road," and reference to the reservation as an "island"—which Neihardt did not originate but did use—also appear in *Crazy Horse.* And accounts such as "Crazy Horse teasing his young relative, who is a little afraid of him" and "Black Elk coming to visit Crazy Horse and finding his teepee empty and his cousin gone" reappear in Sandoz's text (9). Also important, in Stauffer's view, is the influence of certain attitudes in *Black Elk Speaks*: distrust of Spotted Tail, who is perceived as becoming soft, for example (9–10). Stauffer notes, too, that Sandoz uses aspects of Neihardt's description of Crazy Horse's appearance and character (10).

The connection between Sandoz's and Neihardt's books may be more involved, however, engaging the very specific as well as the general. In diction, image, and the description of scenes, other overlaps in text appear. For example, Sandoz uses long phrases-as-nouns, or clausal substantives, as does Neihardt: the title of one section is "Many Things Thrown Away" (225); another is "Many Soldiers Falling into Camp" (317). Echoes from *Black Elk Speaks* resound when Custer is called "Long Hair," cavalry are "horse soldiers" (275), and the sun makes "himself great fires" (353). Remembering Neihardt's description of Wounded Knee, Sandoz applies it to Custer, who on the Washita "left the women and children butchered in the snow" (275). Other aspects of language reflect *Black Elk Speaks,* for example the repeated use of "and" in run-on sentences: "They knew the soldier chief by his yellow hair and went out to meet him, riding like wild men, so hot to fight him that they couldn't wait and helped spoil the ambush the Hunkpapas and No Bows had planned" (275).

Moreover, nearly direct equivalence appears in Crazy Horse's talk with the elder Black Elk. It is a word-for-word retelling of the *Black Elk Speaks* episode, as we saw earlier: "'Uncle,' he said, 'you notice the way I act, but do not worry. There are caves and holes for me to live in, and perhaps out here the powers will help me. The time is short, and I must plan for the good of my people'" (359).

Action, too, receives similar description. For example, the fight with General Crook in which Crazy Horse rouses his people contains these phrases in a Neihardtian paragraph: "Hold on, my friends! Be strong! Remember the helpless ones at home!" . . . "This is a good day to die!" . . . "Hoka hey" (319). A similar passage appears in the description of the Custer fight: "'Remember the helpless ones down there! This is a good day to die!' Crazy Horse said to his Oglalas. But they needed no heating words now. 'Hoka hey!'" (328). Now here is Iron Hawk's commentary on the Crook Fight as it appears in *Black Elk Speaks,* replete with similar phrasing, as Neihardt casts into English the Oglala idiom: "It looked bad for us. Then I heard voices crying in our language: 'Take courage! This is a good day to die! Think of the children and the helpless at home!' So we all yelled 'Hoka hey!' and charged on the cavalrymen and began shooting them off their horses, for they turned and ran" (101).

For additional comparison, a section of *Black Elk Speaks* narrating the Custer Fight also includes diction familiar in *Crazy Horse*: "Then another great cry went up out in the dust: 'Crazy Horse is coming! Crazy Horse is coming!' Off toward the west and north they were yelling 'Hoka hey!' like a big wind roaring, and making the tremolo; and you could hear eagle bone whistles screaming" (110–111). Similar diction, extended idiom, and rhythm of sentences describe the same subjects in Neihardt and Sandoz. Even the great central image of *Black Elk Speaks* recurs in *Crazy Horse*; Sandoz describes "the camp circles smaller, the great hoop of the people scattered and broken" (230). An early pupil, herself writing a poetic account of a great man with a great vision, has been well schooled in the Neihardt "tradition."

From archetype to artifact, *Black Elk Speaks* lives in Sandoz's work. This does not mean *Crazy Horse* is a derivative extension of *Black Elk Speaks* but that the books are cousins, sharing the same field of word and image, drawing upon a common store as the Celtic poets drew from the cauldron or as the Anglo-Saxon poets drew from their word hoard. And yet this common store, the union of an Indian idiom with American English, is a product of the innovative collaboration between Black Elk and Neihardt—the creation of an authentic American epic language. We shall see how others use this language nurtured by Neihardt and tended by Sandoz.

WE MIGHT CALL OUR SECOND CASE "HIS SCHOOLMASTER'S VOICE: WIN Blevins and *Stone Song*." One might almost guess from the book's subject matter—Crazy Horse—that this writer of energetic western novels studied in a class taught by Neihardt, sought counsel and assistance from Neihardt, was commended by Neihardt, and even asked Neihardt to read the galleys of his first novel. That first book on the mountain men covered a subject in which Blevins acknowledged that Neihardt was better versed than he.

The correspondence in c3778 tells the story. First is a July 23, 1972, three-page letter addressed to Neihardt from Blevins in which Blevins reintroduces himself. It seems he had taken a poetry class from Neihardt in 1959 and had been to Neihardt's house twice. Blevins asks his old teacher for a telephone or personal interview as a source for his first novel and mentions that he is once more studying Neihardt's *Cycle of the West* (c3778 f61). A September 13, 1972, letter from Neihardt to Blevins expresses interest in Blevins's project and suggests he look at *The Splendid Wayfaring, The Song of Hugh Glass, The Song of Jed Smith,* and *The Song of Three Friends.* It urges a personal rather than a telephone interview and asks whether Blevins has read *Black Elk Speaks* (c3778 f61). A May 8, 1973, letter from Blevins explains that there had been no time to visit and that Blevins's book, *Give Your Heart to the Hawks,* had been helped by Neihardt's poems. Blevins tells Neihardt he will be acknowledged and explains that Neihardt's course, performances, and discussions at his home deeply affected Blevins's art and life (c3778 f71). Three other letters from Neihardt, all in c3778, illuminate his role in Blevins's first book. A May 30, 1973, note to Blevins wishes him success, again asks him to visit, and directs his attention to *Black Elk Speaks* and *When the Tree Flowered* (c3778 f72). A June 11, 1973, letter to Blevins's publisher explains that Neihardt is too ill to read the entire set of proofs of the book but that Neihardt would try to get someone to read parts of it to him for commentary (c3778 f73). On July 11, 1973, Neihardt again wrote to Blevins's publisher commending the work (c3778 f73). Neihardt died November 3, 1973.

WHETHER BETSY HEARNE WOULD APPROVE OR NOT, AS ONE WOULD EXPECT of a novel, *Stone Song* does not footnote either Neihardt or Sandoz. Pages 525–526 recommend additional reading, however, telling Blevins's audience to start with *Crazy Horse: The Strange Man of the Oglalas*—although providing a variant title form. This section also suggests *Black Elk Speaks* as a preliminary vehicle for understanding the Lakota and calls DeMallie's *The Sixth Grandfather* a version of *Black Elk Speaks* the author believes particularly helpful (525).

The book is full of echoes of Neihardt, for it partakes of the legacy we have examined in its choice of diction, image, and theme. Its doing so is virtually unavoidable, for it is written about Plains Indians—in English—after Neihardt wrote and by a former student of the man who wrote to acknowledge his debt to his teacher. As with Sandoz, a number of general manifestations of Neihardt occur. Pages 158, 277, 407, 414, and 421 use the image of the hoop and the tree. The horse of Crazy Horse's vision changes into different colors (166); horses of different hues are in Black Elk's vision. And the excruciating emptiness of the first part of Crazy Horse's vision quest in pages 12–25 and 163 reminds one of Eagle Voice's quest in *When the Tree Flowered*; Spirit does not manifest itself by presence but by absence until the seeker has given up. The odd inverse relationship between physical and spiritual triumphs (158) reminds one of Sitanka's fate in *Twilight of the Sioux.* Black Elk's and Neihardt's belief in the cyclical nature of history reappears in pages 362–363 and 421. Other aspects of diction reappear as well—Lakota battle cries, for example, on page 399.

Most striking in detail are the three episodes we saw in which Sandoz had borrowed from Neihardt: Crazy Horse's dialogue with the elder Black Elk outside of camp, the description of the stand against General Crook, and portions of the Custer Fight. Here again is Neihardt's rendition of the conversation between Crazy Horse and the senior Black Elk: "Uncle, you have noticed me the way I act. But do not worry; there are caves and holes for me to live in, and out here the spirits may help me. I am making plans for the good of my people" (136). Blevins's paraphrase follows Neihardt's order and incorporates Crazy Horse's request that Black Elk not be concerned, his statement that caves are good enough shelter for him, and his hope that the supernaturals will assist him. It also includes, as does Sandoz's account, a closing statement of urgency; events are moving fast (417). Blevins's account of the fight with Crook, especially from pages 390–392, contains much diction redolent of *Black Elk Speaks*—and, by extension, of Sandoz's book as well. Through pages 390 and 391 we find the admonition not to forget those unable to fight, the battle cry affirming that death today would be welcome, and—although spelled differently—two *hoka heys*. Similar diction appears in the account of the Custer Fight; page 399 contains three standard battle phrases. And note this section of *Black Elk Speaks,* in which underlining denotes words that also appear in a similar passage of *Stone Song* (399). *Black Elk Speaks* remembers

> a very pretty young woman among a band of warriors about to go up to the battle on the hill, and she was singing like this:
>
> "Brothers, now your friends have come!
> Be brave! Be brave!
> Would you see me taken captive?" (112)

The transcripts and DeMallie record "Brothers-in-law" for the generic "Brothers" and "Take courage" for "Be brave" (DeMallie, *Sixth* 183); so does *Stone Song* (399). As for being beholden to Black Elk and Neihardt, the text speaks for itself. Is there an echo in the empty classroom?

OUR THIRD CASE CONCERNS THE PROLIFERATION OF AN INHERITANCE. WE might title it "His Grandchildren's Voices: Red Hawk and Brave Eagle." For similar Neihardtian reverberations appear in two books for children by Paul Goble, acknowledged in current editions in short, prefatory essays discussing Goble's debt to Neihardt. Goble tells us that "readers who know the literature will recognize my influences: the echoes of *Black Elk Speaks* by John G. Neihardt are plain" in the "Author's Note to the Bison Book Edition" preceding either volume (*Red* 8; *Brave* 7). Both in *Red Hawk's Account of Custer's Last Battle* and in *Brave Eagle's Account of the Fetterman Fight*, Goble employs Neihardt's narrative strategies while displaying images central to *Black Elk Speaks*.

In essence, both books simulate the features of the "as told to" genre of *Black Elk Speaks* in which an "author" introduces the narrative with a foreword or preface; interposes from time to time, providing historical commentary to enhance the reader's understanding; and closes with a postscript or authorial commentary on the events that have just been "told." The "teller" in both instances is a fictional character with a plausible name. "Red Hawk" is especially plausible because there is a Red Hawk in the "High Noon on the Little Horn" section of Neihardt's *The Twilight of the Sioux*, although that character is an older foil to young Running Wolf (136–137). In both books Goble is careful to maintain the illusion of the first-person narrator who tells the story of his youth from the perspective of the high hill of maturity; Red Hawk closes with a more-than-fifty-years-hence reminiscence (57), whereas Brave Eagle tells us, "I have sent my heart back over the years; the fight has come back as from the dead" (58). The books also contain subheadings that remind one of artifacts in *Black Elk Speaks*: "Brave Eagle Begins" heads page 17 of *Brave Eagle's Account*; "Red Hawk Begins" appears on page 15 of *Red Hawk's Account*—emulating the "Fire Thunder Speaks," "Black Elk Continues," and "Standing Bear Speaks" of the book named for one of its own subheadings, *Black Elk Speaks*.

Also, diction and imagery appear as they are used in *Black Elk Speaks*. Once again we find phrases characteristic of Neihardt's and Black Elk's collaboration. *Red Hawk's Account*, for example, states, "'Soldiers are coming! Horse-soldiers are attacking!' You could hear the cry going from camp to camp down the valley" (24); compare "The chargers are coming! They are charging! The chargers are coming! . . . We could hear the cry going from camp to camp northward" in *Black Elk Speaks* (109). Red Hawk's grandfather hands him the arrows he had made for his grandson, a detail from *Black Elk Speaks* (18), and tells Red Hawk, "Take courage, grandson! . . . The earth is all that lasts" (24–25). A cry of "Crazy Horse is coming! Crazy Horse is coming!" announces the arrival of the leader, who says, "*Hetchetu*! Be strong, my friends!" and yells, "Remember the helpless ones" (25). Red Hawk describes the actions of the Indians when Reno breaks his line: "'*Hoka hey! Hoka hey!*' . . . At once everyone was shouting and all around me there was the shriek of eagle-bone whistles and the thunder of horses' hooves on the dry earth" (29). Remember *Black Elk Speaks,* which follows battle cries with

> Then another great cry went up out in the dust: "Crazy Horse is coming! Crazy Horse is coming!" Off toward the west and north they were yelling "Hoka hey!" like a big wind roaring, and making the tremolo; and you could hear eagle bone whistles screaming.
>
> The valley went darker with dust and smoke, and there were only shadows and a big noise of many cries and hoofs and guns. (110–111)

Goble has Red Hawk acknowledge that "my memory now is clouded with the dust and noise and the smell of fighting" (54). Emulating the description of the Wagon-Box Fight in *Black Elk Speaks,* Goble has Red Hawk describe the cavalry, who "shot their guns with a sound like the tearing of a blanket" (39); *Black Elk Speaks* describes the sound of breech-loaded guns being fired as "like tearing a blanket" (16).

Whereas Goble's text mostly discusses war, his beautiful illustrations—redolent of ledger art and carrying the burden of Standing Bear's paintings in the original printing of Neihardt's book—also present the theme of potential peace and unity pervading *Black Elk Speaks.* Pages 16–17 depict a camp circle in unity, with the opening toward the east; this illustration complements text on page 17 discussing the strong, unified camp. Pages 20–21 communicate the circular theme of unity and peace in the drawing of a scene inside and outside a tipi. Nevertheless, Goble's narrator reminds us that unity and peace have been shattered: "Once all the earth was ours; now there is only a small piece left which the white people did not want" (59). One sees similar sentiments in *Black Elk Speaks* 9, 18, 146, 196, 213–214, 229, 231.

Brave Eagle's Account of the Fetterman Fight employs a similar strategy in conveying its message: pages 28–29 depict a Sun Dance, emblematic of the sacred hoop and the unity of all things; page 30 presents a camp scene in which a ceremonial fire—hoop-shaped—appears in the foreground. And this book, too, uses phrasing similar to that of the battle descriptions in *Black Elk Speaks*: page 55 has "only the rocks live forever," "now is a good time to die," and "*Hoka Hey.*" But the book also contains a superb juxtaposition of illustration and text. Page 21 depicts the military's treacherous council. Its overarching symbol, looming above the conference, is a boxlike building at Fort Laramie with sharp-cornered, staring windows. On the following page, in contrast, is roundness—Red Cloud's prayer as the meeting begins, a directional prayer redolent of *Black Elk Speaks*: "to the west which is the power of the thunder and the life-giving rain; to the north from where the purifying winds come with the snow; to the east with the day-break star" (22). It is a prayer incomprehensible to the grasping soldiers.

Zena Sutherland, in *Children and Books*, praises Goble's writing for its adherence to factual exactitude (392); Judith Saltman, in *The Riverside Anthology of Children's Literature*, extols its refusal to simplify issues of history in the telling of a complex, emotional story (1020). On those pages both quote the "small piece" passage from Goble (*Red* 59) as an example of a character's understanding of his people's fate. But are they not praising the speech of the grandson remembering his grandfather?

NOTE

1. The pagination referenced in this chapter is that of the 1988 Bison edition of *Black Elk Speaks*.

6
BLACK ELK *Speaks Today*

EMULATED, VALUED, DERIDED, AND ALMOST WORSHIPED, *BLACK ELK SPEAKS* has definitely been a touchstone for cultural and spiritual movements since its completion. The book resembles *Hamlet* or the United States Constitution in that it will always be interpreted differently depending on the attitudes of its readers and those who comment on it.

An examination of the way some commentators have reacted to *Black Elk Speaks* has highlighted the interplay between the book's poetics and its diverse contemporary readers. This aspect of the legacy of *Black Elk Speaks* is evident in anthologies and related productions. For example, when *Black Elk Speaks* goes to school in a college text, giving students perhaps their only look at part of this book, odd permutations may appear. *The HarperCollins World Reader*'s first edition, edited by Mary Ann Caws and Christopher Prendergast, announced that Black Elk's visionary account was taken down by "Niehardt" [sic], an "anthropologist." Three of the four ascents discussed in *Black Elk Speaks* appeared, although they lacked detailed context (2399–2401). Was there reluctance to include the Fourth Ascent because of a critical misconception?

The Norton Anthology of American Literature, fifth edition, Volume 2, tells its readers that after December 6, 1904, Black Elk "never engaged in traditional healing practices again" (924), one of the issues currently debated and a far-from-closed topic. Rather than discuss Enid Neihardt's ability to record the material and Ben's bilingualism, the *Norton* introduction says, "Enid wrote it all down as best she could" (924). The editor states that "it was on the basis of a number of such sessions that Neihardt produced the book known as *Black Elk Speaks*" without describing the extensive process of interviewing and transcription, the lengthy periods involved, or the overarching ceremonial and familial context into which the Neihardts were integrated and that also educated them. One might receive the impression that only a few interviews were conducted, and one should know that the book has a long title that helps to explain the collaboration. Rather than report Neihardt insisting that his role was creative and that he wrote the very beginning and the very end of the book, the *Norton Anthology* says, "Neihardt himself acknowledged" writing these parts—making it appear as if Neihardt were reluctant to do so, in the manner of "Nixon himself acknowledged that he tape-recorded John Dean." Furthermore, the editor introduces accusations of a "strong mystical Christianity" alleged to be Neihardt's, another point in the current debate. The closing paragraph of the introduction to the excerpt on Black Elk leaves the student unsure as to which of Neihardt's daughters recorded what (925).

When *Black Elk Speaks* appears as a reference in a quarterly read by students of myth, its telling of the story of the White Buffalo Calf Woman is attacked in Glenn Schiffman's letter to the editor castigating Joseph Bruchac for retelling it in a similar way—as if either Black Elk's or Neihardt's contact with the story renders it suspect. Yet as Bruchac indicates in his reply to the author of the letter, several versions of the story exist, and Bruchac's form of the narrative was set down well before Black Elk talked to Neihardt. Nor is it necessarily the case, Bruchac adds, that Christian beliefs influenced the telling of the events in this way (120–122, 122–124).

And the scholarly quarterlies often contain a view that Neihardt was a "bad collector" of material, as if he were a contemporary anthropologist or his purpose were to create modern ethnography. Thus Mick McAllister, writing in *Western American Literature,* cites *Black Elk Speaks* as the "best known instance of collector intervention" (4). McAllister calls Neihardt "a minor anachronism of a poet" and says the book "rises like an oak from the weedy thicket of his romantic novels and epic poems" (15). Nevertheless, McAllister concludes, by what the book has inspired, it is surely "true" (16).

A recent anthology of commentary on Black Elk and Neihardt is *The Black Elk Reader*, edited by Clyde Holler. This book is useful in its presentation of different perspectives on Black Elk but perhaps more so for providing a snapshot of the late-twentieth-century academic—from dedicated bibliographer to passionate partisan to somewhat bewildered observer. Any such collection is inherently restrictive. Although this one's title implies definitiveness, its contents would benefit from the extended participation of many important speakers left out of the dialogue, including Michael Castro, Sally McCluskey, Robert Sayre, Scott Momaday, Raymond DeMallie, and Black Elk's descendants. In this collection one finds some impoliteness and extrapolation from sources far removed. Certainly, it should not be a question of whom one likes or whether one is personally atheist, agnostic, Protestant, Catholic, Marxist, new-age, or authentic Lakota traditionalist in belief. One can still, in absolute civility, examine a piece of literature and ask whether it works, how it works, why it works, and for whom it works.

Those who deny that someone from a particular cultural or genetic background can enter into a special collaboration with another from a different background will probably never accept that such collaboration *can* work, that there could be any level of authenticity in the project of Neihardt and Black Elk. But a history and philosophy surround *Black Elk Speaks* that explain much in the book's approach and structure. For example, no discussion of Neihardt's "religion" or "philosophy" can ignore *Poetic Values*, the *Laureate Address, Patterns and Coincidences, All Is But a Beginning,* and his correspondence, notes, and marginalia. In addition, Black Elk took pains to transmit fact and feeling to Neihardt, whom he regarded as receptive. Those serious about understanding what Black Elk tried to do must study the context of the 1930 encounter and the 1931 interviews and must confront an eclectic Black Elk who taught different listeners differently. They will view a teacher who used ceremony and displays of community as well as narrative, who did not just educate the Neihardts but instructed others as well, and who, regardless of outward forms of expression, maintained integrity in the face of what can only be described as the cultural genocide of his people.

Also, any illusion that *Black Elk Speaks* was not art but was either sloppy ethnography or the sermon of a fundamentalist fanatic has trouble standing in the presence of the history and the manuscripts, which plainly reveal a poet in the careful and deliberative work of an artist creating art. Reading these documents we observe Neihardt grappling with the task of conveying Black

Elk's eloquence to an audience from the dominant culture that historically had been, was then, and still is far from receptive to such communication. The book's draft consistently shows an attempt to articulate its narrative in cogent and emotionally powerful language and reveals the process used in choosing its evocative phrasing. This is the poetic process, not the act of writing ethnography.

The phrasing itself has become an expected way of communicating issues across cultures. The study of such technique and of Neihardt's followers in prose helps us understand the extent to which an American epic language did in fact emerge from Neihardt and Black Elk's project and how that language could be used as well. An ironic aspect of this linguistic heritage is that some later writers have exploited what Neihardt accomplished, damaging the credibility of Neihardt's writing by their misuse of it. One now finds Neihardt echoes in bad film and pulp novels. One may learn and reproduce the attributes of Neihardt's style without having any sense of their application. Of course, since Neihardt's book, American popular culture has been looking for wise old Indians to reveal spiritual mysteries; and presses, scribblers, and artificial visionaries have been eager to oblige. We thus see an influence of the present on perceptions of the past.

One issue is clear, regardless of whether one believes Black Elk was influenced by other traditions in his own narration of vision and life. Black Elk *was* influenced by the desire to be recorded. As did James R. Walker's friends and informants, Black Elk wanted his narrative preserved in writing. Black Elk's collaboration with John Neihardt resulted in the spoken expression of belief being transformed into a new "religion of the book" in the way of Judaism, Christianity, and Islam—preserved first in tellings and then disseminated in written, heightened language. Perhaps this was Black Elk's hope—that his insight would "go out" to the world through the medium so successful with other spiritual traditions and that the vision could be performed for everyone.

The books central to these teachings—*Black Elk Speaks, The Sacred Pipe, When the Tree Flowered,* and the transcripts publicized by Raymond DeMallie in *The Sixth Grandfather*—are now bolstered by supporting publications, including reminiscences and derivations. And as with other religions of the book, there are accompanying exegetical commentators. As one of those commentators, Kenneth Lincoln, points out, when Black Elk and Neihardt collaborated, "literature as both men knew it changed. An Indian oral tradition of medicine, religion, winter count history, and tribal ceremony bridged from living ritual performance into the marketplace of print" (82). Lincoln's comment is apt because he notices that *Black Elk Speaks* is not merely a conversion of words into words. Rather, *Black Elk Speaks* encompasses a wide range of cultural communication, much of which it seeks to evoke. The vehicle of print has certainly stimulated interest in *Black Elk Speaks*, and as Vine Deloria Jr. notes in his introduction to its 1988 Bison edition, it resonates whenever the subject of first peoples' beliefs is discussed (xiii).

The fact that print has been thus prolific in presenting Black Elk to the public results from Black Elk's inspired selection of a medium—John G. Neihardt. Black Elk could have perfunctorily dismissed Neihardt. But Neihardt was philosophically attuned to exploring spiritual values, and he esteemed art as a means to access them. Over three decades of writing, beginning in adolescence after his own vision, had reinforced Neihardt's spirituality and his craft. By the time he met Black Elk, Neihardt had written lyrics, epics, dramas, stories—and journalistic pieces in which he sought to change the heart of the dominant culture. He had traveled the country reciting his poetry, feeling its cadence and its effect on audiences. His work with translations helped him present the sense and sound of one language in the form of another. His time with the Omaha, whose Siouan language contains similarities to Lakota, elicited a mutual respect and prepared him for his work with Black Elk.

That work was a book of prose written by a practicing and long-schooled poet, accustomed to the use of figure, technical device, and rhythm in both iambic and free-verse lines. In fact, Neihardt never abandoned free verse. Rather, he just expanded its field of operation, moving from the lyric to the narrative domain and teaching Mari Sandoz how to do the same for her own epic in free verse—her biography of Crazy Horse. *Black Elk Speaks* represents not only a new kind of book in American literature but a new use of free verse as well.

What has been the reaction to this historic effort? Every possible opinion has been expressed, both of Neihardt and of Black Elk. What is the collaboration's legacy? Carefully preserved documents and memorabilia. A prose poem intended to inspire, teach, and unite those of all cultures. A book defying categorization, the product of a unique artistic and spiritual enterprise, undertaken as the sacred insights of a holy person were shared with a writer to transmit to the world. A focal point for social renewal. The ongoing conversation and attempt to understand.

Without that sharing, there might now be only silence.

Annotated Bibliography

THE CONNECTIONS BETWEEN *BLACK ELK SPEAKS* AND OTHER WRITINGS ARE nearly infinite, and it is with reluctance that I limit annotations only to those works cited in my text. I want to mention some additional materials, as they might assist the general reader interested in topics this book covers.

Certainly, works such as Alvin M. Josephy's *Now That the Buffalo's Gone: A Study of Today's American Indian* (New York: Knopf, 1985) and his *The Indian Heritage of America* (Boston: Houghton Mifflin, 1991 [1968]) will provide the general reader with a large, overarching context. Josephy's papers also reference many primary and secondary sources of value. An index to the *Alvin M. Josephy, Jr. Papers,* in the Special Collections and University Archives, University of Oregon Library System, may be found currently at <http://libweb.uoregon.edu/speccoll/mss/injoseph.html>.

Those wishing for information about the Lakota and related peoples should visit the *Lakota Wowapi Oti Kin,* a project of Martin Broken Leg and Raymond

Bucko, S.J., and peruse the extensive bibliography available at that site: <http://maple.lemoyne.edu/~bucko/lakota.html>. The site links with electronic texts of writings by Zitkala-Sa, Charles Eastman, and others; statements of legal issues, including the texts of treaties; religious concerns; historical data; tribal and tribally chartered college information; and a rich assortment of other contemporary and past resources.

In addition, ethnographic material collected by James R. Walker in the early reservation era has been edited and published in three print volumes; a fine starting point mentioned in the works cited is *Lakota Belief and Ritual*, edited by Raymond DeMallie and Elaine A. Jahner (Lincoln: University of Nebraska Press, 1991), which offers a glimpse into the sometimes contradictory practices and beliefs of those older than Black Elk. An interesting correlative briefly referenced in my text but worthy of study is *The Medicine Men: Oglala Sioux Ceremony and Healing* (Lincoln: University of Nebraska Press, 1990). In it, Thomas H. Lewis discusses the many textures of belief and ceremony observed in the 1960s and early 1970s. He records that one of his informants, besides being a medicine man and active in the Catholic Church, served in the Native American Church—a classic example of eclecticism that would truly aggravate the particularist. Similarly, William K. Powers's *Oglala Religion* (Lincoln: University of Nebraska Press, Bison edition, 1982) speaks of the Jesuit attempts to integrate elements of traditional Oglala belief into late-twentieth-century church services at Pine Ridge. Powers notes that such acts, intended to "reach" the congregation, had an unexpected effect on traditional spiritual practitioners in the congregation, who apparently were gratified that the clergy was finally beginning to come around to *their* point of view (115–116).

Several other books are of interest to the general reader for their portrayal of Lakota religious issues. For example, Stephen E. Feraca's *Wakinyan: Lakota Religion in the Twentieth Century* reprints his 1963 material with extended commentary (Lincoln: University of Nebraska Press, 1998). William K. Powers has written *Yuwipi: Vision and Experience in Oglala Ritual* (Lincoln: University of Nebraska Press, 1984 [1982]), depicting the detail and context of this ceremony as run by George Plenty Wolf. A book seeking to restore the perspective on holy women in Lakota culture is *Walking in the Sacred Manner: Healers, Dreamers, and Pipe Carriers—Medicine Women of the Plains Indians* by Mark St. Pierre and Tilda Long Soldier (New York: Simon and Schuster, 1995). An informative look at practitioners in their culture, this book erases misconceptions and illuminates the activities of holy women. Finally, Lee Irwin's *The Dream Seekers: Native American Visionary Traditions of the Great Plains* (Norman:

University of Oklahoma Press, 1994) speaks clearly about the visionary role in Plains cultures. Irwin's chapter "Mythic Discourse" covers the central issues of communicating, reenacting, and evoking the sacred associated with the visionary in ways aligned with my discussion, although using different terminology. The book provides detailed and copious examples of visions and discusses their contexts.

Both Royal B. Hassrick's *The Sioux: Life and Customs of a Warrior Society* (Norman: University of Oklahoma Press, 1964) and the older book by George E. Hyde, *Red Cloud's Folk: A History of the Oglala Sioux Indians* (Norman: University of Oklahoma Press, 1975 [1937]) provide readable historical background. These authors' agendas are transparent in the text and should pose no difficulty for the reader seeking information. Catherine Price has written a fine cultural and political description in *The Oglala People, 1841–1879: A Political History* (Lincoln: University of Nebraska Press, 1996). Luther Standing Bear's *Land of the Spotted Eagle* (Lincoln: University of Nebraska Press, 1978 [1933]) continues to provide social and spiritual descriptions that are interesting, detailed, and at times passionate counterpoints to the academic books discussed earlier. In addition, Ella Deloria's *Speaking of Indians* (Lincoln: University of Nebraska Press, 1998 [1944]) was gently written to dissolve the standard stereotyping of Native Americans that continued to flourish long after *Black Elk Speaks.*

Moreover, writings by Zitkala Sa and Charles Alexander Eastman tirelessly explained to a largely indifferent dominant culture some Indian points of view; these can be accessed in *Lakota Wowapi Oti Kin,* listed earlier, or in print. Zitkala Sa's *American Indian Stories* (Lincoln: University of Nebraska Press, 1985 [1921]) depicts the pressure on young people to deacculturate and adopt the modalities of the dominant culture. Her *Old Indian Legends* (Lincoln: University of Nebraska Press, 1985 [1901]) retells many traditional stories to show a commonality of ethics and attitudes with those of the general readership. Eastman's *The Soul of the Indian: An Interpretation* (Lincoln: University of Nebraska Press, 1980 [1911]) contains an empathetic explication, and yet prefigurings of even further ethnic destruction appear throughout the book.

Cultural and physical genocide is crystallized in Wounded Knee, but that tragedy has long and shameful antecedents. The history student should read Francis Jennings's *The Invasion of America: Indians, Colonialism, and the Cant of Conquest* (New York: Norton, 1976), which traces and dissects the ideology of the conquerors and their self-justifications, drawing upon information similar to that in Gary B. Nash's *Red, White, and Black: The Peoples of Early America*

(Englewood Cliffs, N.J.: Prentice Hall, 1974). Although neither of these texts discusses the Plains Indians, the reader can perceive an ominous foreshadowing of what was to come to them. Robert M. Utley's *The Indian Frontier of the American West, 1846–1890* (Albuquerque: University of New Mexico Press, 1984) depicts the radical transformations facing those peoples.

Dover has issued an inexpensive two-volume edition of George Catlin's *Letters and Notes on the Manners, Customs, and Conditions of the North American Indians* (New York: 1973 [1844]) that contains Catlin's verbose but searing assessment of what he correctly surmised would be the dominant culture's policy of conquest and oppression. Two widely read books include accounts of cultural genocide affecting the young. Mary Brave Bird and Richard Erdoes have written *Lakota Woman* (New York: Harper, 1990), which chronicles poverty on the postwar reservation, interactions with disillusioned peers, repressive schools attempting to eradicate heritage, the American Indian Movement, and traditional religious practices. Renee Sansom Flood has produced *Lost Bird of Wounded Knee* (New York: Scribner, 1995), an account of Zintkala Noni, a child rescued at Wounded Knee in 1890 and then taken from her relatives by a military man as a trophy, never to know or reclaim her roots. Flood dissects the socially institutionalized racism, the dysfunctional adoptive family, and the internal anxieties that drove Zintkala Noni to an early death. Those passing through the Freeport, Illinois, Memorial Library might ask the kind volunteers in the Frances Woodhouse Local History Room to show them the material on file concerning Zintkala Noni, some of which is referenced in *Lost Bird*; the old newspaper articles about her, dating from 1891 to 1897, are astonishingly patronizing and bigoted—ample evidence of the "cant of conquest" as manifested in journalism. In the language of these articles, not only is the little girl a human trophy, she becomes an "it," a nonperson.

James Mooney's account of the Ghost Dance movements that responded to U.S. pressure and of the Wounded Knee Massacre is available as an inexpensive reprint, *The Ghost Dance Religion and Wounded Knee* (New York: Dover, 1973 [1896]), which should also be studied by those surveying U.S. history. Alice Beck Kehoe, in *The Ghost Dance: Ethnohistory and Revitalization* (Chicago: Holt, 1989), has generally followed DeMallie in interpreting Black Elk. Her work is detailed in its depiction of the Ghost Dance religion and discusses a group of Ghost Dancers active in the 1960s in Canada who were organized as a church—descendants of Lakota who stayed in Grandmother's Land as the army tried to round up all "hostiles."

The commentary on Black Elk or *Black Elk Speaks* that I have directly cited is annotated in the next section. The material in this genre is uneven, some of it on the fringes being groupie-like adulation of Neihardt-as-guru and some of it possessing a tantrum-like petulance attacking Neihardt-as-ogre. A new derivative appears to invoke Black Elk as a saint for devotional practice. As an example of an intentionally overcomplicating extremist position, one text I have not cited asserts that Neihardt was a master trickster who plotted the whole course of dialogic reaction to *Black Elk Speaks* to teach us that speech and writing are different. But in general and without too much simplification, current controversy about the book divides into the different positions discussed in my text, which seem sincerely held and which have been endlessly catalogued and reviewed by other writers. An entire compendium of them is available in Clyde Holler's *The Black Elk Reader,* cited in the next section. Many of these positions are cleverly argued; certain ones seem to me to be partially true extrapolations from secondary or tertiary writing. Definitely, Esther Black Elk DeSersa, Olivia Black Elk Pourier, and Aaron and Clifton DeSersa's book *Black Elk Lives,* edited by Hilda Neihardt and Lori Utecht, which recalls Black Elk and the familial context, will assist future writers in carefully depicting events and motivations.

Hilda Neihardt and I have had several discussions concerning her father's respect for and use of the poetics of traditional masters, whether ancient Greeks, writers of Vedic verses, or William Wordsworth. The poems of Wordsworth and Milton are easily accessed in many new and old editions. Neihardt's poetics, employed in *Black Elk Speaks,* were linked to his belief that the universe is itself poetic, fundamentally composed of energy and therefore nonmaterial. He regarded the cosmos as an idea, thereby inviting comparison with Einstein's thought and with some Eastern religions to which he was exposed.

A number of books discuss this view of the universe, some of which are written by scientists. I recommend Fritjof Capra's *The Tao of Physics* (New York: Bantam, 1977 [1976]) as a good starting point. Although not a scientist but a reporter on science, Gary Zukav has written *The Dancing Wu Li Masters: An Overview of the New Physics* (New York: Bantam, 1980 [1979]), which is informative. Neihardt would have delighted in the narrative of attempts to verify Bell's Theorem and its predictions about nonlocal interconnectedness and would have been most interested in theories interpreting apparently chaotic systems as complexly ordered ones. A curious connection exists between Neihardt and Postmodernism in the poet's belief in the nonphysical nature of the universe and in its undogmatic fluidity. Neihardt, as we have seen, thought we even invent our versions of "science" so they mirror our perceptions. Lori Utecht, who is studying Neihardt's essays and reviews, and Tim

Anderson, who is writing a new biography of Neihardt, no doubt will elaborate on Neihardt and science in their publications.

WORKS CITED

Anderson, Tim. "The Poetry of John G. Neihardt." *Neihardt Journal* 1 (1999): 4–13. Tim Anderson is working on a new biography of Neihardt and has collected information not previously available. He is especially interested in the development of Neihardt's poetry over time and in critical reactions to it.

Bataille, Gretchen M. "Black Elk: New World Prophet." In *A Sender of Words: Essays in Memory of John G. Neihardt.* Ed. Vine Deloria Jr. Salt Lake City: Howe, 1984, 135–142. An essay that examines the role of *Black Elk Speaks,* including Black Elk as prophet in his community.

"Black Elk." In *The Norton Anthology of American Literature,* Vol. 2. Ed. Nina Baym. New York: Norton, 1998, 924–937. Perhaps this entry signals a trend that *Black Elk Speaks* will receive increasing exposure. The introduction to the excerpt reflects ambivalence about the work, however.

Blevins, Win. *Stone Song: A Novel of the Life of Crazy Horse.* New York: Forge, 1996 [1995]. A work of speculative fiction that adds to what is known about Crazy Horse interpolations about his spirit guardian, extrapolations about his family, and presentations of other aspects of Lakota culture.

Born, David O. "Black Elk and the Duhamel Sioux Indian Pageant." *North Dakota History: Journal of the Northern Plains* 61 (1994): 22–29. A singularly valuable article based on extensive interviews with Bud Duhamel and Charlotte Black Elk. Born explains the origin of the pageant, the role of Black Elk within it, and the implications for our assessment of Black Elk's activities.

Brown, Joseph Epes, ed. *The Sacred Pipe: Black Elk's Account of the Seven Rites of the Oglala Sioux.* Norman: University of Oklahoma Press, 1989 [1953]. The classic exposition of sacred rites, copiously annotated by Brown to show links to other world religions, and a "poetic" book in its own right.

Bruchac, Joseph. Reply to Schiffman. *Parabola* (spring 1998): 120–124. This letter exchange in *Parabola* points out that controversy continues over which version of the White Buffalo Calf Woman story is to be preferred and shows how the one in Black Elk's telling has been drawn into the discussion.

Brumble, H. David. *American Indian Autobiography.* Berkeley: University of California Press, 1990 [1988]. The systematic study of a cross-cultural genre and its features.

Buechel, Eugene, S.J. A *Grammar of Lakota: The Language of the Teton Sioux Indians.* St. Louis: Swift, n.d. [1970; 1939]. Of interest is Buechel's translation of second-person personal pronouns, which is closer to the transcripts of the interviews with Black Elk (using "thou," for example) but farther from DeMallie's edited version. Buechel's discussion of "clausal substantives" also provides important context for understanding their use in *Black Elk Speaks.*

Campbell, Joseph. *The Flight of the Wild Gander: Explorations in the Mythological Dimension.* New York: Harper, 1995 [1990]. One of many books by Campbell explicating his understanding of the role of myth.

Castro, Michael. *Interpreting the Indian: Twentieth-Century Poets and the Native American.* Norman: University of Oklahoma Press, 1991. An excellent study of several writers who use or interpret Native American issues. Castro discusses Neihardt as an editor and artist who employed Black Elk's diction and imagery to crystallize issues for the reader when necessary but who remained faithful to his collaborator.

Caws, Mary Ann, and Christopher Prendergast, eds. *The HarperCollins World Reader, Single Volume Edition.* New York: HarperCollins, 1994, 2399–2401. Another anthology containing a piece of *Black Elk Speaks.*

Curtis, Natalie (Burlin), ed. *The Indians' Book: Songs and Legends of the American Indians,* 2d ed. New York: Dover, 1968 [1923]. A valuable book, although religious-progressivist overtones intrude on the collection and presentation of Short Bull's material.

Deloria, Vine. "Introduction." In *Black Elk Speaks: Being the Life Story of a Holy Man of the Oglala Sioux as Told Through John G. Neihardt (Flaming Rainbow).* By John G. Neihardt. Lincoln: University of Nebraska Press, 1988 [1932], xi–xiv. Deloria's introduction to the 1988 edition of *Black Elk Speaks* responds to those uncomfortable with Neihardt's mediation of Black Elk's message.

DeMallie, Raymond J. "John G. Neihardt's Lakota Legacy." In *A Sender of Words: Essays in Memory of John G. Neihardt.* Salt Lake City: Howe, 1984, 110–134.

——, ed. *The Sixth Grandfather: Black Elk's Teachings Given to John G. Neihardt.* Lincoln: University of Nebraska Press, 1984. DeMallie's article shows how Neihardt was uniquely qualified to mediate between the Lakota and white cultures. *The Sixth Grandfather* presents the transcripts and stenographic notes of the 1931 interviews with Black Elk, although edited to adjust the English. Much helpful information and analysis precede this material in the text, and it is a fine book in its own right.

DeSersa, Esther Black Elk, Olivia Black Elk Pourier, Aaron DeSersa Jr., and Clifton DeSersa. *Black Elk Lives: Conversations with the Black Elk Family.* Ed. Hilda Neihardt and Lori Utecht. Lincoln: University of Nebraska Press, 2000. Reminiscences of the holy man, the family context, and the social issues impinging on Nicholas Black Elk. See Stover, later in this section.

Eliade, Mircea. *Patterns in Comparative Religion.* Trans. Rosemary Sheed. New York: Meridian, 1974 [1958]. Useful for comparing key symbols in other religions.

Elliott, J. H. *The Old World and the New: 1492–1650.* Cambridge Studies in Early Modern History. London: Cambridge University Press, 1970. Elliott explains how Europeans grappled with concepts of social evolution in rationalizing their encounters with the "New World."

Forbes, Bruce David. "Which Religion Is Right? Five Answers in the Historical Encounter Between Christianity and Traditional Native American Spiritualities." *Neihardt Journal* 2 (2000): 18–26. Forbes uses a classifying schematic that identifies patterns of belief possessed by different critics of *Black Elk Speaks.* See also Holler, who has done some classification as well.

Fultz, Jay. Introduction. In *The End of the Dream and Other Stories.* By John G. Neihardt. Lincoln: University of Nebraska Press, 1991, ix–xxv. A well-written piece exploring the features and intent of John Neihardt's early stories.

Goble, Paul. *Brave Eagle's Account of the Fetterman Fight.* Lincoln: University of Nebraska Press, 1992 [1972].

——. *Red Hawk's Account of Custer's Last Battle.* Lincoln: University of Nebraska Press, 1992 [1969]. Both books are beautifully illustrated works for children written in a Neihardtian style, with drawings reminiscent of ledger art.

Green, Norma Kidd. *Iron Eye's Family: The Children of Joseph La Flesche.* Lincoln: Johnsen, 1969. Describes the history of a distinguished family and illuminates the milieu in which the young Neihardt became familiar with Indians.

Grinnell, George Bird. *The Fighting Cheyennes.* North Dighton, Mass.: J G Press, 1995 [1915]. A classic and influential work. The diction of this book, like that of *Black Elk Speaks,* has left a mark on subsequent writers working with similar material.

Hearne, Betsy. "Cite the Source: Reducing Cultural Chaos in Picture Books, Part One." *School Library Journal* 39 (1993): 22–27. *Academic Abstracts Full Text.* CD-ROM. Ebsco, July 1993. Argues for standards of source attribution in children's fiction; her argument can be extended to literature of all kinds, including the historical novel for adults. Hearne's article has been somewhat predictive, as in recent years a similar controversy has emerged concerning "popular histories" for adult readers.

Hebard, Grace Raymond. *Sacajawea: A Guide and Interpreter of the Lewis and Clark Expedition, With an Account of the Travels of Toussaint Charbonneau, and of Jean Baptiste, the Expedition Papoose.* Glendale: Clark, 1933. One of the works in the Neihardt Memorial Library, University of Missouri, Columbia, Missouri, which contains explanatory inserts added by Neihardt and photos with handwritten captions by the author (see Marginalia under "John G. Neihardt," later in this section).

Hittman, Michael. *Wovoka and the Ghost Dance.* Ed. Don Lynch. Expanded ed. Lincoln: University of Nebraska Press, 1997. A compendium of material about Wovoka, including evidence that the government monitored his doings long after the Ghost Dance furor had died down. The book reproduces government correspondence on the subject.

Holler, Clyde. *Black Elk's Religion: The Sun Dance and Lakota Catholicism.* New York: Syracuse University Press, 1995. Holler's analysis of Black Elk's religion is based on his research and his steering a course between Rice and Steltenkamp. This position is well argued. See Stover, "Eurocentrism," for a reply.

——, ed. *The Black Elk Reader.* New York: Syracuse University Press, 2000. A substantial collection of criticism, both positive and negative, focused on Neihardt and Black Elk. It is by no means exhaustive but provides an interesting group of perspectives. See Forbes's article earlier in this section.

Holloway, Brian R. "*Black Elk Speaks* and Some Discontents." *Neihardt Journal* 1 (1999): 14–21. Looks at several critical positions regarding *Black Elk Speaks.*

Iser, Wolfgang. *The Act of Reading: A Theory of Aesthetic Response.* Baltimore: Johns Hopkins University Press, 1980 [1978]. I use Iser to discuss the reader's assembling of meaning when interacting with a text.

Jennings, Francis. *The Invasion of America: Indians, Colonialism, and the Cant of Conquest.* New York: Norton, 1976. A thorough dissection of early Indian/colonist interaction.

Krupat, Arnold. *Ethnocriticism: Ethnography, History, Literature.* Berkeley: University of California Press, 1992. Studies the dialogue and dialectic created at the boundary of culture between Indian and white communicators.

Lame Deer, John, and Richard Erdoes. *Lame Deer, Seeker of Visions.* New York: Simon and Schuster, 1972. A classic book at the boundary of culture between Indian and white communicators and an important exposition for the mainstream culture of the 1970s. This work uses many of Neihardt's editorial strategies, including composite first person, polyvocality, and chronological material punctuated with set pieces and thus evokes oral literature.

Lewis, Thomas H. *The Medicine Men: Oglala Sioux Ceremony and Healing.* Studies in the Anthropology of North American Indians. Lincoln: University of Nebraska Press, 1990. An account of beliefs and practices Lewis encountered while working at Pine Ridge during the 1960s and early 1970s. An informative text written from a physician's point of view.

Lincoln, Kenneth. *Native American Renaissance.* Berkeley: University of California Press, 1985. In discussing *Black Elk Speaks,* Lincoln recognizes that it is a "collective telling" and that Black Elk's "healing quest" became one seeking the restoration of his people. Some of Lincoln's language bears examination: Black Elk is referred to as "purblind" (87), and Neihardt's work with Black Elk is called "field anthropology" (28). Elsewhere Lincoln is particularly apt in his admonishment not to stereotype such discourse.

Mails, Thomas E. *Fools Crow.* Lincoln: University of Nebraska Press, 1990 [1979]. Fools Crow as told through Mails via Dallas Chief Eagle. Mails seems to view himself in a Neihardtian role throughout his discussions with Fools Crow. Fools Crow offers commentary on Black Elk's role as his mentor.

Maslow, Abraham H. *Religions, Values, and Peak-Experiences.* 1964. New York: Viking-Compass, 1970. I use Maslow in discussing the concept of art that originates from and attempts to evoke mystical experience.

McAllister, Mick. "Native Sources: American Indian Autobiography." *Western American Literature* 32 (1997): 3–23. A bibliographic essay demonstrating unconcealed dislike of Neihardt but nevertheless grudging respect for *Black Elk Speaks*—which, says the author, is true in an essential way.

McCluskey, Sally. "Black Elk Speaks: And So Does John Neihardt." *Western American Literature* 6 (1972): 231–242. McCluskey's article, based on textual analysis and interviews with Neihardt, seeks to center critical understanding of *Black Elk Speaks* on the book as a function of both collaborators, as it was intended to be. Neihardt gave McCluskey a definitive statement about his role in *Black Elk Speaks.*

Milton, John. Book IX. *Paradise Lost.* Project Gutenberg. Urbana, Illinois, 1991 [1667–1674]. August 5, 2002 <ub/docs/books/gutenberg/etext91/plboss10.txt>. This e-text appears to conflate part of Book VIII and Book IX. The cited lines are actually from Book IX. I have adjusted the spelling in the part quoted and provided an approximate line numbering.

Modern Language Association. "Statement on the Significance of Primary Records." *Profession* 95 (1995): 27–28. The subtle differences between the transcripts and the published rendition of them alone justify the MLA statement, let alone the chance to watch Neihardt turn the raw material into polished text—right down to the smallest strikeovers and erasures the original manuscript drafts provide.

Momaday, N. Scott. "To Save a Great Vision." In *A Sender of Words: Essays in Memory of John G. Neihardt*. Ed. Vine Deloria Jr. Salt Lake City: Howe, 1984, 30–38. A strong identification of *Black Elk Speaks* as participant in the oral tradition.

M. Slade Kendrick Papers, 1951–1973. Western Historical Manuscript Collection, Columbia, Missouri. Collection c628 f2 contains commentary in a letter from John G. Neihardt to Kendrick. Used by permission of the Western Historical Manuscript Collection, Columbia, Missouri, and the John G. Neihardt Trust.

Neihardt, Hilda. *Black Elk and Flaming Rainbow: Personal Memories of the Lakota Holy Man and John Neihardt*. Lincoln: University of Nebraska Press, 1995.

——. Personal interview, Bancroft and Tekemah, Nebraska, June 17, 19–20, 1996. Hilda Neihardt clarifies many items concerning the interviews, the family's relationship with the Black Elks, the final beliefs of Lucy Looks Twice, and other issues on which secondary or tertiary sources have commented.

Neihardt, John G. *All Is But a Beginning: Youth Remembered, 1881–1901*. Lincoln: University of Nebraska Press, 1986 [1972]. An anecdotal remembrance exploring particular incidents as emblematic of larger patterns.

——. *Black Elk Speaks: Being the Life Story of a Holy Man of the Oglala Sioux as Told Through John G. Neihardt (Flaming Rainbow)*. Lincoln: University of Nebraska Press, 1988 [1932]. The "Bison" edition I have used in citations, since, although it has been superseded by a later edition, it is the text usually appearing in references by critics. Unfortunately, it does not contain the Preface of the 1972 Pocket Edition or the sequence of paintings by Standing Bear as they were intended to appear in *Black Elk Speaks*. My quoting from *Black Elk Speaks* is courtesy of the University of Nebraska Press and the John G. Neihardt Trust, as follows: Reprinted from *Black Elk Speaks* by John G. Neihardt by permission of the University of Nebraska Press. Copyright 1932, 1959, 1972, by John G. Neihardt. © 1961 by the John G. Neihardt Trust.

——. *Black Elk Speaks: Being the Life Story of a Holy Man of the Oglala Sioux as Told Through John G. Neihardt (Flaming Rainbow) by Nicholas Black Elk.*

Twenty-First Century ed. Lincoln: University of Nebraska Press, 2000 [1932]. This new edition carries on its spine the authorial indication "Neihardt & Black Elk." It contains preface material and much of the art missing from the paperback Bison edition. I would like to think that my discussions with the Neihardt family about the importance of such items helped to reintroduce them to the text.

——. *The Divine Enchantment: A Mystical Poem; Poetic Values: Their Reality and Our Need of Them.* Lincoln: University of Nebraska Press, 1989 [1900, 1925]. I have normally cited *Poetic Values* in this edition.

——. Interview, June 12, 1971. *The Dick Cavett Show.* ABC. Tape in Neihardt Center, Bancroft, Nebraska. This program helped to catalyze national interest in *Black Elk Speaks.*

——. John G. Neihardt Papers, c. 1858–1974. Western Historical Manuscript Collection, Columbia, Missouri. The collection contains original drafts, transcriptions, letters, tapes, and miscellaneous materials and is indexed by a list of finding aids. The collection is housed at the Ellis Library and is available on microfilm. Items cited in the collection are used by permission of the Western Historical Manuscript Collection and the John G. Neihardt Trust. Throughout my text they are identified by their collection number—for example, c3716, c3778—plus a folder number if there is one.

——. *Laureate Address.* 1921. C3716 f485, John G. Neihardt Papers, c. 1858–1974. Western Historical Manuscript Collection, Columbia, Missouri.

——. Letters to M. Slade Kendrick. See entry under M. Slade Kendrick Papers.

——. Letters to Stanley C. Smith. See entry under Stanley C. Smith Papers.

——. Letters to George Sterling. See entry under Sterling Correspondence.

——. Marginalia. Neihardt reacted to the works of others, writing notes in the margins of his books and occasionally inserting descriptive or explanatory pieces into the text. Examples appear in the volumes in his personal library, donated to the University of Missouri–Columbia. The Neihardt Memorial Library is currently not in Ellis Library but in Tate Hall, University of Missouri–Columbia. Neihardt's personal library is not part of the Western Historical Manuscript Collection.

——. *Patterns and Coincidences: A Sequel to* All Is But a Beginning. Columbia: University of Missouri Press, 1978. See note to *All Is But a Beginning,* earlier in this section.

——. *Poetic Values.* Ed. Dr. Sisirkumar Ghose. New York: Macmillan, 1925. I have cited this early edition to stress that the concepts expressed in *Poetic Values* preceded Neihardt's encounter with Black Elk.

——. "Preface: The Book That Would Not Die." In *Black Elk Speaks.* New York: Pocket Books, 1972 [1932], ix–xiii. Neihardt's Preface, written in 1971, makes explicit his role as poetic collaborator and his sense that Black Elk was a prophet.

——. *The Twilight of the Sioux: The Song of the Indian Wars–The Song of the Messiah.* A Cycle of the West, Vol. II. Lincoln: University of Nebraska Press, 1971 [1925–1953]. The cycle has been mined as source material by many writers but is itself a masterpiece; "The Song of the Messiah" should be read aloud by those skeptical about employing the iambic line in contemporary poetry. I quote from *The Twilight of the Sioux* courtesy of the John G. Neihardt Trust, and such quotation is by permission of the University of Nebraska Press as follows: Reprinted from *The Twilight of the Sioux* by John G. Neihardt by permission of the University of Nebraska Press. Copyright 1943, 1946, 1953, by John G. Neihardt.

——. *When the Tree Flowered: The Story of Eagle Voice, a Sioux Indian.* Lincoln: University of Nebraska Press, 1991 [1951]. Not really a novel but a synthesis of later interviews with Lakota set into a frame plot. It features material from Eagle Elk, Andrew Knife, and Black Elk set into a frame story.

——. "The White Radiance." In *The Giving Earth: A John G. Neihardt Reader.* Ed. Hilda Neihardt Petri. Lincoln: University of Nebraska Press, 1991, 287–291. Poetics, mysticism, and social commentary. Neihardt views different social and artistic perceptions as constituting portions of a spectrum, not a hierarchy, yet each only partially interpretive of the "white radiance" itself—total perception, mystical union.

Rice, Julian. *Black Elk's Story: Distinguishing Its Lakota Purpose.* Albuquerque: University of New Mexico Press, 1991. The initial sections criticize Neihardt as an incompetent auditor and collector of information, insensitive to the possibility that Black Elk would use whatever means he could to help his people. Later sections of the book—almost a separate work, really—constitute an interesting self-contained exposition of different Lakota contexts for Black Elk's tellings.

Rosenberg, Ruth. "Introduction." In *Lame Deer, Seeker of Visions.* By John Fire Lame Deer and Richard Erdoes. 1972. New York: Washington Square–Pocket, 1994, i–xxix. Rosenberg, apparently using DeMallie, not the transcripts, castigates *Black Elk Speaks* for its "biblical cadences" and holds up *Lame Deer, Seeker of Visions* as a proper bicultural document.

Russell, Bertrand. *Mysticism and Logic.* New York: Norton, 1929. A volume in the Neihardt Memorial Library that contains Neihardt's marginalia reacting to Russell's argument.

Saltman, Judith, ed. *The Riverside Anthology of Children's Literature,* 6th ed. Boston: Houghton Mifflin, 1985. Praises Goble's work for its verisimilitude.

Sandoz, Mari. *Crazy Horse: The Strange Man of the Oglalas.* Lincoln: University of Nebraska Press, 1992 [1942]. Sandoz's experimental biography using Neihardt's strategies of diction and point of view. It should be read together with *Stone Song* by Win Blevins for comparison.

Schiffman, Glenn. Letter to the editor. *Parabola* (spring 1998): 120–122. See Bruchac, earlier in this section.

Scott, Jamie, and Paul Simpson-Housley, eds. *Sacred Places and Profane Spaces: Essays in the Geographics of Judaism, Christianity, and Islam.* Contributions to the Study of Religion. New York: Greenwood, 1991. Contains chapters discussing the spiritual topography in religious tellings (see my notes to Figure 4.10). Some topographical analogues can be compared to material in *Black Elk Speaks.* The editors, working from the foundations established by Eliade, wish to create a forum for the exploration of spiritual geography rather than to fixate upon the study of dichotomy or "spiritual evolution."

Stanley C. Smith Papers, 1951–1971. Western Historical Manuscript Collection, Columbia, Missouri. Letters to Smith from Neihardt contain particularly detailed discussions. These, in c3607 (particularly f6, f7, f16), reveal Neihardt's opinions about a wide range of issues, including the function of art and the artist. Used by permission of the Western Historical Manuscript Collection, Columbia, Missouri, and the John G. Neihardt Trust.

Stauffer, Helen Winter. *Sandoz, Neihardt, and Crazy Horse.* Distinguished Lecture Series for the Mari Sandoz Heritage Society, Vol. 1. Chadron: Mari Sandoz Heritage Society, 1992. A close discussion of the interrelationship of these two authors.

Steltenkamp, Michael F. *Black Elk: Holy Man of the Oglala.* Norman: University of Oklahoma Press, 1993. A book limning Black Elk as Catholic; some statements are contradicted by Hilda Neihardt's *Black Elk and Flaming Rainbow,* earlier in this section. Steltenkamp's and Rice's books are best read together with Holler's for a survey of views critical of Neihardt and of each other. Steltenkamp's book ultimately seems to leave unanswered the extent to which Black Elk abjured all traditional beliefs.

Sterling Correspondence, 1916–1924. Huntington Library, Sterling Letters. Originals of Neihardt's correspondence with the poet George Sterling, 1916–1924, are in the Huntington Library, San Marino, California; the Western Historical Manuscript Collection, Columbia, Missouri, has copies in c3074. They are used by permission of both parties and by the John G.

Neihardt Trust. These letters are valuable for their discussion of cyclical views of history, poetics, and social issues.

Stover, Dale. "Eurocentrism and Native Americans." *CrossCurrents: The Journal of the Association for Religion and Intellectual Life* (fall 1997). Available at <http://aril.org/fall_1997.htm/>.

——. Interview of Esther DeSersa and Olivia Pourier, "Black Elk's Granddaughters Speak." Special session of the Great Plains Regional Meeting of the American Academy of Religion, Omaha, Nebraska, 1998. Viewable at the John G. Neihardt Center, Bancroft, Nebraska.

——. Interview of Francis "Bud" Duhamel, January 28, 1998. Produced by KOTA, Rapid City, South Dakota. Viewed at the Neihardt Center, Bancroft, Nebraska, April 26, 1998. Stover's article replies to Holler's work and addresses as well the academic world's creation of edifices of thought based on syntheses of other academic sources, an endless process that can move quite far from direct, primary experience. Stover's discussion with Esther DeSersa and Olivia Pourier corroborates the findings of DeMallie and Born. Stover's interview of Bud Duhamel corroborates Born's, extends the description at times, and has implications similar to those of Born's research.

Sutherland, Zena. *Children and Books,* 9th ed. New York: Longman, 1996. Sutherland admires Goble's writing.

Tibbles, Thomas Henry. *Buckskin and Blanket Days: Memoirs of a Friend of the Indians.* New York: Doubleday, 1957. A volume in the Neihardt Memorial Library. Although Neihardt's marginalia are unevenly distributed throughout the collection, this book provides not merely marginal commentary but, in addition, a four-page letter to posterity in the interest of factual exactitude.

Utecht, Lori. "John G. Neihardt as Essayist." *Neihardt Journal* 1 (1999): 22–28. Neihardt wrote thousands of essays, many of which were book reviews. These express Neihardt's thoughts on a large variety of subjects and help the scholar seeking to identify key expressions of the poet's beliefs.

Walker, James R. *Lakota Belief and Ritual.* Ed. Raymond J. DeMallie and Elaine A. Jahner. Lincoln: University of Nebraska Press, 1991 [1980]. A useful compendium of material Lakota religious and other leaders gave Walker so it would be preserved. It reveals some of the variety of beliefs held by those leaders.

Washburn, Wilcomb E. *The Indian in America.* The New American Nation Series. New York: Harper, 1975. Washburn surveys different cultures and reactions to them by the United States.

"White Buffalo Woman." In *I Become Part of It: Sacred Dimensions in Native American Life.* Ed. D. M. Dooling and Paul Jordan-Smith. San Francisco: Harper, 1992, 204–205, 280. *Black Elk Speaks* anthologized.

Wong, Hertha Dawn. *Sending My Heart Back Across the Years: Tradition and Innovation in Native American Autobiography.* New York: Oxford, 1992. Wong seems to have misinterpreted Castro (see listing earlier in this section) in her statement about Neihardt's text.

Wordsworth, William. "Ode on Intimations of Immortality, From Recollections of Early Childhood." Stanza One. In *Palgrave's The Golden Treasury.* Ed. Walter Barnes. Chicago: Row, Peterson, 1915, 414–420. The various versions of *The Golden Treasury* once served as arbiters of poetic taste. Wordsworth's ubiquitous appearance in such early-twentieth-century anthologies suggests his continual background influence on Neihardt.

Zaleski, Philip. "*Black Elk Speaks* in the Top Ten Spiritual Books of the Century." *Neihardt Journal* 2 (2000): 9. The book was voted in the top 10 of the top 100 such books selected by a panel that assisted Zaleski, editor of The Best Spiritual Writing series, HarperSanFrancisco.

Index

Page numbers in italics indicate photographs, transcript pages, or manuscript pages.